Cyberdemocracy

Information technology has long been thought by scholars, politicians and activists to be a tool that could be used to enhance democracy. Computer networks, the Internet and information and communications technology could have the capacity to challenge the monopoly of existing political hierarchies.

Cyberdemocracy is a new study of the potential for 'electronic democracy' through the examination of case studies and civic projects in US and European cities. It aims to strike a balance between enthusiastic and dismissive approaches to 'electronic democracy'. The authors consider the impact of new technology in the political process and examine in particular the ways in which the principles and requirements of public service and universal access will, or will not, be maintained as the new electronic media become integrated in local politics and civic networking.

Cyberdemocracy is a vigorous contribution to a vital debate about the state of democracy and the impact of communications technologies. It will be essential reading for both students and policy-makers.

Roza Tsagarousianou is a lecturer and researcher at the Centre for Communication and Information Studies of the University of Westminster. **Damian Tambini** is a research fellow at Humboldt University, Berlin. **Cathy Bryan** is a researcher at Informed Sources and is concerned with developments in media and communications technologies.

Acknowledgements

The editors would like to thank colleagues at the Centre for Communication and Information Studies at the University of Westminster for their valuable comments and support during various stages in the preparation of this book. The CCIS seminars in which some of the issues raised in this book were discussed have proved an invaluable source of ideas and solutions to the problems arising in our research.

Drafts of some of the contributions in this book were presented and discussed at the *9th Colloquium on Communication and Culture*, Piran, Slovenia, April 1996. We are grateful to the organisers and participants for giving us the opportunity to air and discuss our work at that stage.

Cyberdemocracy
Technology, cities and civic networks

Edited by Roza Tsagarousianou,
Damian Tambini and Cathy Bryan

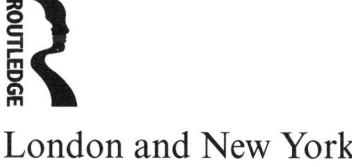

London and New York

First published 1998
by Routledge
11 New Fetter Lane, London EC4P 4EE

Simultaneously published in the USA and Canada
by Routledge
29 West 35th Street, New York, NY 10001

© 1998 selection and editorial matter, Roza Tsagarousianou, Damian Tambini and Cathy Bryan; individual chapters, the contributors

Typeset in Times by M Rules
Printed and bound in Great Britain by T. J. International Ltd, Padstow, Cornwall

All rights reserved. No part of this book may be reprinted or reproduced or utilised in any form or by any electronic, mechanical, or other means, now known or hereafter invented, including photocopying and recording, or in any information storage or retrieval system, without permission in writing from the publishers.

British Library Cataloguing in Publication Data
A catalogue record for this book is available from the British Library

Library of Congress Cataloguing in Publication Data
Cyberdemocracy: Technology, cities and civic networks / edited by Roza Tsagarousianou, Damian Tambini, and Cathy Bryan.
Includes bibliographical references and index.
1. Political participation – Computer network resources. 2. Local area networks (Computer networks). 3. Democracy. 4. Community development, Urban. 5. Community Organization.
I. Tsagarousianou, Roza. II. Tambini, Damian.
III. Bryan, Cathy.
JF799.C93 1998
321.8′0285′468–dc21 97–14243

ISBN 0–415–17134–2 (hbk)
ISBN 0–415–17135–0 (pbk)

Contents

	Figures and tables	vii
	Contributors	viii
	Abbreviations	x
1	**Electronic democracy and the civic networking movement in context** *Cathy Bryan, Roza Tsagarousianou and Damian Tambini*	1
2	**Virtually going places: square-hopping in Amsterdam's Digital City** *Letty Francissen and Kees Brants*	18
3	**Back to the future of democracy? New technologies, civic networks and direct democracy in Greece** *Roza Tsagarousianou*	41
4	**Berlin in the Net: prospects for cyberdemocracy from above and from below** *Oliver Schmidtke*	60
5	**Civic networking and universal rights to connectivity: Bologna** *Damian Tambini*	84
6	**An Internet resource for neighbourhoods** *Ed Schwartz*	110
7	**The First Amendment online: Santa Monica's Public Electronic Network** *Sharon Docter and William H. Dutton*	125

8 Manchester: democratic implications of an economic initiative? 152
Cathy Bryan

9 Electronic democracy and the public sphere: opportunities and challenges 167
Roza Tsagarousianou

Index 179

Figures and tables

FIGURES

2.1	Map of Amsterdam's Digital City	19
2.2	Europa Plein (Europe Square) in Amsterdam's Digital City	27
2.3	User diagram for Amsterdam's Digital City	29
3.1	Homepage of 'Direct Democracy'	50
3.2	Project Pericles: diagram of local authority electronic network	51
5.1	City council connections	92
7.1	Registration and use of PEN (1990–96)	131
7.2	Diagram of the Public Electronic Network (PEN), City of Santa Monica	148

TABLES

4.1	Means of access to the Internet	62
4.2	Internet users by education and occupation	77
5.1	Use of E-mail by IperBolE users	94
5.2	Use of discussion groups by IperBolE users	95
5.3	IperBolE users by age	98
5.4	IperBolE users by gender	99
5.5	IperBolE users by profession	99
5.6	Planned and current services in Bologna's IperBolE project	104
5.7	Universal versus partial cyber citizenship	104
7.1	PEN's menu of information and communication services	130

Contributors

Dr Kees Brants is a member of the Euromedia Research Group and Lecturer at the Department of Communication, University of Amsterdam. His research focuses on communication policy and political communication.

Cathy Bryan completed her first degree in Politics and Parliamentary Studies at the University of Leeds in 1992 and was awarded her second degree, an MA in the Theory and Practice of Human Rights from the University of Essex in 1994. Cathy has worked on a number of projects on a voluntary basis with the civil liberties organisation Liberty. She has previously worked as a researcher for Graham Allen, MP, formerly shadow minister with responsibility for the media and the Information Superhighway, and for the University of Westminster. She is currently employed as a researcher at Informed Sources, a specialist consultancy addressing developments in media and communications technologies.

Sharon Docter (JD, University of California, Los Angeles School of Law, 1988) is a Ph.D. candidate at the Annenberg School for Communication, University of Southern California. She currently serves as a Lecturer in Communication Arts at California Lutheran University in Thousand Oaks, California. Her research concerns the way in which the First Amendment may be applied to the regulation of information and communication technology as well as the degree to which First Amendment considerations have shaped the design of new technologies and policy governing use.

William H. Dutton, Professor at the Annenberg School for Communication at the University of Southern California, Los Angeles, was National Director of the UK's Programme on Information and Communications Technologies while a Visiting Professor at Brunel

University. He is editor of *Information and Communication Technologies – Visions and Realities* (1966) and *Wired Cities* (1987).

Dr Letty Francissen taught until 1996 at the Department of Communication, University of Amsterdam and currently works as a freelance communication researcher. She has published on new media and citizen participation.

Dr Oliver Schmidtke studied political science, sociology and philosophy at Hamburg University, Toronto University and Philipps University, Marburg. He holds a Diploma in Political Science (1991). In 1995 he was research fellow at the European University Institute at Florence and is now a lecturer at Humboldt University, Berlin.

Ed Schwartz is the creator of Neighborhoods Online and founder and President of the Institute for the Study of Civic Values in Philadelphia. He has also served as an at-large member of the Philadelphia City Council (1984–87) and as Philadelphia's Director of Housing and Community Development (1987–92). He holds a Ph.D. in Political Science from Rutgers University and is the author of *NetActivism: How Citizens Use the Internet* (1996).

Damian Tambini is from London. His main research interests are social movements, nationalism and the history of citizenship. He received his Ph.D. in Social and Political Sciences from the European University Institute in Florence in 1996 and he is currently Research Fellow at Humboldt University, Berlin, working on the emergence of social and political citizenship in Britain and Germany. While working on this book he was based at the University of Westminster, London.

Roza Tsagarousianou is Lecturer and Researcher at the Centre for Communication and Information Studies of the University of Westminster. She has a Ph.D. in Sociology from the University of Kent at Canterbury. Her research focuses on the relationship between citizenship, the public sphere and mass communication. She is currently writing a book on this theme, entitled *Civic Landscapes and Public Spaces: Citizenship and Communication in Contemporary Democracies*.

Abbreviations

CAB	Citizens' Advice Bureaux (UK)
CDC	Community Development Corporation (USA)
CMC	computer-mediated communication
ESD	electronic service delivery
ESRC	Economic and Social Research Council
FCC	Federal Communications Commission (USA)
FEFC	Further Education Funding Council (UK)
GED	General Education Diploma
ICT	information and communications technology
IGC	International Global Communications
LETS	Local Exchange Trade System (UK)
MCC	Manchester City Council (UK)
NII	National Information Infrastructure (USA)
NTIA	National Telecommunications Information and Assistance
PICT	Programme on Information and Communication Technologies (UK)
URL	universal resource locator
WWW	World Wide Web

1 Electronic democracy and the civic networking movement in context

Cathy Bryan, Roza Tsagarousianou and Damian Tambini

The urban landscapes – physical and social – of (post-) industrial societies are rapidly transformed as we approach the new millennium. Our making sense of space, time, the social, the political, the urban and the rural, the private and the public are also deeply affected by this whirlwind of change. To a significant extent, the development of communications and informations technologies is central to this transformation and to all the functions that combine to make up contemporary cities (Graham and Marvin, 1996: 2–4).

As far as urban politics are concerned, the transformation of cities into electronic hubs for telecommunications and telematics networks has been coupled with attempts at the grassroots and local or regional authority levels, to introduce versions of 'electronic democracy'. 'Electronic democracy' is a concept with a relatively long history. It has been a central feature of the technological Utopias proposed by scholars, politicians and activists since the 1960s. Today, over a 1,000 towns and cities in the US have homepages on the World Wide Web. More than 200 already have civic networking projects,[1] using networked computers to provide new channels for access to local political information and participation in decision-making. The trend is spreading in Europe now, as public funding is made available for the exploration of the potential of the utilisation of new technologies in civic networking and municipal administration in local government and at the European Union level. In the Netherlands alone, sixty towns have embraced computer-mediated communication (CMC) and have civic networks of some kind. At the European level, the Telecities project has been funded by the EU to enable European local governments to pool resources and experience in the application of information and communications technologies, and every month new projects are launched. Interest in electronic democracy is also growing at the supranational level. Many involved in the European movement view new communications technologies as a way of bypassing sceptical national media and providing EU-related information directly to citizens in the hope of overcoming the 'democratic deficit' of the EU.[2] Civic networking initiatives are not, however, merely government-led; they also have a growing base of grassroots support, particularly in the US. Political parties of all sizes and ideological hues, voluntary organisations, pressure groups and other organisations in civil society are exploring computer-mediated communication as a means not only to reach potential supporters and bypass the traditional media filters, but to network with one another, sharing information and resources. For many, CMC holds the key to the enhancement of the democratic aspects of the political process and to the creation of new opportunities for citizen participation in the local and national political spheres.

The civic networking ideal is linked to a series of interdependent technological, socio-economic and infrastructural developments that have made the turn of the century a moment of particular historical opportunity. The development of increased capacity cabling and satellite telecommunications has led to the convergence of different media (e.g. television and telephony) and to more scope for interactivity. This has sparked the search for new uses for the media and new justifications for public and private investment in them. Coupled with the widespread use of PC networks in economies that are increasingly based on information industries, the new communications context has permitted the proliferation of networks such as the Internet, and the 1990s are witnessing a scramble among media and telecommunications companies for strategic advantages under the new conditions.

While technological innovation alone does not facilitate social and political change, there are certain technological developments upon which the rhetoric of the policy-makers is premised and the hopes of the civic networking movement are founded. These include:

- the digitisation of data, allowing sound, text and images to be transmitted over a single network, thereby eroding boundaries between different types of communication;
- digital compression technologies, allowing greater quantities of these data to be transmitted;
- the introduction of high-capacity networks, both wired (fibre-optic cables, Integrated Services Digital Network or ISDN) and wireless (broadcast satellites, microwave transmission);
- the development of advanced switching technologies, such as Asymmetric Digital Subscriber Loop (ADSL), allowing data to flow

in both directions at high speeds, facilitating high-bandwidth interactive communications;
- the evolution of network transmission protocols, principally those associated with the Internet, allowing new forms of content to be universally received by television and PC users at home and in the office.

These technical changes occur at a time of huge upheaval in the telecommunications and media industries. All national telecommunications providers and all the main public broadcasting companies in Europe are engaged in the dual transitions of privatisation and deregulation. Although national telecommunications providers tend to do well commercially under market conditions, fierce debate rages over the degree to which these private utilities can be expected to provide universal services in the public interest. Public service broadcasting is generally perceived to be in crisis, and the ideals that governed it in the name of the public interest are now also thrown into question. Citizens' rights in the areas of telecommunications and public service broadcasting are replaced with consumer rights, and ideals other than market ones have a minor role in the debates in the press and media. Where other voices are heard, however, the most popular and widespread conviction is that the traditional political communication structures and the old media are failing democracy, and the implication is, somehow, that the new media, properly steered, can provide the solution. Thus, the civic networking movement is driven by two separate forces: those who are looking for a solution to these problems of democracy, and those who are looking for new uses and new markets for new technology.

MEDIA AND THE CRISIS OF POLITICAL PARTICIPATION

In all the Western democracies, voter apathy has been rising steadily in the post-war period. From as early as the 1950s, a series of large-scale voting studies indicated increasing voter indifference or even hostility to politics and found that citizens were often apathetic and uninformed about public issues (cf. Berelson *et al.*, 1954; Campbell *et al.*, 1960; Crozier *et al.*, 1975). This trend has continued and today there are substantial rates of citizen abstention from elections and increasing citizen detachment from politics. Membership of the main mass parties has been in decline, as has the active participation of those members in fundraising and meetings. Commentators have explained this decline in civic engagement in terms of a lack of trust of the main political parties and the break-up of the old class identities that party systems had evolved to reflect.

As party political affiliations become more fluid, voluntary organisations, pressure groups and lobbies attract greater membership. Greenpeace, Amnesty International and the like are fast developing into huge impersonal organisations, in which members have little say or involvement, simply throwing signatures or cheques at causes that seem remote from everyday life. They do little to provide the empowerment, the control or sense of control over local environment and everyday life that politics should provide. Indeed, whereas many in the past conceived of democratisation in terms of the extension of civil and political rights to more and more of the population, the debate more recently has concerned how to get those who do have rights to exercise them or to fulfil their duty to participate in political life. Despite this revival of communitarian and civic republican ideals among intellectuals, apathy seems to be spreading also to local politics, leading to nostalgic calls for a return to community involvement and town meetings.

What are the implications of these developments as far as politics is concerned? How can people forge solidarities and associations in order to debate and improve their lives? Or to reverse the question, why do people appear to be failing to co-operate – with their neighbours, their fellow citizens, with the people who share their economic interests or their vision of a better way of life? There are many answers to this problem; perhaps the most commonly heard is that the key factor is the lack of proper public spaces, of a public sphere not colonised by the state and political parties and not subjected to the logics of commercialisation and commodification prevalent in contemporary Western societies – a public sphere in which citizens could freely engage in deliberation and public debate. Generations of political thinkers have identified these trends of commercialisation, spectacularisation, trivialisation and state colonisation of the public sphere, from members of the Frankfurt School – Horkheimer and Adorno (1979) and more recently Habermas (1989) – through to contemporary media analysts concerned with the impact of the transformation of public service broadcasting at the end of the millennium (Blumler and Gurevich, 1995; Garnham, 1990).

A complex regulatory machinery and a set of delicate rules of genre have moulded existing media systems according, at least in part, to the requirements of democratic communication. Indeed, Blumler and Gurevich (1995), Garnham (1990: 111–114), and others have read current media changes in terms of a concern with the decline of public service broadcasting, which they see as an (albeit imperfect) twentieth-century equivalent of the public sphere, threatened by commercialisation.[3] The regulative ideals of impartiality, public service and universality of access governing public media, they argue, are not safe in the hands of private media. Given the current crisis of public service media and a corresponding expansion of commercial media in most European countries, there is cause for concern about how public service ideals might be protected, and further commercialisation and trivialisation of democratic communication prevented.

James Fishkin has laid the blame for the shallowness of American political debate squarely with the pernicious effects of what he calls the 'soundbite media', calculating that the average time given to a political spokesperson on primetime TV declined from 42 seconds in 1968 to 9 seconds in 1988 (Fishkin 1992). He argues that we already live in an electronic democracy due to the influence of media, and in particular media polling, talk shows and focus groups. He argues that we need to redesign electronic democracy, making it more representative and more deliberative in order to serve democratic ideals. Douglas Kellner (1985) stressed the failure of television to provide the information necessary for public debate in the US in the 1980s and also its role in spectacularising political debate and building a conservative hegemony. He called for media to be used in alternative, and more democratic, ways, a move which, he argues, would necessarily involve regulating for improved public access and accountability.

These writers differ in the details of their diagnosis of the crisis of modern democracies, but share a general premiss that the existing social infrastructure for the support and encouragement of public debate and political action has been severely eroded and undermined. The projects that this book examines hold a related assumption: that by altering the form of communication the content can be changed, and more participation encouraged.

There may, therefore, be a silver lining in the cloud launched by the critics of the media: the media as we know them are passing. Massbroadcast, one-to-many TV is a medium of the past. Newspapers will be replaced by interactive bulletins that we will be able to read and publish from the tops of our desks on the machine that will replace our TV and our PC. New media, and particularly computer-mediated communication, it is hoped, will undo the damage done to politics by the old media. Far from the telescreen dystopias, new media technology hails a rebirth of democratic life. It is envisaged that new public spheres will open up and that technologies will permit social actors to find or forge common political interests. People will actively access information from an infinite, free virtual library rather than receiving half-digested 'programming', and interactive media will institutionalise a right to reply.

THE IDEOLOGY OF THE CIVIC NETWORKING MOVEMENT

Supporters of CMC-based initiatives and activists involved in civic networking argue that not only can the new media be harnessed to reverse the decline of public communication due to commercialisation and bias, but that they offer new possibilities to surpass all that was previously achieved using old media. What are the claims being made for teledemocracy? The following have been isolated as the hopes of the movement:

1 Efficiency and ease of access to information. New media increase the scale and speed of information provision, and give citizens more control over their information diet. Thereby they better arm citizens with the information they need in order to participate (Arterton, 1987: 21). This theme has been taken up by politicians as part of the spirit of public efficiency. In the US, the National Information Infrastructure (NII) Agenda for Action, stresses the provision of easy and equitable access to government information, while in other cases, such as that of Bologna, the civic network was created partly as a response to a new Italian law on the need for transparency in public services.

2 New technology can be harnessed to measure citizens' preferences in representative democracies, and will thus make it easier for citizens to respond, thus making political participation (access to information, deliberation, debate and voting) easier, and thereby resolving the perceived crisis of participation (citizen alienation, abstention and apathy) in liberal democracies. Often implicit rather than developed, this assumption was clearly important in Amsterdam, where the ability to discuss issues with other citizens and communicate with city hall officials without visiting a meeting, telephone or postbox was seen as a virtue in itself. A related hope, therefore, is to empower to the shy, the disabled, and carers, by offering them both a platform for political voice and opportunities for previously impractical access to employment and educational facilities. CMC will include in the process of democratic participation people who are socially disadvantaged, obliged to stay at home or otherwise have little voice.[4]

3 CMC can transform the conditions for collective political action by, for example, creating new organisational possibilities through subject-specific discussion groups, dramatically reduced 'publishing' and communication costs, and so on. This was the aim behind Philadelphia's Neighborhoods-Online, which focused on group rather than individual participation (see also Rheingold, 1995). This will

increase existing tendencies towards the fragmentation and reflexivisation of political movements. New media technologies such as satellite transmission of digitalised data have been deployed by groups seeking to draw attention to their protest activities. In the UK, Greenpeace, Reclaim the Streets and the M11 protesters have used information and communications technology (ICT) in such innovative ways.

4 The Net itself is a metaphor and/or precursor of a new anarchic political community in which traditional political identities linked to territorial and sectional interests are undermined, and new forms of politics emerge free of state coercion. The new communications revolution can lead to more 'horizontal' and less 'vertical' communication. The American magazine *Wired* voiced this hope: 'although originally founded by government . . . the Internet's decentralised co-operative structure has been, ironically, the closest thing to a functioning large-scale anarchist society that human culture has ever seen' (Kinney, 1995: 94). Such an interpretation of the impact of CMC reflects a widespread tendency to conflate communications, society and politics, ignoring the complexity of the relationship between the three.[5]

5 The received wisdom will no longer simply be received. It is more likely to be contested, since the 'audience' and subjects of the information can immediately respond to it, and also because passive reception of information will be replaced by active discovery of it. Interactivity was perhaps the buzzword most often heard in support of the Amsterdam projects, both the Digital City project and the City Talks project that preceded it. The implication is that through interaction enabled by new media, citizens will shape the ideas that shape their city.

6 CMC will bring about the removal of 'distorting' mediators (journalists, parliamentary representatives, even parties) from the process of political communication and decision-making. CMC is more direct, with less scope for political censorship or secrecy. Thus, the 'bias' of the media – i.e., their use to serve the political projects of those who control them, and of other mediators will be eliminated, thereby offering the possibility of more direct representation of citizens' preferences and interests.

7 Efficiency of service provision. New technology offers the possibility of tailoring public services to citizen/consumer needs/desires, using tools such as polling, referenda and forms of public performance review. This resonates with the philosophy of so-called 'new public management'. In the new age of pollster democracy, information

and communications technology will enable politics to take its true place as a form of market research, getting the people what they want, unfettered by distorting ideologies.
8 CMC can solve some of the key problems and dilemmas of representative democracy in practice. This idea, discussed mainly within political theory, uses new computer technology to provide hypothetical responses to what have emerged in the democratic theory literature as problems for the theory and practice of democracy (such as proportional representation, strategic voting, agenda-setting, the territorial basis of constituencies, cycles, etc.) (McLean, 1986).

There are of course a variety of other arguments in favour of civic networking, notably economic ones (Bryan, 1996; Dutton, 1992). Supporters of civic networks are quick to voice the advantages of new media in terms of efficiency and competitiveness of the local economy and so on, and to argue that access to the Information Superhighway, like the right of mobility, should be a universal one. Many explicitly make reference to a broader Habermasian view of the new media as providing hope for a new arena of communication, a new public sphere that can replace the old one now crippled by commodification and fragmentation. The 'Center for Civic Networking', a US advocacy group titles its homepage 'Information Infrastructure: Public Spaces for the 21st Century'.

All the above arguments tend to isolate the new technologies of CMC from their socio-historical context. It is not technological possibility alone that will decide if hopes placed in teledemocracy are to be dashed. What, then, in practice determines the degree to which new CMC technology is harnessed to benefit active citizenship? Are we witnessing a carve-up of new market possibilities by telecommunications service providers and computer firms? An attempt to make the democratic process dependent on their technology? Do the hopes held in electronic democracy simply overestimate the democratic potentials of the technology? Is the degree of political will the determining factor in the future of teledemocracy? Or does the whole utopian hope of teledemocracy misconstrue the current 'crisis of democracy'? This book will offer no hard and fast answers to these questions, but it should at least place them more firmly on the agenda.

THE CONTEXT: POLICY DEBATE ON NEW MEDIA

Such hopes for new media consider the media in an abstract sense, divorced from their socio-political and economic context. As the

Electronic democracy and the civic networking movement 9

introduction of other media in the past have shown, however, cultural context, regulation and economic factors generally blunt our ability to exploit media to the maximum of their potential (de Sola Pool, 1983). In fact, the policy debate on how to regulate new CMC has hardly raised the problem of democratic communication as a separate issue. Discussion has been dominated by metaphors such as 'information infrastructure' and 'Information Superhighway' or slogans, such as 'information society', that are often devoid of content (Sawnhey, 1996). At the same time, the culture of the Internet has infected civic networking with a strange allergy to any form of state regulation (Barbrook, 1996), though some intervention is obviously necessary to guarantee the degree of public service, and universality of access, that civic networks desperately need. In public debate, however, new technology is more often used as a slogan. Ironic, then, that the 'soundbite politics', the evil networkers most want to overcome, itself excludes complex discussions of democratic communication from policy debates on new media.

The term 'Information Superhighway' can be credited to US Vice-President, Al Gore, who coined the phrase in the early 1990s as a piece of political rhetoric to capture the imagination of the US electorate. This is not the first time that technology has been heralded as the bringer of jobs, reviver of industry and saviour of a politician's flagging popularity. In 1963 Harold Wilson told a British Labour Party conference that 'We are redefining and we are re-stating our socialism in terms of the scientific revolution'. Through this scientific revolution industry was to be radically changed, creating an environment which would be inappropriate 'for restrictive trade practices or out-dated methods on either side of industry' (quoted in Butler and Butler, 1994: 272). Developments in cable television in the 1960s promised the possibility of a greater diversity of voices reaching the television screen plus the potential for interactivity. In the 1970s and 1980s the utopian idea of the information city inspired several projects such as the QUBE project in Columbus, USA and Hi-Ovis in Japan (Arterton, 1989: 445). These projects developed out of the combined interests of utopians seeking to rebuild community networks within cities and telecommunications companies seeking to test out fledgling services such as video-on-demand and interactivity.

With the Superhighway rhetoric came a set of policy initiatives including the NII Agenda for Action in September 1993. The Agenda for Action defines the NII as 'a seamless web of communications networks, computers, databases, and consumer electronics that will put vast amounts of information at users' fingertips'. The NII is regarded by the Clinton administration as the blueprint for the Information Superhighway which will 'unleash an information revolution that will change forever the way people live, work, and interact with each other' (United States National Information Infrastructure, 1993: 2).

Taking the example of the UK, where deregulation and privatisation have gone further than elsewhere in Europe, the Programme on Information and Communication Technologies (PICT) was set up in 1994 and funded by the Economic and Social Research Council (ESRC) to bring precision to the term 'Information Superhighway'. The PICT group decided that the government's definition, articulated in the House of Commons Trade and Industry Select Committee report, provided a generally acceptable basis from which to explore the concept, which it conceived as 'a broadband telecommunications service with the ability to carry enormous quantities of information at high speed; the capacity for two-way (interactive) communication; and the ability to deliver any media, including video, audio and text' (House of Commons Trade and Industry Committee, 1994).

In addition to this, the PICT paper suggests three further characteristics which could be expected from a national Information Superhighway. The first of these is 'seamless interconnection' and the second, that the highway will be a network of networks. The onus will therefore be on fast, digital switching to keep information moving through the network with as few hold-ups as possible. The third incorporates a notion of an 'open environment' whereby the regulatory framework should ensure that the network of networks allows for competition in the provision of services to business and domestic consumers. If these conditions were met, the infrastructure would indeed be in place for civic networks to move beyond their current stage of experimentation and take a more central place in democratic communication.

Yet what has become increasingly apparent is that the money and the political will to build such a network is less in evidence. Little has been said by Tony Blair since the announcement of his deal with BT at the 1995 Labour Party conference. This deal, in which BT pledged to install fibre-optic cable to every school and hospital in the UK in return for the lifting of the 'asymmetry' rules which prevent them from using their network for the provision of entertainment services while allowing cable television companies to push their services on the back of telephony, is hardly the stuff of revolutions.

The National Heritage Committee began its report on the future of the BBC with the words The media revolution is nigh!, explaining that

the world stands on the threshold of an extraordinary technological revolution. The box in the corner of the living room, for forty years or so the source of a limited choice of entertainment, will not only provide an almost unlimited quantity of entertainment but will also become, for millions, the workplace, the shopping centre, perhaps eventually even the polling booth.

(National Heritage Committee, 1993: v)

In the same way that the white heat of technology was to forge a new set of relations between employers and workers, thereby redirecting the Labour government's intractable problems of industrial relations policy, the Information Superhighway is being used to circumvent the policy problematic of media ownership restrictions. Convergence is a convenient concept for policy-makers unable to decide how to regulate media industries. By arguing that current restrictions are anachronistic in the light of technological developments, high-profile media professionals such as Michael Grade can argue for the abolition of all restrictions on ownership. The recent government proposals (HMSO, 1995) for reform of the media ownership regulations has accepted the argument for treating the media industry as a single cake, and the Labour Party has also made informal indications that this is the way their policy will evolve.

The EU's Information Society project shares, at least at the level of rhetoric, many of the democratic aims of the civic networking movement. In February 1995 the Economic and Social Committee of the EU published an 'Opinion on Europe's Way to the Information Society. An Action Plan' (European Commission, 1995), drawing on and developing the recommendations in the Bangemann report entitled 'Europe and the Global Information Society'. The main thrust of both documents is that infrastructures should be liberalised, 'with public service obligations shared out among all operators offering services to the public'. The desire to create a regulatory framework that permits a competitive environment led to the publication of the Green Paper on the liberalisation of infrastructure (COM(94)440 final), which set 1 January 1998 as the target date for the completion of telecommunications liberalisation across Europe. Other goals, including the social and political changes which Blair and Gore had picked up on, have not escaped the attention of European policy-makers, and a recent statement by the EU's high-level group of experts, 'First Reflections Report', states that 'The Information Society should be about people. We must put people in charge of the information, rather than it being used to control them.'

Discussions of civic uses of new interactive media have not, however, been adequately linked to these concerns, for several reasons. First, decision-making in the field of science and technology has been historically, and remains less democratic than other types of policy-making (Sclove, 1995). The technical nature of policy formulation in this area continues to exclude many lay people from engaging with the issues at hand. While policy areas such as defence, transport, health and education are the subject of the critique and influence of numerous highly organised pressure groups, often deploying the language of human rights and civil liberties to argue on behalf of the public interest, there has until recently been no similar entry point for lay people with opinions on scientific or technical matters. The growth of organisations such as the Campaign for Civic Networking and the Electronic Frontier Foundation in the US have introduced civil libertarian issues into the Superhighway debate and are attempting to provide an organisational impetus for public interest. This fledgling movement is constrained by its own preoccupation with the Internet – using E-mail as a lobbying device and conducting online discussions which have little resonance with the wider public or the political elite, and, as the contributions to this book show, have little adequate conception of the needs of democratic communication in the new media age.

Second, these policy initiatives, while utilising the language of democracy, have not been based upon a body of academic research from which critical theories of cyberdemocracy might evolve. The lack of an intellectual critique of the democratic claims being made for new technologies stems in part from the lack of empirical studies upon which to found this debate and upon a related failure of the academic community to acknowledge that this is an area worthy of their sustained attention. As a result of this neglect, political discourse around democracy and new media demonstrates a naive attempt to transpose existing concepts, such as 'universal service' or 'public interest broadcasting', into this new environment. Indeed, a revised formula for universal service has yet to be defined by US regulator the Federal Communications Commission (FCC) following the enactment of the Telecommunications Act in February 1996. The existence of high-bandwidth capability has been taken to imply interactivity and greater two-way communication. Initial research, however, suggests that information traffic flow on high-bandwidth networks is skewed toward downstream movement. Trade Unions, voluntary organisations and political parties use the Internet to send information, rather than receive it, implying that it is a monologue not a dialogue which is being facilitated by technological developments.

Third, the technological developments outlined above are taking place in a distinct political atmosphere, where government control of the organisations which develop and roll out these technologies is no longer accepted as the most efficient control structure. The investment required to keep up with what is perceived to be an increasingly rapid set of technological developments is beyond the purse of most governments. Monetarist economic thinking, with its emphasis on strict control of public expenditure, dictates that it should be private capital which funds these developments.

The revisiting of debates on civic networking and electronic democracy, the emerging of hopes for democracy similar to those of the 1960s and 1970s, albeit within a new terminological framework, suggests that a critical investigation of the empirical basis for the claims of advocates of electronic democracy, such as that undertaken by the contributors to this volume, is a necessary and valuable exercise.

Our research suggests that civic networking will not realise its objectives unless it becomes more realistic in its goals and methods. Most of the hopes expressed by activists are unrealisable without fundamental changes in the way communications technologies are regulated, and many depend on local conditions of public access and political culture. The culture of civic networking, due particularly to its relationship to the culture of the Internet, tends to reject any form of regulation or intervention, and amounts to a refusal to allow regulation for organised 'public'- (i.e., not market-) oriented uses of this technology.

Beneath the metaphors that shape the broader debate, some more concrete aspects of media policy are also under discussion. It is important to understand the wider political and economic context in which these proposals have evolved and the combined and, in some cases, conflicting demands of international competitiveness, competing domestic interests and the perceived need for democratic regeneration which have influenced the funding and support for these local projects.

In what ways is the national policy setting important to these city initiatives? Generally, national politicians can create as well as respond to media interest, and the policy climate will affect the media reception of local initiatives. More specifically, initiatives such as those featured in *Cyberdemocracy* rely heavily upon centrally approved funding. Not, as a rule, part of a distinct and structured national policy, many of the initiatives are hybrids: neither truly voluntary in nature nor firmly enmeshed within a state-sponsored framework. Projects with more secure long-term funding, such as that in Bologna, are the exception rather than the rule and raise the question of whether a more nation-wide approach needs be taken to regulate emerging civic networks. This means that the long-term objectives of each initiative can appear to lack clarity as the implementation of explicit long-term objectives is at the mercy of external funding sources. Leaving aside the broader question of infrastructure which we have just discussed, the national and supranational policy context impinges on the civic networks in two main areas: content regulation and universal/public service.

Free speech is central to the civic networking movement's hopes, but governments and regulators are wary that new communications technologies may be used for the publication of terrorist literature, hate speech and pornography, as well as libellous or copyright-infringing materials. While the balance between competing freedoms has always proved difficult to strike, with the requirements of national security, public morality and law and order pitted against the demands of sexual difference, political dissent and diversity, the digitalisation of information undermines many of the legislative tools which are currently in place. To this end policy-makers have been debating how to protect citizens from subversive, pornographic or otherwise offensive material in the digital environment, with most emphasis placed on the protection of children. This legislation will also govern civic networks where they compete as public Internet providers. The legal battles which will define these issues have already begun, as we read in the next chapter, on Amsterdam. In 1996 the European Commission adopted a Green Paper on the protection of minors and human dignity in the electronic and information media, and drew up a communication outlining measures that might be taken to fight against harmful and illegal information on the Internet. The aim of the Green Paper is to create a framework for self-regulation and to harmonise existing national legislation, rather than imposing new legislation in this area. The communication is similarly focused on the need for practical measures to combat the circulation of criminal material on the Internet. Some of the practices regarded as problematic include the ability of servers to offer anonymous addresses for Internet users and the problem of encryption. The Bangemann report seems to favour a system that would enable users to choose what they wanted to see, to use filters, and in which the industry should establish its own code of conduct as a means of stemming illegal works.

A second complex issue is that of the inadequacy of the existing principles of public service and universal access as mechanisms for ensuring a degree of parity in the calibre of information/communication service received and the ability to use and pay for that information or service. Just as the hopes of the civic networking movement no doubt increase with every new home connected, a simultaneous concern grows among representatives of the poor that an information underclass is being created. The deregulation and privatisation of the telecommunications sector across Europe and the US has led to the birth of many new telephony providers and broadcasters. Some argue that this competition will reduce costs for everyone, but others fear the development of a two-tier system. There is already some evidence that this is taking place – a number of Internet access providers are giving customers a choice of paying a higher monthly Internet connection fee in return for guaranteed high-speed brown-out free Internet access. Even the Internet has a fast lane and a slow lane. The question of access is critical to the hopes of the civic networking movement, because, if certain groups either cannot or simply do not participate in the electronic public sphere – women, the poor, etc. – ICTs will mirror problems of old media – i.e., exclusion.

The hopes of the civic networking movement thus rely upon a conviction that the means of taking part in communication of a civic or political nature are at the disposal of all those that want to make use of them. Aside from the issue of 'wanting' to take part and the factors influencing the desire to participate, the ability to make use of new technologies will be constrained primarily by availability and cost of services. At the pre-convergence stage, two main principles could be found in both Europe and the US – that of universal access to telecommunications networks and of a state-supported public service function for television.

It is apparent that the norms governing the development of telecommunications policy underwent a rapid and profound change in the 1980s and, while the technological developments outlined above are no doubt critical to this development, it would be overly simplistic to attribute such a paradigmatic shift simply to technological change. Paradigm changes in other policy areas, such as education and welfare provision, reflect a similar ideological approach to the provision of formerly public goods. The burden of fulfilling obligations entailed by the implementation of citizens' rights is proving too onerous a task even for nominally left-wing administrations to sustain. In the UK, the use of citizens' charters employing the language of consumer rights rather than that of citizenship is indicative of this shift in what is perceived by the state to be the just returns for an individual's loyalty and obedience. Within this context the liberalisation of telecommunications, which is taking place throughout Europe, the US and, less rapidly, but none the less steadily throughout much of the developing and developed worlds, is part of a wider political and economic trend.

Government policies in the area of telecommunications provision, including the development of the communications infrastructure and the control of pricing and provision of services via this infrastructure, have traditionally been governed by notions of public interest. The privatisation of telecommunications pays tribute to the principle of public interest, and its political proponents argue that competition is the most efficient method of meeting criteria such as freedom of communication and opportunity to derive equally social and economic benefits – but the accusation has been levelled that it is material gain in the form of profits for telecommunications companies rather than public interest incentives which are driving these policy changes (Garnham, 1990). Civic networking advocates and activists, therefore, need to take account of the broader picture. The initiatives covered in our study have tried to take advantage of what they perceive to be a moment of historical opportunity. It is too early for us to try to judge whether or not they have been successful – but what follows are a series of detailed reports of how they have set about achieving their goals, the obstacles they have faced and the reactions they have met from users and observers.

NOTES

1 For listings of civic networking projects see the documents of the Center for Civic Networking (http://www.civic.net:2401/ccm.html); the listings of Community Computer Networks and Free-Net Websites (http://www.freenet.victoria.bc.ca.freenets.html).
2 See for example 'Rewiring Democracy', a pamphlet put out by Maclennan Ward Research Ltd, with a foreword by Alan Donnelly, MEP.
3 'I want to argue that . . . changes in media structure and media policy, whether these stem from economic developments or from public intervention, are properly political questions of as much importance as the question of whether or not to introduce proportional representation, of relations between local and national government, . . . that the policy of western European governments towards cable TV and satellite broadcasting is as important as their attitude towards the development of a United Europe; . . . that political scientists and citizens concerned with the health and future of democracy neglect these issues at their peril' (Garnham, 1990: 104).
4 See Mary S. Furlong, 'An Electronic Community for Older Adults: The SeniorNet Network', *Journal of Communication*, 39 (3): 145–153. According to N. Negroponte, '30% of all Americans over 70 have a PC' (interview in *International Herald Tribune*, 14 March 1996).
5 According to Williams, for example, 'the political order of nations is being rapidly transformed from the written document and spoken word to an electronic communications network enveloping everyone. The new political order is the communications structure' (quoted in Arterton, 1989: 439).

REFERENCES

Arterton, C. (1987) *Teledemocracy: Can Technology Protect Democracy?*, London and New York: Sage.
—— (1989) 'Teledemocracy: Reconsidered', pp. 438–450 in T. Forester (ed.)

Computers in the Human Context: Information Technology, Productivity and People, Oxford: Blackwell.
Barbrook, R. (1996) Media Freedom, London: Pluto Press.
Berelson, B. et al. (1954) Voting, Chicago: University of Chicago Press.
Blumler, J. and M. Gurevich (1995) The Crisis of Public Communication, London and New York: Routledge.
Bryan, C. (1996) 'Manchester: Democratic Implications of an Economic Initiative?', Javnost, III (1): 103–116.
Butler, D. and G. Butler (1994) British Political Facts 1900–1994, Basingstoke: Macmillan (seventh edition).
Campbell, A. et al. (1960) The American Voter, New York: John Wiley.
Crozier, M. et al. (eds) (1975) The Crisis of Democracy, New York: New York University Press.
Dutton, W.H. (1992) 'Political Science Research on Teledemocracy', Social Science Computer Review, 10 (4): 505–523.
European Commission (1995): 'Action Plan on the Liberalization of the Telecommunications Infrastructure' (Com (94) 347 final).
—— (1996) 'Green Paper on the Liberalization of the Telecommunications Infrastructure' (Com (94) 440 final).
Fishkin, J. (1992) 'Talk of the Tube: How to get Teledemocracy Right', The American Prospect, Fall (11): 46–52.
Garnham, N. (1990) 'The Media and the Public Sphere', pp. 104–114 in N. Garnham (ed.) Capitalism and Communication: Global Culture and the Economics of Information, London and Newbury Park, CA: Sage.
Graham, S. and S. Marvin (1996) Telecommunications and the City: Electronic Spaces, Urban Places, London: Routledge.
Habermas, J. (1989) The Structural Transformation of the Public Sphere, Cambridge: Polity.
Horkheimer, M. and T. Adorno (1979) Dialectic of Enlightenment, London: New Left Books.
HMSO (1995) Media Ownership: The Government's Proposals (Cm 2872), London: HMSO.
House of Commons Trade and Industry Committee (1994) Optical Fibre Networks, London: HMSO.
Kellner, D. (1985) 'Public Access Television: Alternative Views', Radical Science Journal, 16.
Kinney, J. (1995) '"Anarcho-Emergentist Republicans"', Wired (September): 94.
McLean, I. (1986) 'Mechanisms for Democracy', in D. Held and C. Pollitt (eds) New Forms of Democracy, London: Sage.
National Heritage Committee (1993) The Future of the BBC, Second Report: Volume 1, London: HMSO.
Rheingold, H. (1995) The Virtual Community, London: Minerva.
Sawhney, H.S. (1996) 'Information Superhighway: Metaphors as Midwives', unpublished paper, May.
Sclove, R. (1995) Democracy and Technology, London: The Guildford Press.
de Sola Pool, I. (1983) Technologies of Freedom, Cambridge, MA and London: Harvard University Press.
United States National Information Infrastructure (1993) 'Agenda for Action', version 1.0, Washington, DC (September).

2 Virtually going places
Square-hopping in Amsterdam's Digital City

Letty Francissen and Kees Brants

Next to the dykes, the polders below sea level, the picturesque houses on the quiet canals and the images of farmers and fishermen in traditional costumes and wooden shoes, a second Netherlands is springing up. It is a virtual Netherlands, not built on poles in sandy soil, but constructed with bytes and digits, up in the air. Some seventy Digital Cities now exist, more or less advanced sites on the Internet with some 100,000 inhabitants and many more visitors. And the number is still growing.

The virtual communities vary in size – from the Digital Island in the (real) village of Urk, which, at the moment, has only visitors and no inhabitants, to Amsterdam's Digital City, which claims a population of more than 40,000 and thousands of visitors per day. The cities and villages also differ in the kinds of services they provide. In some, via a fancy graphic interface, users can collect and produce information, participate in discussions and debates, send electronic mail all over the world or build their own houses. But most of the cities are small and simple, with only one-way streets in which to collect information from the city council or the local tourist office. Many of these smaller villages function merely as annexes and subsidiaries of the local town hall and they lack proper funding to set up the infrastructure necessary to really go interactive.

The Digital City of Amsterdam (De Digitale Stad) can be seen as the capital of the new virtual Netherlands; not only because it was the first such community when it started in January 1994 and has since remained the largest and most popular, it was also an example and adviser to the other cities when they began their experiment and a 'Godfather' to some of the Digital Cities abroad when it advised in the organisational set-up of the ones in Berlin and Antwerp. Moreover, Amsterdam's Digital City seems to attract so many computer and software whizzkids that it is always one step ahead of the others.

Technically speaking, the Digital City is a computer connected to a

Figure 2.1 Map of Amsterdam's Digital City

world-wide network, a site on the Internet comparable to the FreeNets in the US. The city metaphor was chosen to create both a recognisable and true-to-life frame of reference and an applicable and user-friendly interface. The concept is simple: the virtual city is based on the features of an ordinary one. For the information providers there are different theme-based squares, serving as meeting places for people interested in particular themes (see Figure 2.1). There is, for example, an environmental square, a news square, a health square, a book square and a gay square, each with eight buildings occupied by thematic information providers. The users can, like real citizens, build 'houses' between the octagonal 'squares', homepages containing personal or other information. In the 'public spaces' of the squares and in bars discussions take place on a wide range of topics. The metaphor has, in short, become both really virtual and virtually real.

The Digital City presents itself as a pilot project for the Electronic Highway, in which the outlines of the future 'digital society' are becoming visible. It began as a grassroots initiative, an interactive answer to a growing gap between politics and the public. It hoped to turn politics upside down; not only politicians telling the electorate what they have decided and gaining support by explaining and persuading, but citizens telling them what is on their mind and what to do: a return to an Athenian style of direct democracy, only this time electronic. In its relatively short existence it is, however, developing into much more than an electronic medium that provides easy access to government-held information at the local and the national level, and to that of social organisations and of citizens' groups. It seeks to educate us and prepare us for the computer-based information society, contribute to the speed of Amsterdam's economic development and at the same time create new channels for discussion and the shaping of opinion.

In this chapter we will try to distinguish fact from fiction, heaven from hype, so to speak, in a sketch of the aims, services and development of the Digital City of Amsterdam.[1] We will evaluate the actual practice, access and participation in the light of its objectives while putting its claims and output in the wider context of what has been called a new public sphere.

A SHORT HISTORY OF THE FUTURE

The context in which the Digital City started was one of gloom and even desperation. At the 1990 local elections, less than two-thirds of the national electorate and no more than 50 per cent of Amsterdammers voted. This downward trend was confirmed the next year when a mere

43 per cent of the Amsterdammers showed up for the provincial elections. In fact, these elections were considered to show a more general, longer existing and at the same time growing gap between politics and the public. More proof for this assessment was found in the, seemingly contradictory, support for extreme right-wing, anti-system parties on the one hand and a decline of party membership in favour of single-issue (notably environmental) movements on the other.

According to Frissen (1996: 128) this development is the result of a 'democratic paradox': the parliamentary system, open to individual articulations and claims, creates high expectations which it can only modestly fulfil because its finances are limited and it has to address the general and not the individual interest, and thus must compromise. No wonder there is widespread cynicism towards vested politics and politicians; the local political system in particular, in spite of its apparent proximity to the people, is considered inaccessible. All these developments have coincided, since the fall of the Berlin wall, with the diminishing importance of political ideologies as the 'cement' of society and growing fragmentation and individualisation of the public.

In this democratic 'darkness', the interactive potential of new multimedia were seen as the proverbial light at the end of the tunnel. It should be noted that the Netherlands likes to see itself as a European forerunner in the field of telematics. As one of the most densely cabled countries (90 per cent), with a computer in almost every other house, a modem in one in twelve, and a traditionally strong, R&D-focused electronics industry (Philips), there has been a government tradition of technology push, expecting this to trigger a demand pull. With a strong knowledge-based industry and still-growing service sector, information is considered an important economic resource. The most recent (1995) illustration of this is the investment by the Ministry of Economic Affairs of Dfl 70 million to position the Netherlands as the electronic 'gateway to Europe' and to get a million Dutch users connected to the Electronic Highway by 1997 (Bekker, 1996). In this telematic euphoria, Amsterdam sees itself as the centre, as this would profit the city both economically and culturally. This vision, combined with a Social Democratic mayor with a political science background, a Centre-Left municipality that not only worried about the growing gap between politics and citizens but also believed that technology is there for the people and that its use should thus be democratised, has formed the breeding ground for two experiments with local electronic democracy that were initiated by the local municipality (for more details and discussion see Brants, Huizenga and van Meerten, 1996).

The so-called City Talks (*Stadsgesprekken*) were a series of live discussion programmes on 'hot' issues on the local public-access TV channel, with a limited form of two-way communication. In the City Talks politicians and representatives of non-political organisations discussed a chosen topic (drugs, crime, housing) while the home audience could get extra background information via teletext and react to the opinions voiced (through telephone when the experiments started in 1989, later via computers in public places). These reactions were then put to the discussants and included in the debate, while the viewers could also vote for certain statements or policy options. It was a politics-initiated form of input democracy, with wants and desires articulated bottom-up, but most of those involved were not really happy with the way things went. Politicians complained that they did not get enough space to make their point, while citizens were dissatisfied with the lack of political consequences, which the politicians in turn explained by pointing to the non-representativity of the participants.

The City Consultations (*Stadsberaad*) were designed by the municipality in 1993 as a sort of interactive electronic questionnaire accessible via interactive teletext (combined with telephone) and first tested on the budget allocation of a sub-local authority. Inhabitants were asked to give their opinions and preferences and were then 'led' through the whole decision-making process in the form of 'choice trees'. They could rank options and preferences and be confronted with the result of specific choices. After being shown the outcome of the decision-making process and comparing them with choices of others, the respondent could revise his or her own. Ideally, city councillors would take stock of the outcome, but the technology was not yet up to fulfilling all the expectations of the participants. After one more experiment, which attracted only a few hundred participants, the City Consultations were aborted.

It was in this combination of political panic, electronic optimism and actual experimenting with interactive communication that, in early 1994 the Digital City was launched. It was inspired by the FreeNets in the US and Canada but the timing coincided with forthcoming local elections. Contrary to the other Amsterdam experiments, this was a bottom-up initiative, started by an independent political-cultural centre, De Balie, and the Hacktic Network Foundation (now called XS4ALL), a group of former computer activists. Originally, the Digital City of Amsterdam was set up as a ten-week experiment, aimed at providing a new forum for political debate at future local elections. In the first year the city council and the Ministries of Home and Economic Affairs supported the initiative with Dfl 600,000 (US$ 350,000).

The initiators of the Digital City more or less copied the basic principles and aims of the FreeNets and expanded the idea by creating the city metaphor. In their application for subsidy from the local authority they formulated a whole range of objectives. They saw that multiple aims could be achieved and in a way many of the aims were prompted by this new medium, but they had to be further developed by the prospective users, as the Digital City had to be built by its inhabitants and not by its initiators. The Digital City had in mind:

- to initiate and stimulate public debate between citizens and between citizens and local government in electronic discussion groups;
- to create a platform for distributing (local) government information as well as administrative and public information;
- to assist and support citizens and social organisations in order for them to offer their information electronically and to participate in telematics projects;
- to stimulate debate about citizens rights and their obligations on the Electronic Highway and to look after the interests of consumers;
- to advise on the development of community information services;
- to provide opportunities for and connections between new projects and information providers, nationally and internationally;
- to develop instruments (such as graphical interfaces, help-desks and user manuals) enabling users access to all kinds of information services;
- to maintain and expand contacts with international community networks.

The success of the Digital City of Amsterdam was evident from day one. Widespread media attention placed it in the spotlight and immediately scores of people tried to find their way in, creating long traffic jams. The original twenty modem lines were insufficient and even the hastily laid extra telephone lines could only slightly diminish the congestion created by some 1,700 daily 'visits'. In the first ten weeks of its existence, the Digital City registered 13,000 inhabitants and over 100,000 visits.[2] Early research indicated that the users were mainly young, male, well educated and politically aware. As the majority were either students, private sector employees or civil servants, entry to the City was often sought at the university or at work, be it initially 'just to look around' (Schalken and Tops, 1994).

The immediate success and euphoria made stopping after the planned ten-week trial virtually impossible. In mid-1994 the organisation began to work towards a more permanent structure and shortly afterwards the new Digital City version 2.0 was unveiled, integrating text, pictures and sound, using the World Wide Web standard. In January 1995 the initiators founded their own Digital Foundation, which took over legal responsibility from De Balie. The objectives became more specific, but certainly no less ambitious. They were idealistically formulated as a tri-functionality aiming at democratic, innovative and economic success.

First, the Digital City wanted to stimulate democratic processes and participation in order to arrive at a well-balanced electronic community. Everyone wishing to take part in the economic, political and cultural potential created by the Electronic Highway should be able to do so. The development of the public domain in the electronic society is considered vitally important for the furtherance of democracy and for economic development.

Second, the Digital City wanted to contribute to the development and dissemination of knowledge. As part of the Internet, it participates in its research, both to further Internet development and to share information with users. New technical possibilities and expertise should be handed over to citizens, project partners, providers of services, community organisations and other digital cities in the Netherlands and in Europe.

Finally, the Digital City wanted to fulfil a platform function for product development in small- and medium-sized companies in order to strengthen the regional economic structure. As globalisation and technological development threaten employment and social cohesion, organisations like the Digital City should indirectly aid people to look for new possibilities and services. The Electronic Highway represents such an opportunity.

These aims, which point to a trend of more information and service provision without abandoning the ideal of interactive debate, are also the basis of the third and most recent version of the Digital City (3.0), introduced in June 1995.

CITY LIFE

To explain how the Digital City works, we will begin by describing the technological infrastructure that lays at the heart of the city plan. Next, there are two kinds of inhabitants: the information providers who 'work', so to speak, from the buildings on the different squares, and the information seekers, who 'live' in houses and hop from square to square, enter buildings in search of information or chat in the cafés and discussion groups.

A technical excursion

One of the main concerns of town planners in general and cybertown planners in particular, is the building of an appropriate infrastructure. In general, the infrastructure of a Digital City consists of one or more servers (computers), modems (for access through normal telephone lines), portmasters (connected to the server while bringing all the incoming telephone lines together), routers (connecting the Digital City to the Internet), hired telephone lines and terminal servers (Schalken and Flint, 1995). The terminal servers are used to control the server and program the software to operate the system. Finally, there must be an agreement with an Internet provider who connects the City to the rest of the Internet.

The Digital City of Amsterdam started with one server (a SUN-clone), a Unix operating system, twenty modem lines, a portmaster, a router, the infrastructure of the Internet provider XS4ALL and practically no terminal servers of its own. They were borrowed from De Balie, or were private property of two employees or the volunteers. At the end of 1996, the Digital City ran on six powerful servers (e.g. a SUN-Sparc 1000 and a SUN Ultra Sparc 170), which are placed at two different locations in Amsterdam. There are over thirty modem lines and the Digital City Foundation has now around ten terminal servers.

The infrastructure here described is, to keep up the city metaphor, nothing more than a building site with a network of roads and pavements, but without traffic rules and traffic. The users being the traffic, rules are found in a computer operating system telling what can be done and what not and showing the way. For that, an advanced software program is necessary.

The Digital City and its inhabitants could hardly keep up with the rapid development of the software. The first version of the City was based upon the software program Freeport, which was available on the Internet. It was used as a basis to connect several Internet protocols, such as 'Telnet', 'Gopher' and 'ftp'. In this way, the programmers of the Digital City created their own software. Initially, the City provided information and communication in a text-based environment (version 1.0). Soon after the start it became clear that Freeport was not sufficient for all the functions the initiators had in mind and it also failed in providing a minimum security of privacy. Therefore, in October 1994, the step was made to the World Wide Web (WWW) and version 2.0 of the City was presented. Those with the required hard- and software could now visit a city in which text, sound and moving pictures were integrated. Again, the City's programmers adjusted the WWW software to their goals and objectives. For those lacking the necessary hard- and software, the text version of the Digital City was still available. Although the second version offered many new possibilities, there were still limits to the communication opportunities. For instance, it was not possible to provide two-way communication traffic within the Web. So, in order to communicate, one had to leave the WWW-environment temporarily. These limitations called for the development of the third version of the Digital City, which started in early 1995. It is based upon the latest techniques of the Internet, whereby information and communication functions are integrated. The software for this interface was largely designed by the programers of the Digital City. The development will not end here, as work on the design of a three-dimensional city has already begun. If it ever gets off the ground, a text version will still be available, albeit as a sort of anachronism.

WORKING IN THE CITY

Looking at the participation in and use of the Digital City of Amsterdam, the initial success of the ten-week experiment did not die down. Both with information seekers and information providers we see a sharp increase, resulting in a total City population comparable to a mid-size Dutch city. Since 1995 a whole range of new services has been developed. In the early days, by entering the City the user was offered a limited menu with, for example, a post office, central station, library, public forum, town hall, and so on. People could collect information, have access to the Internet, send and receive electronic mail, and participate in discussions. Access was also provided to the administrative information system BISA, formerly exclusively reserved for municipal employees and politicians, and the public information system PIGA, previously only for municipal press officers.

As part of the 'economic development' aim, small- and medium-sized businesses have been stimulated to open sites in the City and advertise cheaply. Because of the poor 'visibility' of the original city plan, not many businesses enrolled. That changed with the third version, which improved the city metaphor and accessibility considerably. The 1996 plan of the City consists of thirty-one squares, each with its own theme, i.e., a sports square, a tourist information square, a news square, several cultural squares, political squares and Internet-related squares, a travel square, an environment square, and so on. There is a Europa square, where the Dutch bureau of the European Commission 'sells' integration of the European Union while at the same time stimulating discussions on its form and problematics.

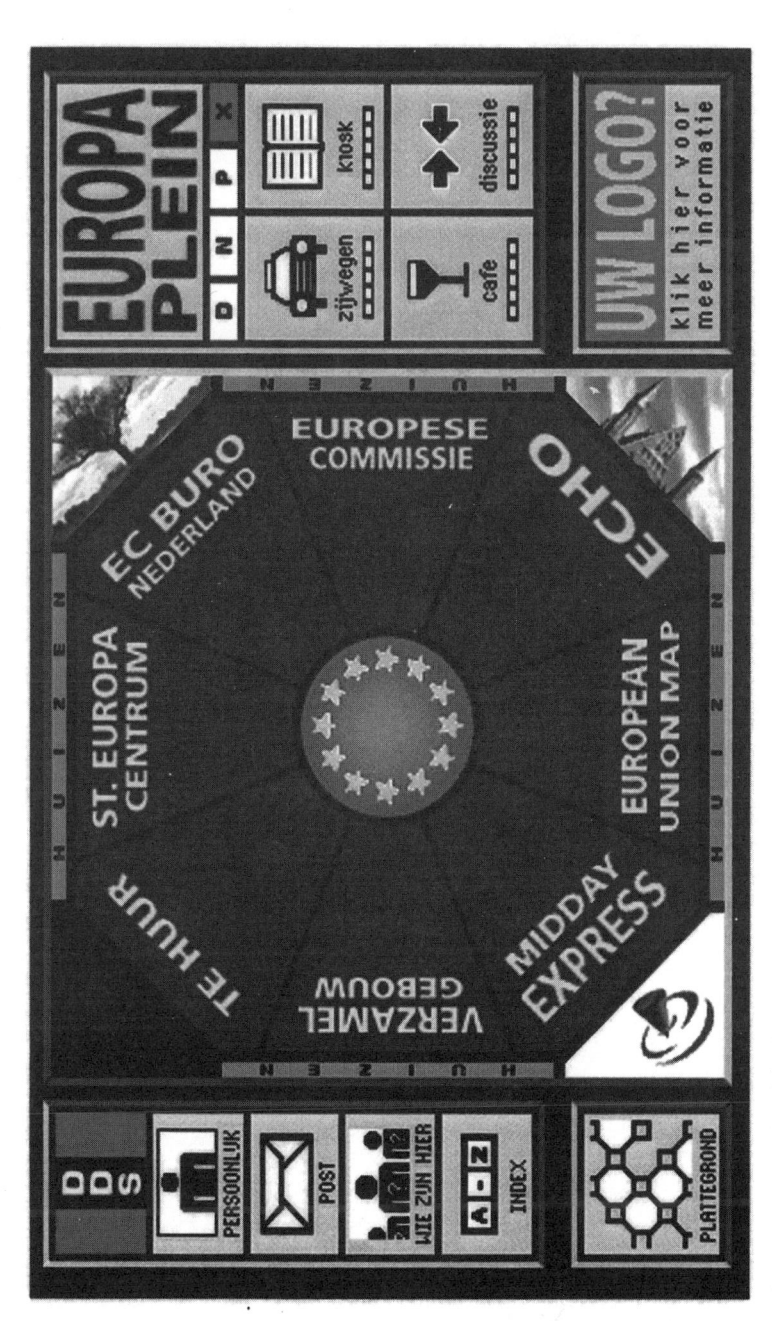

Figure 2.2 Europa Plein (Europe Square) in Amsterdam's Digital City

Each square has eight buildings that can be rented by businesses, non-profit organisations and government or municipal departments and institutions (see Figure 2.2). On the education square, for example, there is a building (BVE site) where teachers can find and add to a knowledge data-base. This so-called BVE-Net was developed by the City as part of its contribution to the development and dissemination of knowledge and supported by the Ministry of Education. One of the eight buildings on a square is an assembly building where smaller organisations can rent flats. Organisations can also obtain temporary buildings for conferences or exhibitions. A billboard or webvertisement (from US$200–$1,750) for the businesses or organisations adds to the visibility of the (paying) information providers. The initial cost of a building (of 10-MB disk space) is around US$235 with a monthly rent of around US$175 (including E-mail and Internet visibility). The assembly building is cheaper, with a monthly rent of around US$30 per flat.

The squares fulfil the role of meeting-places for like-minded people to gather specific information or chat in the special bar. They can also visit a kiosk with information on square-related literature available via the Internet, one or more discussion groups on the square's theme, or take a side road via a hyperlink for information on theme-related places elsewhere on the Internet. The architecture of the square is completed with extra click-functions for calls and announcements, personal mail and information on who else is in the square at that moment. There are several extras for the paying information providers, like more search functions, statistical information on visitors to their building or flat, survey possibilities and the ability to close your building to 'outsiders'. In spite of these gadgets, the number of commercial information providers is only slowly growing, despite the popularity of opening up commercial sites on the Internet. At the end of 1996 there were about 200 information providers, of which the majority were non-profit making (see Figure 2.3). Most squares are to be found around cultural (with separate books, art, film and music squares), travel and political themes.

Living in the City

The users of the Digital City spend most of their time searching for information on the buildings in the different squares. They live, so to speak, outside. To support the 'democratic process' aim, potential participation of the citizens was improved in the second and extended in the third version of the Digital City. Registered inhabitants can now

Virtually going places: Amsterdam

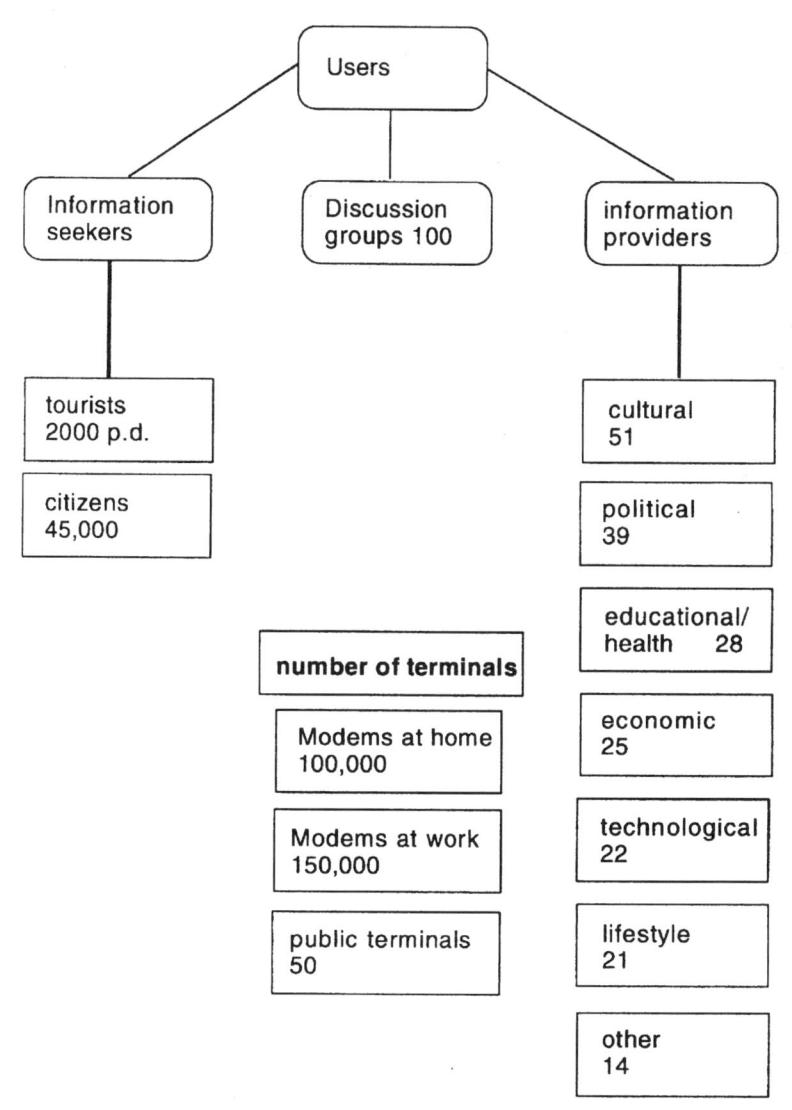

```
                              Users
                ┌───────────────┼───────────────┐
        Information        Discussion       information
        seekers            groups 100       providers
            │                                   │
    ┌───────┤                           ┌───────┼───────┐
  tourists                            cultural
  2000 p.d.                              51
  citizens                            political
  45,000                                 39
                                      educational/
                    number of terminals  health  28
                    Modems at home    economic
                    100,000              25
                    Modems at work    technological
                    150,000              22
                    public terminals  lifestyle
                    50                   21
                                      other
                                        14
```

Figure 2.3 User diagram for Amsterdam's Digital City

build 'houses' between the squares, Websites or homepages with information, personal stories, hyperlinks to other Websites, etc. Information citizens can offer has two limits: no advertising and no pornography. There is one place where citizens have their own rules: the metro or underground, initiated by one of the original hackers, further developed by the citizens and more and more leading a life of its own. What began as a game has grown so large and opaque that even the City programers have difficulties finding their way.

The population of the real Amsterdam is hardly growing any more; the Digital City, however, is proliferating as never before (see Figure 2.3). Every day between 100 and 200 new citizens register (free of charge; in contrast to the information providers, inhabitants pay no subscription), bringing the mid-1996 total to around 45,000.[3] On average, they enter the City once a week, according to the City 'authorities', while 2,000 non-registered 'tourists' pay a visit every day, bringing the total of entries to over 8,000 per day. Judging from a regular check of who is in the City, this seems a very optimistic estimate; half that number would probably be more realistic. A quarter of a million 'pages' are consulted every week; more than three-quarters of these, however, are visited by people who live outside Amsterdam (Beckers, in print). It is not known, however, whether the 4,000 to 8,000 visits are made by different people or by a much smaller number of, say, political activists or cyber-enthusiasts.

What is known about the users comes from two successive surveys in 1994 and 1996 with voluntary questionnaires added onto the main menu of the City. It is unlikely that the representative respondents (1,197 and 1,300, respectively) are truly representative and it is not known whether visitors (inhabitants and tourists) have filled in questionnaires more than once. But, with these reservations in mind, an initial user profile is emerging. In the experimental period in 1994 the picture of the City visitor was more or less similar to that of the FreeNets in the US and Canada: he was male (91 per cent), young (73 per cent under 35 years old), well-educated (almost half were university graduates or students) and, if not studying, with a good job, politically aware (77 per cent) and using the City mainly for 'browsing', the Internet and E-mail or to chat in the (then only one) café (Schalken and Tops, 1994).

In two years the population did not change much, although the number of female visitors to the Digital City rose in 1996 to 16 per cent and the inhabitants get younger and younger: 71 per cent were under 30 in 1996. The users are still politically aware, well-educated, with more than half still following a further education; 3 per cent are unemployed (Beckers, in print). This profile of the inhabitant of what could well be called a student city is hardly the picture of the average Amsterdammer. The population of Amsterdam is more or less equally divided between the sexes (365,000 are female and 352,000 male) and across the age range, has on average a considerably lower level of education than the inhabitants of the Digital City. The average Amsterdammer also stands a fair chance of being unemployed (20 per cent), especially if he is young and from an ethnic minority (32 per cent of the population), nor is he much interested in party politics (Jaarboek Amsterdam, 1995). But then, half the inhabitants come from outside Amsterdam.

Compared to the rest of the Netherlands, however, another survey shows that the Amsterdammer has good access to the Internet or the Digital City. Of the Amsterdam population 13 per cent say they sometimes visit the latter and 30 per cent the former. According to the municipal statistical office an amazing 27 per cent of the Amsterdammers (193,000, equally divided between the sexes) claim to have a computer with modem at home and 39 per cent (280,000) say they have them at work (O+S Omnibus 40, 1996). Looking at the profile of the average Amsterdammer, a modem in every two households is highly unlikely. Although most computers and modems in the Netherlands are indeed to be found in the capital, 100,000 and 150,000, respectively, would be more realistic.

Access to the Digital City for those with no modems at work or at home, was made possible in the beginning by a few dozens public terminals, placed in municipal buildings, public libraries and homes for the elderly. The maintenance, however, was poor, and with the elderly in particular the terminals stood mostly idle. Early in 1996, some ten public terminals were left, turning access to Digital City and other interactive channels into an elitist affair and specifically denying access to minorities, the unemployed and women (at home) who are said to profit from public terminals (Collins-Jarvis, 1993). Realising the painful contradiction with its own aims, the local government at the end of 1996 decided to subsidise some forty new terminals which, after application, will be placed in similar and more public places. In co-operation with the PTT, several have now (mid-1997) been placed next to public telephone booths.

Talking in the City

The City's inhabitants can also visit and participate in the discussion groups on the different squares. Originally, the groups on computer technology, art and culture had a larger and more active participation than those on specific political issues, strengthening suspicion that the Digital City was more a playground for computer fanatics than an Athenian-style agora for a new democracy. The discussions on the Internet, technology and computers, however, deal in part with democratic use, unequal participation and how to improve that. At the end of

1996 there were more than 100 discussion groups, sometimes very small, sometimes 'sleeping'. The majority were based on travel, countries and cultural themes, while City- and Internet-related issues were still strongly present. A categorisation looks something like this: one-third of the discussion groups are on cultural and lifestyle themes, one-third leisure, one-fifth civic issues (including local politics) and one-eighth on the City and the Internet.

On average, there are about ten large groups, with more than ten regular participants, the majority City-related with a civic 'undertone'. In 1996, for example, the European Movement Netherlands started a discussion on the EMU with political parties both contributing and reacting to other participants. Discussions can be lively, intense and substantial, as with the 'multicultural city and racism' discussion group which sprung up in 1994 after a participant announced that he would vote for an extreme right-wing party (Centrum Democraten). The discussion lasted for several weeks and covered government policies on migration, personal experiences and emotional statements (Brants *et al.*, 1996: 242).

Sometimes heated discussions tend to trigger so-called 'flame wars', whereby unwelcome views or participants are 'burnt away' by verbal and/or technological means. A still rarely applied way of controlling these debates and at the same time shunning the unwelcome or the superfluous and allowing for a plurality of views, is the use of a 'moderator'. This balancing act is not unproblematic, as is shown in the case of a government-initiated debate on a report with proposals on how to use technology in communications between government and citizens (BIOS-3, 1995).

High on the Dutch government's agenda is the implementation of instruction projects in the public sector that make use of information technology. In the BIOS-plan itself this is judged a way to improve the client-orientation of public services and thereby enhance the democratic awareness of citizens and increase the transparency of government. The BIOS-3 report got its own 'room' in the virtual government building on the political square of the Digital City and inhabitants were asked to read and discuss it over a period of two months. A hundred and fifty people registered and some fifty participated actively (only three of them women). Government and party political participation was minimal, which resulted more in citizens discussing with each other than with politicians.

The Ministry of Home Affairs asked the Digital City to appoint a moderator and the board in the end appointed one of its members. Although the evaluation report is written by the moderator himself

(Ministerie van Binnenlandse Zaken, 1995), what he says about his role proves its problematic character. All contributions to the debate first entered his mail-box; he decided which ones were relevant or asked participants to be clearer or more to the point. After only two days he felt he had to introduce a form of 'netiquette', as the electronic discussions showed signs of *ad hominem* arguments so familiar in flame wars. Critical reactions to his restricting role prompted others to ask for elimination of these kinds of criticisms. Both participants and the moderator in his report expressed the need for (and at the same time see the practical impossibility of) detailed and reasonable criteria for moderating the content of the debate, which should be made clear at the outset (ibid.: 16–17).

ORGANISING THE UNORGANISABLE

Contrary to the associational structure of the FreeNets in the US, where members regularly elect supervisory boards, the organisation of the Digital City is surprisingly undemocratic and the decision-making structure rather opaque. But although citizens sometimes protest over decisions taken and discuss the level of democracy in town, the structure itself is hardly challenged (Schalken and Moorman, 1995: 249). What began as an experimental, grassroots initiative has turned into a substantial, self-supporting, non-profit organisation, with a paid staff of sixteen, several freelancers and numerous volunteers, all of whom divide their work and attention between the clients, citizens and R&D issues. The tri-functionality, and particularly the focus on client services, is said to necessitate a more professional organisation that need not consult everyone on every occasion.

Because of the experimental character and the limited time-span it was planned for, the organisation of the City was never a big issue. The initiators, Hactick (XS4ALL) volunteers and Balie employees shared an enthusiasm for the interactive potential of the Internet and worried more about hard- and software and the funding of these, than about organisational structure. The initiators were, moreover, located in different parts of Amsterdam.

The first year's subsidy was used to set up the experiment technically. After the subsidy stopped – for the municipality and the government because they only wanted to contribute to the initial costs and for the City because they wanted to be independent from politics – more attention was paid to the organisation. In spite of the grassroots philosophy of 'bottom-up' democratic procedures, a foundation structure was chosen with a supervisory board and a paid staff. The supervisory board, which governs from a distance, consists of one member appointed by De Balie, one by XS4ALL, one representing the local municipality and/or industry, one the social and/or cultural groups in Amsterdam and one the new media and/or technology policy. Apart from the first two members, appointments are by co-optation and not via nomination. There are plans to limit the composition of the board to members of the last three categories. Representatives of the Digital Citizens are conspicuously absent, but according to the Articles of the Digital City Foundation, they have someone in an advisory council which is chosen and appointed by the supervisory board. Other members of this council include representatives of the government, institutions, business, social and cultural organisations, employees and volunteers. However, it does not exist. The advisory council never got beyond the Articles.

The City's staff in a way, form an executive board – although the name does not do justice to the ideally flat structure of the organisation. This board consists of all sixteen paid employees, more or less headed by a coordinating manager and assisted by coordinators for complaints and external contacts, and the running of the office. The rest of the staff are involved in system operating, research, software development and general assistance. The manager, sometimes referred to as the mayor of the City, is responsible for policy and – as there is no clear decision-taking structure nor regular staff meetings – generally has a final say in decisions with regard to allowing new providers, setting up projects, closing down accounts, etc. In a way, he oversees the anarchistic organisation of a, by definition, anarchistic medium. On an irregular basis 'quarterly' reports are published on the Net and live meetings with citizens are organised.

With the professionalisation of the organisation, the emphasis and activities also change. Where, traditionally, the democratic aim was at the forefront, client-orientation and economic aims have become more important. The major source of income is service to businesses and organisations: renting out disk space, Internet advice, designing of homepages, income of which, in the first half of 1996, half was spent on overheads in service provision, one-third on community services and the rest on innovation. In the future the City wants its activities to be less interdependent, by making the users more responsible for the organisation of community services and by combining forces with external partners for further innovations. The relation with local and national governments has changed too. The original partners and subsidy providers have become clients who pay for buildings and squares, for special projects and technical and other assistance. This is problematic

Virtually going places: Amsterdam 35

for the City, as governments discover also other service providers who have entered the market and the Digital City finds itself in a real market situation competing for clients/consumers. According to its 1996 policy plan, the future of the City lies in innovative projects (the implementation of a professional data-base, experimenting with 3D, experiments with electronic banking), in making the City more accessible for foreigners (by providing an English language navigation structure) and in extending the democratic aim (terminals in libraries, Internet via the cable, experiments whereby citizens can experiment in their houses with audio and video). In all, one can distinguish a slight shift from the traditional democratic ideals towards innovation and more commercial thinking.

ISSUES AND PROBLEMS

The development of the Digital City did not only provide new opportunities for participation and democracy, it also posed new problems and raised new issues, particularly in the discussion groups. Some of these issues have to do with the generally unorganised, even anarchistic, nature of the Internet and are thus not unfamiliar outside the City too. What binds them is that they touch on questions of freedom and control.

A first issue, however, is the potential gap the rapid development threatens to create between what is technically possible and what is actually demanded. Since its start in early 1994, the interface of the City has already undergone three metamorphoses, from a text version to a very advanced WWW version, while 3D is lurking around the corner. On the one hand, the research of the whizzkids is contributing to a more user-friendly interface and enlarges the possibilities and development of the Internet as a whole; there is no future for experiments like the Digital City without pioneering research. On the other hand, the enthusiasm of the initiators runs the risk of turning the City into a playground for software developers who spend more time behind their electronic drawing-boards than they do listening to users' needs and technical limitations. The text version of the City is still available, but to be 'with it' and to make use of everything that is available and possible, the citizen will have to spend more and more money on stronger computers, or get left behind. What is technically possible might well get in the way of what is (notably in the City's own aims) socially desirable.

The second issue is of a legal nature. Actions by a German prosecutor in 1995 resulting in CompuServe denying access to all newsgroups with the prefix 'sex', and the telecommunications content regulation in the 1996 US Communications Decency Act, have pointed to what some consider a moral panic over the difficulty in controlling the Internet (Brants, 1996). The legally complicated question is whether access providers can be held responsible for the origination or nature of the content on the Internet. The Digital City is in the midst of controversies over this issue as well (be it that pornography is not so much the problem), and so far they have been given the benefit of the doubt. In a law suit in March 1996 by the Church of Scientology over supposed copyright violation in putting Church documents on the net, the president of the District Court of The Hague in summary proceedings decided that access providers like Digital City cannot 'influence or even know what others, whom they allow access to the Internet, propagate or publish' and that they can thus not be held accountable (Visser, 1996). The Minister of Justice, however, has stated that if they are aware or could reasonably be expected to be aware of criminal offences being committed, providers *are* responsible. A case with regard to alleged racism in one of the City's discussion groups, 'dds.multcult', is still in the hands of the prosecutor.

What these examples show is the specificity of legal problems in the Netherlands: copyright and racism, not pornography, are the problems. The rule not to allow pornography on the homepage of citizens has been introduced merely for practical reasons: such sites tend to create traffic jams in the system. The proverbial Dutch tolerance (which, it should be noted, borders on pragmatism and indifference) seems to have its effect on 'netiquette' as well. On the whole, freedom of expression and self-regulation is the starting-point and basic philosophy, partly out of fear of triggering the sort of actions regulations try to control. Originally, the City refused to take action against racism in discussions on the grounds that the discussion groups are considered to be a public domain where people can freely debate with each other. Complaints should be dealt with by participants themselves, assisted, if necessary, by City officials. There is an emerging discussion about the pros and cons of discussion moderators and who might appoint such persons, but a definite decision is still far off. Moreover, a Digital Citizens' movement is supporting – and in a way lobbying against any attempt to restrict – the unregulated, non-hierarchical and free exchange of opinions.

But however much they are open to contention, the City has introduced certain 'rules of the game'. More than in discussion groups, in some of the cafés racism and particularly sexism have been virulent and the board has (on average some fifteen times per year) blocked the accounts of certain citizens, often on the grounds that these discussants use false identities. A controllable name and address is now a first prerequisite for a (free) account. Refusing entry to the City has to be reasoned and openly reported, and citizens can vote on whether they want to turn back the decision, except when the City is legally liable.

It is our impression that, thus far, 'netiquette' is a minor issue and 'flaming' more the exception than the rule. This has probably to do with Dutch tolerance as well as with the tradition of consensual politics known as 'pillarisation', which dominated the Netherlands until the 1970s and which was famous for suppressing controversies and seeking compromises. To put it differently: City inhabitants seem to be able and willing to combine tolerance with self-control; note also the actual absence of moderators in discussion groups. Even the limited discussion on the role of the moderator in the BIOS-3 debate gives the impression of being fed more by intellectual irritation over paternalism than a matter of principle, let alone legal concern over restricting freedom of speech.

TOWARDS A NEW PUBLIC DOMAIN?

The Digital City started shortly before the 1994 local elections, in reaction to what was considered to be a growing gap between politics and the public. In political discourse (with little empirical evidence of a trend, however) the citizen was increasingly pictured as a cynic who considered the political system inaccessible for claims, ideas and debate and the politician incapable and only interested in his or her own wellbeing. In a way, the need of the population for interactive new media was postulated. Not being inhibited by time and space, with low thresholds and (because of their asynchronous character) with more room for reflexivity, consultation and consideration, they were seen as the remedy for local democracy in a mid-life crisis. How, then, is one to assess this new city in the light of the aims it has set for itself, the political context which triggered it and the place it is claiming as a new public domain?

The Digital City wanted, first, to enhance democratic processes and participation in order to arrive at a truly balanced electronic community. Its success within weeks is remarkable, given the generally slow acceptance of new electronic media, and it points to a – not yet clear – mixture of curiosity and need. The latter seems to have the upper hand as the population is growing, both in 'ordinary' citizens and in information providers. Access as a first prerequisite for participation is improved by a user-friendly interface and the (re)instalment of terminals in public places. But where the City has attracted a new generation which has extended the notion of 'the political', the majority of the inhabitants is already blessed with political efficacy and knows his or her way into the decision-making arena. In spite of an increase in women users, it is still a gendered medium, as well as a class- and ethnically divided one. However, discussions about the lack of representativity and low participation – notably by politicians who originally hailed the new medium as the cure for an ailing democracy – reflect the expectation that citizens be (party) political animals and remain interested as long as information is provided. As this is certainly not the case with the population of any city or country, one not only creates an in-built disappointment, but also confuses the issue of the democratic level of the Digital City.

The city metaphor and the actual building of 'houses' has enhanced the freedom of expression by turning citizens into information providers themselves and in that sense has contributed to the second aim of developing and disseminating knowledge. The growing number of both squares and buildings, and daily visits, point to a mutual need for knowledge sharing. Moreover, the City board and programers have assisted in setting up educational sites and have shared their expertise with newcomers both nationally and internationally. But where the software allows for advanced visual information and is user-friendly, the cost of hardware and data traffic goes up simultaneously. In relation to the democratic process, local government has become more transparent with the provision of access to the administrative and public information systems. In spite of the first aim, the risk here might well be a deepening of the democratic paradox: advanced interactivity gives the impression that more claims can be placed on the political agenda, that they are taken seriously and are, ideally, seen to. But dramatically increasing the claims made on a financially limited political system not only threatens to overload the system, but could also create an in-built disappointment for citizens, which in turn breeds cynicism. Besides, transparency which turns politics into a glass house makes politicians wary and the public suspicious.

Third, the Digital City wanted to contribute to the economic development of Amsterdam in general and to that of small- and medium-sized businesses in particular. Technical support has been given in developing attractive interfaces for business sites, but for the Digital City this was as much a part of their knowledge-sharing philosophy as it was prompted by the sheer necessity of generating income. Without proper empirical or economic research it is hard to assess what the contribution to the local economy has been. Certainly, a number of businesses have opened up buildings and received visitors, but the other side of the coin is that being less dependent on government subsidies has made the City more dependent on information providers' money.

So, is the Digital City an example of what Dahlgren (1991) has called the emergence of dynamic alternative public spheres, next to those of the corporate state and the existing mass media? There is no clear-cut answer to this question. The City seems to have the capacity to function as a community network, an audio-visual space where temporary communities can discuss certain themes as part of an existing local community. But its voluntary nature is both its strength and its weakness: everyone is free to participate, but no one is committed to the outcome. Further, the democratic aim and the non-hierarchical, 'bottom-up' structure of the City contrast heavily with its undemocratic, co-optation-based and opaque organisational and decision-making structure. The lack of a strict 'netiquette', however, points to a general acceptance of and a pragmatic approach of this set up: the City works, so to speak, and its population is generally happy.

The urban metaphor has presented a recognisable frame of reference which might well strengthen the idea of community. The discussion groups on the provider squares may be non-committal and debates in the cafés sometimes clouded by discriminatory contributions, but at least they are a means of attaching people to the City. In that sense, they form an Athenian-style agora, the marketplace where people come both for the purchase of goods and the exchange of ideas. On the other hand, the metaphor might also strengthen the cacophony of city noises, the compartmentalisation of debate and the fragmentation of social reality; and thus add to the loneliness of the square-hopper or, in the worst case, to agoraphobia.

NOTES

1 Unless otherwise indicated, information about the Digital City is based on their own official documents, board meeting reports, their regular news 'flashes', the virtual magazine *De Digitale Stedeling* and interviews with two City 'officials'.
2 The exact number of visitors is not known, as logging in as a 'tourist' is anonymous and can be done more than once.
3 Officially more than 50,000 are registered, but in practice only 80 per cent of these are active. If one enters less than once every two months, one loses one's citizenship.

REFERENCES

Beckers, D. (in print) *Digital Communications: Use and Users of the Amsterdam Digital City*, Amsterdam: University of Amsterdam Press.

Bekker, V. (1996) 'The Playground of the Electronic Superhighway', pp. 9–27 in V. Bekkers *et al. Emerging Electronic Highways*, The Hague: Kluwer Law International.

BIOS-3 (1995) Ministerie van Buitenlandse Zaken, *Terug naar de Toekomst. Over het Gebruik van Informatie en Informatie- en Communicatietechnologie in de Openbare Sector*, Beleidsplan Informatievoorziening Openbare Sector No. 3, The Hague.

Brants, K. (1996) 'Policing Democracy: Communication Freedom in the Age of Internet', *Javnost/The Public*, 3 (1): 57–71.

Brants, K., M. Huizenga and R. van Meerten (1996) 'The New Canals of Amsterdam: An Exercise in Local Electronic Democracy', *Media, Culture & Society*, 18 (2): 233–247.

Collins-Jarvis, L. (1993) 'Gender Representation in an Electronic City Hall: Female Adoption of Santa Monica's PEN System', *Journal of Broadcasting & Electronic Media*, Winter: 49–65.

Dahlgren, P. (1991) 'Introduction', pp. 1–27 in P. Dahlgren and C. Sparks (eds) *Communication and Citizenship*, London: Routledge.

Frissen, P. (1996) *De Virtuele Staat. Politiek, Bestuur, Technologie: Een Postmodern Verhaal*, Schoonhoven: Academic Service.

Jaarboek 1995 Amsterdam in Cijfers, Amsterdam: Het Amsterdams Bureau voor Onderzoek en Statistiek, 1996.

Ministerie van Binnenlandse Zaken (1995) *Eén Maand Binnenlandse Zaken Discussie @ Internet*, Verslag van een door de Digitale Stad georganiseerde discussie op het Internet over Beleidsnota Informatiebeleid Openbare Sector 3 'Terug naar de toekomst'. Den Haag: Ministerie van Binnenlandse Zaken.

O+S Omnibus 40 (1996), *Bureau Stadspas*, Projectnr. 6767. Het Amsterdams Bureau voor Onderzoek en Statistiek.

Schalken, K. and J. Flint (1995) *Handboek Digitale Steden*, Amsterdam: Stichting De Digitale Stad.

Schalken, K. and M. Moorman (1995) 'De Digitale Steden', pp. 225–277 in Rathenau Instituut, *Toeval of Noodzaak? Geschiedenis van de Overheidsbemoeienis met de Informatievoorziening*, Amsterdam: Otto Cramwinkel Uitgever.

Schalken, K. and P. Tops (1994) 'The Digital City. A Study into the Backgrounds and Opinions of its Residents', paper presented at the Canadian Community Networks Conference, 15-17 August, Carleton University, Ottawa, Canada.

Visser, D. (1996) 'Op de provider rust geen vergewissingsplicht', *Mediaforum*, 8 (4): 61–63.

3 Back to the future of democracy?

New technologies, civic networks and direct democracy in Greece

Roza Tsagarousianou

For over a decade, policy-makers, academics and other social commentators have been debating about existence (or not) of a link between the application of information and communications technology and democracy. Although there seems to have developed a consensus regarding the significance of ICT, there is still a deep divide between the *apocalittici* (cf. Abramson, Arterton and Orren, 1988; Arterton, 1987) and the *integrati* (cf. Barber, 1984; Toffler, 1980), to borrow the terms that Umberto Eco (1964) has used in his discussion of the mass media.

It would be fair to say that the application of ICT in the political process is characterised by ambiguity: it is well documented that governments and private organisations have been using ICT as a means of control and surveillance, extending from the cases of fraud detection, storage and exchange of criminal and financial records to those of political surveillance and control (Gandy, 1994). However, this stored and shared information within the confines of political and economic organisations has been available and accessible to a small number of government and private enterprise employees while the citizens have only exceptionally had access to it. However, during the late 1980s, ICT has been seen increasingly as having the capacity to provide solutions to the growing alienation of the citizenries of advanced industrial societies and has been featuring in demands or proposals for democratisation and reinvigoration of their public spheres. Although public awareness of the potential of ICT was supported by the high-profile embrace of the new technologies by such political figures as Al Gore, Bill Clinton, Newt Gingrich and, to a lesser extent, by the European Union Commission, at the forefront of this shift in the envisaged uses of ICT have been a number of American local government authorities (Glendale, Pasadena, Santa Monica) which sought primarily to improve citizen–local authority contact, delivery of services and, in the longer term to encourage citizen participation in public affairs, a process which can be traced back to the mid-1980s (Dutton and Guthrie, 1991; Guthrie and Dutton, 1992). Similarly, since the early 1990s a number of European local authorities (Amsterdam, Bologna, Manchester) rather than central governments have been engaged in experiments in electronic democracy, often arguing that their embracing of ICTs will resuscitate the declining citizen participation in political life and will give new vigour to local politics.

Among other European attempts to introduce versions of electronic democracy at the level of local government, a rather ambitious project was launched in Greece in 1992 which eventually culminated in the development of a pilot programme of application of ICTs in the political process. This project was Network Pericles, a communications network developed by a team of researchers based at the Communication and Media Laboratory of the National Technical University of Athens, comprising a number of local authorities in Greece, France and Cyprus and partly funded by the European Union MED-URBS programme.

Like other electronic democracy projects, the aim of Network Pericles is to enable citizens to participate directly to the political process of their local authority or region. In addition, although its initial implementation is located at the local authority level, in theory at least, local or regional networks can be linked with each other and form larger networks used by larger constituencies; the program's creators do not discount the possibility of citizens' participation through an enlarged network to the political process of nation-states and even larger entities, such as the European Union.

In a nutshell, according to its creators, Network Pericles is intended to develop and utilise the technological infrastructure that could support and enhance the democratic process. The network has been designed to improve citizens' access to information related to the political process, to help sustain, expand and organise forms of direct political action, such as the launching of citizens' initiatives, referenda and processes of deliberation, and to enable authorities to consult citizens on policy issues and therefore to reinvigorate local democracy. However, unlike other electronic democracy projects, Network Pericles is a network dedicated to the needs of local democracy; it has been conceived as an instrument of political debate and political action alone and it is not envisaged to be a medium of delivery of any other municipal service. What is more, although its creators have not ruled out the possibility, Network Pericles is not linked to the Internet or any other public network and has been designed specifically for the purposes of provision and exchange of public information, debate and voting. As a result of this particular combination of deliberative and plebiscitary functions, it is therefore doubtful if one can draw generalisable conclusions out of an evaluation of Network Pericles, as the relationship between computer-mediated communication and the political process in the former is markedly different from that in other electronic democracy projects.[1] Indeed, as, I hope, will be demonstrated later in this chapter, it is possibly this difference that has affected Network Pericles's process of implementation and realisation, as it presents, or is perceived to present, a challenge to established perceptions and the practice of politics. The aim of this chapter therefore, is not to arrive at generalisable conclusions regarding the application of ICT in local democracy but to assess the merits and shortcomings of a specific case, that of Network Pericles and, more precisely,

- to examine the underlying assumptions of this project regarding the role of new technologies in enhancing democracy and in changing political culture and reversing the trend towards political apathy among the citizenry;
- to situate the project within the current debate regarding citizenship and the public sphere in contemporary (post-)industrial societies.

NETWORK PERICLES: SOME BACKGROUND INFORMATION

Although Network Pericles has not been intended to be an 'exclusively' Greek experiment in electronic democracy,[2] it could be argued that its conception has been influenced by the socio-political conditions in Greece and the debate about the present and future of the democratic process there. Although increasing citizen alienation and disillusionment with the political process have been quite common phenomena in most contemporary democracies, their manifestations in Greek political life have been influenced by a number of factors specific to the political process and political culture in Greece. As this is not the place to refer to these extensively, I will only briefly mention some aspects which I would think are pertinent to the discussion that will follow.

The tradition of *clientelism*, prevalent in Greek politics since the establishment of the Greek state in the 1830s, has consistently subverted and undermined the liberal democratic institutions of the state while, combined with the domination of political parties over political and social life (akin to the phenomenon of *partitocrazia* in Italy), it has discouraged citizens' autonomy and the development of a democratic public sphere and perpetuated the weakness of civil society and grassroots activism in Greek society (Tsagarousianou, 1994: 334–337).

Related to these features of Greek political life, the colonisation of the public sphere by the state and mainstream political parties and private capital has led to a situation in which the only alternative to state/governing party domination of the publicly owned/controlled mass media has been the private media which are, of course, tightly controlled by their owners (Tsagarousianou, 1993).[3]

Whereas voter apathy and citizen alienation have been endemic features of most Western democracies, including Greece, since the 1950s (cf. Berelson *et al.*, 1954; Campbell *et al.*, 1960; Crozier *et al.*, 1975) the expression of political cynicism and disillusionment by ever-increasing numbers of the electorate has been a relatively recent phenomenon in Greek society, as in many other Western European and North American societies. This negative attitude towards politics has been expressed in the rapidly decreasing voter turnout in elections in a country where voting is supposedly compulsory, as well as in public opinion surveys (Mavrogordatos *et al.*, 1988).

It was against this background of increasing political cynicism and disillusionment that Network Pericles was conceived in 1992 by a team of researchers at the National Technical University of Athens. According to Giorgos Kambourakis and Marios Nottas, the leading members of the Network Pericles team, the main reasons for the initiative were what the team members considered to be inherent problems of representative democracy, namely:

- the difficulty of developing a decision-making process that would be responsive to the demands of the electorate due to the size of the latter in contemporary Western societies in general and in Greece in paricular;
- the alienation of the citizen that this entails.

TECHNOLOGY, DEMOCRACY AND COMMUNICATION

As members of the research team have emphasised on several occasions, the Network was designed for exclusively political use; what is more, unlike the case of the Internet or those of other applications of telecommunications and information technology projects where the necessary and relevant technological infrastructure had more or less been already available prior to its specific uses, Network Pericles developed as a result of a political/communicative proposal regarding the enhancement of the democratic process (NTUA, n.d.). It was only after the elaboration of this that the issue of the necessary technology for the realisation of this proposal was explored in detail. The initial research team made a decision to approach specialists in social, political and

Back to the future of democracy? 45

urban issues for their input in the research project and its eventual implementation and, as a result, it was enlarged in order to comprise expertise not only in technological and communications issues, but also in social and political aspects of the project.

Currently, the team includes specialists in information, communications, media management, political communication and representatives of the Ελληνικο Κεντρο Επικοινωνιας (Greek Communications Centre). In addition, the NTUA team has been liaising with Greek and other European Union local authorities, grassroots movements and pressure groups campaigning for direct democracy and ecological pressure groups in order to get advice on issues of common concern and keep them informed of developments. One forum of such social and political organisations in which the advantages and disadvantages of Network Pericles were discussed has already taken place in Delphi and further meetings are planned. The research team has also links with hardware and software developers such as IBM, UNISYS and BULL, as the latter are involved in the design of the hardware and software for the network.

It should, however, be stressed that the concept of Network Pericles has not been the product of widespread social demands or grassroots pressure for the utilisation of CMC in the political process or for the introduction of an element of direct democracy in the Greek, or even other European political systems, nor has it been initiated by local authorities or other public bodies related to the political process. In this sense, the project did not stem out of public debate or concern but was rather the product of a small group of intellectuals and scientists committed to exploring ways to enhance citizenship and the democratic process. The Network Pericles project has, however, been embraced by a small number of municipalities, initially, and, more recently, by the municipality of Athens, the largest local authority in Greece, which is currently using its lobbying and negotiating power in search of further funding from the European Union.

NETWORK PERICLES AND ELECTRONIC DEMOCRACY

The very name of the network, 'Pericles', is indicative of the political model the research team drew upon in the process of conceptualising democracy and visualising its electronic dimension – the Athenian version of direct democracy, associated with the prominent Athenian citizen and politician Pericles. Athenian democracy, premised on a 'notion of an active, involved citizenry in a process of self-government' (Held, 1987: 18), was marked by its distinctive emphasis on the principle of civic virtue whereby citizens were primarily public beings engaged in the institution of a common life (Habermas, 1989; Held, 1987). Indeed, according to the members of the Communication and Media Laboratory of the National Technical University of Athens (NTUA), the creation of Network Pericles does not merely constitute an attempt to implement and test direct democracy in the political process of a number of European municipalities and communes through the use of communications and information technology. It is quite clear that the network aspires to support and resuscitate several of the distinguishing aspects of its classical model, such as direct citizen participation, maintenance of a public sphere and marginalisation of the possible privatising/individualising effects of CMC.

One of the most significant (in terms of citizens' ability to influence the decision-making process) mode of interaction between user/citizen and the local authority is electronic voting. The Network Pericles project enables citizens to register their electronic vote, thus communicating their views on specific issues to their local authority. The network team members argue that, even when voting cannot be binding, the network offers a unique opportunity for the authorities or for citizens to get a clear indication of citizens' opinions on specific issues. This, in their opinion, is a much better and more accurate option than an opinion poll, which is often based on a limited number of respondents. In principle, through the network, citizens are able to engage in three main forms of political decision-making, namely:

Citizens' initiatives, that is, the submission for debate and voting of specific motions by citizens. Such motions (subject to being seconded by a sufficient number of citizens) are automatically entered in the list of issues which are to be decided by vote. The authorities will not be able to sanction or restrict these citizens' initiatives once they determine the percentage of citizens required to second a motion in order for it to be included in the list of issues to be decided by vote. This is considered one of the elements of the network that give it its distinct identity. As Giorgos Kambourakis pointed out 'the ability of the citizen to propose a motion which is then automatically registered for voting is the nodal point of the network; without it there is no network' (Kambourakis, 1995).

Referenda (either binding or consultative). Citizens are able to express their opinion on motions submitted by other citizens (see above) or put to the electorate by the authorities.

Recall, that is, the corrective action of the electorate whereby a previous decision (referring to persons or processes) is annulled. Therefore,

Back to the future of democracy? 47

citizens are in a position to correct, amend or annul previous decisions regarding their preferred course of action with regard to a specific matter or to the election of public officials.

Thus, by participating in the decision-making process, the citizen has the ability to express her/his choice regarding issues that

- have been proposed for consideration by the municipal authority;
- have been proposed by citizens and seconded by a sufficient number of citizens;
- are proposed by the system and refer to use-related issues (e.g. different layout of lists, bigger letter characters to be displayed etc.).

However, the network is not exclusively voting-oriented. The decision-making process is supported by two other main functions of the network: provision of information on the issues for which a vote has been called and provision of facilities for teleconferencing, or citizen conferencing, as it is referred to in the relevant literature. The user of the network is given equal space and time with other interested parties to argue their case regarding issues to be decided by vote, is given unrestricted access to the arguments and information pertinent to a vote to be taken and, more importantly, can register her/his electronic vote. The research team point out that the network is clearly distinct from other teledemocracy networks in that, unlike other systems of electronic democracy where the user primarily is the receiver of information, Network Pericles is premised on the principle that the user/citizen 'provides' information: she/he votes or expresses views in opinion polls, argues for or against specific motions to be debated and carried or rejected.

It is quite clear that the model of democracy to be realised through the operation of the network is one not based merely on the principle of providing the citizen with information or of ensuring transparency of local-authority decision-making processes, but on the principle of giving the opportunity to citizens to obtain information, to deliberate and make decisions. Therefore the goals of the initiative are twofold: the first, to establish and/or improve communication and interaction between citizen and local authority or the state in general; the second, to establish and/or improve these processes among citizens.

It should be emphasised at this point that interviews with the research team made clear that they do not see electronic democracy (and therefore Network Pericles) as being antagonistic to the institutions and processes of representative democracy, as some advocates of plebiscitary models of direct democracy do. Giorgos Kambourakis and Marios

Nottas argue that the coexistence of the two processes will strengthen the institutions and processes of representative democracy as it will enable those involved in the latter to have a better knowledge of the attitudes and opinions of its citizens.

These opinions, however, are not entirely shared by local authority leaders: the mayors of the municipalities of Argostoli and Agioi Anargyroi that are participating in the network, Gerasimos Fortes and Nikos Tambakidis, have admitted that most local authority leaders have been hesitant to embrace the concept as they have been uncertain about the ramifications of the implementation of electronic democracy. They agreed, however, that as the system offered the advantage of keeping local government in touch with its citizens, participating in the network was a risk worth taking.

ISSUES OF ACCESS, PARTICIPATION AND CITIZENSHIP

As already mentioned, unlike other electronic democracy projects, Network Pericles is a network dedicated to the needs of local democracy; it is not, at the time of writing, accessible via the Internet or any other public network, and has been designed specifically for the purposes of public information, debate and voting. The implications of this particular characteristic of the network are quite significant.

As, in addition to providing access to information and scope for debate, the network supports voting, issues regarding accessibility and user-friendliness have acquired urgency and dominated the debate surrounding the network itself as well as its design. Although current legislation in most EU member states, including Greece, makes no provision for electronic voting, the possibility is not that remote, especially as government departments and officials are becoming increasingly interested in the cost-effectiveness, if not democratic potential, of electronic voting. Such a possibility not only renders the network a public service or 'public good' provision medium but also raises a host of issues related to citizenship rights. Access to the network, therefore, is not simply desirable but imperative, as it is potentially a legally sanctioned right.

On the basis of this rationale, accessibility and ease of use have been paramount in decisions regarding the network design.The hardware the user needs in order to have access to the network is installed in special kiosks which are situated in specific central points in the participating municipalities, in order to be easily accessible to the population. With maximum accessibility in mind, the team has estimated that the optimum ratio of kiosks to users is one to 4,500–6,000

Back to the future of democracy? 49

residents. Each kiosk is dedicated to specific functions/activities and is equipped with the appropriate hardware: most kiosks provide facilities for citizen conferencing or for the supply of information, while there are a smaller number of kiosks dedicated to voting. The terminals used are essentially PC terminals specially modified for the needs of the network, while the software has been developed by the research team of NTUA in collaboration with several software companies.

In addition to the terminals situated in the kiosks, access to the network is possible (although not currently available) through private PCs, assuming that the users have the necessary software (to be provided by the municipal authority) and equipment (modem, sound cards, etc.). However, members of the team have stressed that access from private PCs would enable the user to get information and be involved in citizen conferencing but *not to vote*; this restriction was deemed necessary in order to reinforce the 'public' (as opposed to individualistic) character of the democratic process.

The team members interviewed have constantly placed particular emphasis on the need to devise ways of maintaining and reinforcing the public character of the democratic process and therefore of the processes supported by Network Pericles. Marios Nottas defined political involvement of the citizen as one of the main principles on which the network is premised, while Giorgos Kambourakis claimed that the network was developed in such a way so as to overcome problems of similar experiments premised on a logic of privatisation and effort to sustain and enable social/political interaction. Another factor that influenced the provision of public facilities accessible to the citizen was the decision of the team to devise a system with a strong social dimension: thus, voting from home was deemed to perpetuate political inequality by not addressing the issue of social inequality and unequal access to the means of political participation. As access to a PC at home is normally determined by class, income and educational criteria, and as technophobia or a low degree of computer-literacy can be class-related, the team decided that encouraging access from home, especially for the purpose of voting, would be tantamount to empowering the middle classes and contributing to the disenfranchising of lower socioeconomic strata.

Thus, the decision to maintain the public character of the political process and to ensure equal access to the system for all citizens led to the choice of focusing on network access through public kiosks/nodal points in the urban/political landscape.

For the reasons outlined above, the terminals are user-friendly as their designers have based their work on the assumption that a complex system

50   *Roza Tsagarousianou*

might be unattractive to 'technophobic' citizens. After consideration of the options available, the research team opted for the installation of touch-screens (see Figure 3.1) and voice-command equipment, and expressed confidence in the simplicity and user-friendliness of the system, which, according to them, required virtually no computer-literacy and would even enable persons with disabilities to make full use of it.

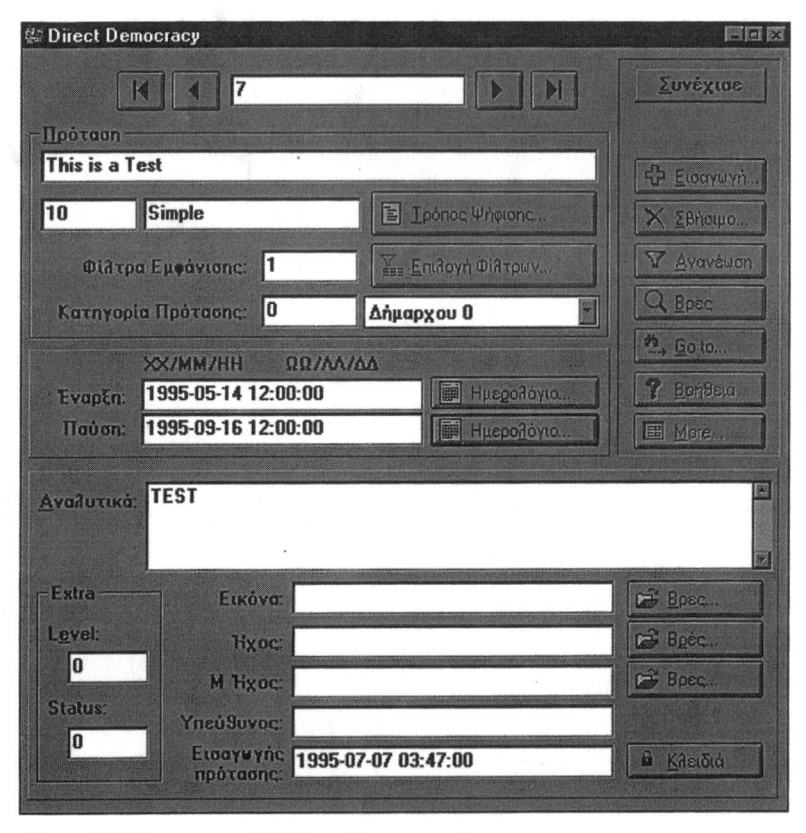

Figure 3.1 Homepage of 'Direct Democracy'
(http://hotwired.dbnet.ece.ntua.gr/LBY/dd.htm)

At the time of writing, the cost of each kiosk is about 5,000,000 drachmas (£13,160) but once it is installed the maintenance costs are expected to be negligible. Scarcity of funds has led to revision of original schedules, in accordance with which a pilot programme would have been in operation in early 1996 in the municipalities of Argostoli, Agioi Anargyroi (Greece), Saint Brieuc (France) and Strovolou (Cyprus) –

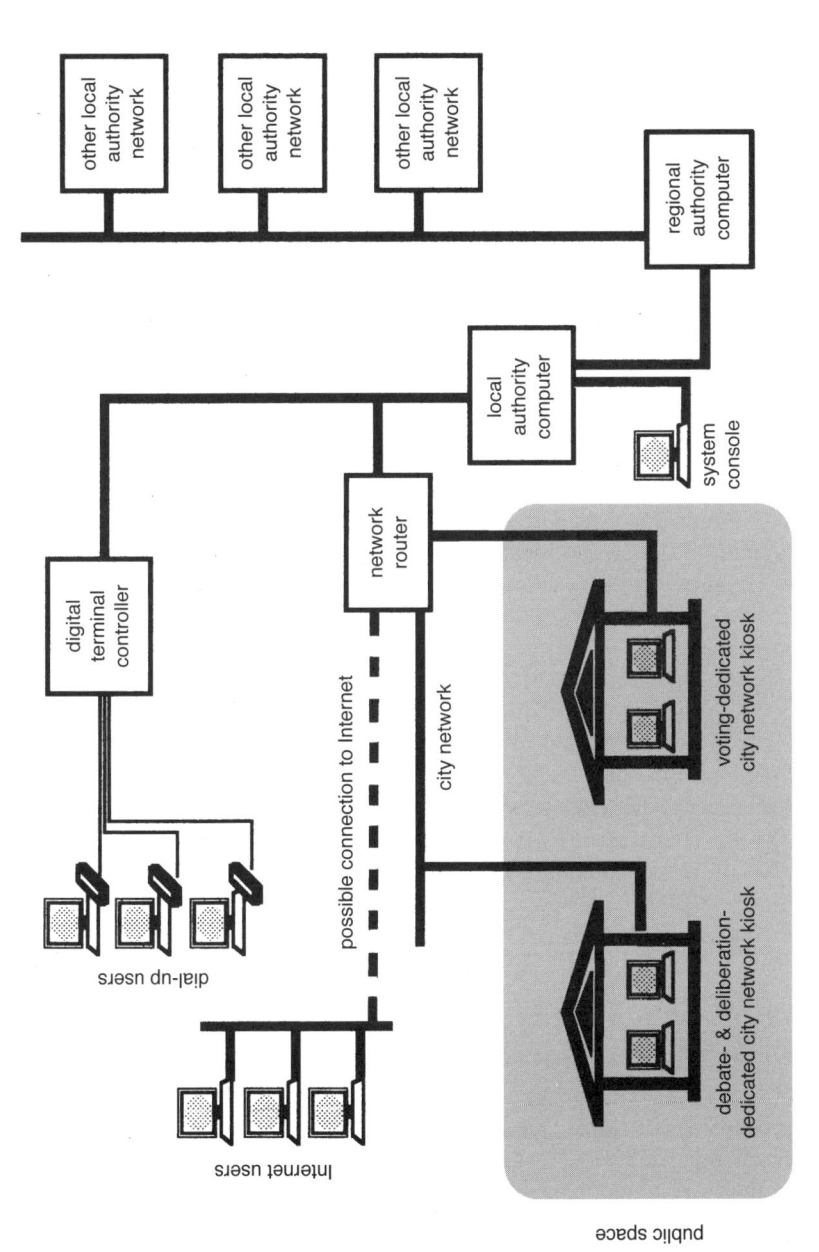

Figure 3.2 Project Pericles: diagram of local authority electronic network

this has not yet been achieved, although at the moment an experimental network is in operation in the NTUA campus. It is also intended that a European village – a network of representative local authorities from all EU countries will be formed shortly. The network is organised in a similar way to the Internet. At the lowest level are the kiosks with their terminals which are linked to the municipal authority (the basic cell of the network), which in turn is linked to the regional centre, which is eventually linked to the centre of the national web (at the moment this is the Ministry of the Interior or any similar authority in the countries participating in the project).

The Network Pericles team have been evaluating technologies that can guarantee the secrecy of voter identity and the non-transferability of their voting entitlement. This is achieved through the combination of a user card and a password with a non-traceable proof of identity (palm-print, voice, etc.). Thus each resident of the municipality is issued with a card which can store information that does not reveal the identity of the user but that refers to his or her characteristics, such as European, national and local citizenship (a European Union, French citizen can, according to current legislation vote in Greece for European (and soon local), but not for national elections). A non-European Union citizen, legally resident in a municipality might be eligible to vote in specific elections, and so on.

This capacity of the network to distinguish between different forms of 'voting rights' through differently encoded user cards introduces flexibility into the processes of public consultation or public referenda – by recognising residents who are registered in local electoral rolls, residents registered elsewhere, residents of adjacent areas who might need or wish to be consulted and residents within a specific age group who might be affected by a specific legislation, different electorates can be defined and invited to vote in the case of local or particular issues.

ELECTRONIC DEMOCRACY, CIVIC TOPOGRAPHY AND THE PUBLIC SPHERE

To evaluate the democratising potential and record of electronic democracy projects, the impact of the latter on the public sphere has to be assessed in order to determine to what extent the latter has been expanded and rendered accessible to citizens. Indeed, democracy has very often been associated with the development of public spaces where the citizens can formulate their political identities and express their political will (Dahlgren and Sparks, 1991; Garnham, 1990; Habermas, 1989; Melucci, 1989). It is clear that the success of electronic democracy

Back to the future of democracy? 53

projects depends on their capacity to support and enable the introduction of new forms of 'publicness' within a public sphere partly dominated by privately owned and controlled media and the state. Therefore, in order to evaluate Network Pericles, just as any other project of electronic or conventional democracy, it is necessary to situate it within the public sphere of contemporary (post-)industrial societies and to assess its contribution to the communicative and political processes unfolding in it.

The centrality given by Network Pericles to the public character of the exercise of citizenship rights is therefore a good point to start, as it raises issues related to 'publicness' and the public sphere. As I pointed out earlier, the political model the research team drew upon in the process of conceptualising democracy and visualising its electronic dimension has been the Athenian version of direct democracy and its central notion of an active, involved citizenry in a process of self-government comprising 'public beings engaged in the institution of a common life' (Habermas, 1989; Held, 1987). On the other hand, it would not be fair to suggest that the inception of the project has been exclusively influenced by civic republican idealism; it has also been pointed out earlier in this paper that the project has been conceived as part of the search for an antidote to citizen heteronomy and apathy. As a result of these two factors, and possibly in view of the lack of notable grassroots initiatives for enhancement of the democratic process and its institutions, the Network Pericles team opted for a solution that would offer reasonable guarantees of the 'socialisation' of the initiative. Throughout the interviews I conducted with members of the Network Pericles team, it was difficult not to notice that the metaphors used to illustrate the functions of the network were related to everyday life practices and settings linked to public spaces in Greek society: the term used to refer to the kiosks dedicated to citizens' deliberation and conferencing – περιπτερα – refers in everyday speech to the small newsagents kiosks situated in nodal points in the Greek urban landscapes, which often serve as convergence points for members of the public who want to peruse the displayed newspaper headlines and engage in discussion with other bystanders. Equally significantly, the metaphor used by Marios Nottas to describe the nature of citizen conferencing sessions – ηλεκτρονικα πηγαδακια (literally 'electronic wells') (Nottas, 1995) – refers to a non-electronic version of this practice known as πηγαδακια (literally 'wells'), that is, the practice of bystanders, often strangers to each other, forming circles next to these kiosks and debating the news that they have just read.

In addition, the very geography of Network Pericles, whereby electronic kiosks will be situated as close as possible to their printed-press era counterparts, reflects the determination of the network team to 'seam' practices and settings related to the actualisation of electronic democracy into the fabric of everyday life. Although, clearly, such decisions cannot guarantee the success of such a project they indicate, nevertheless, that careful thinking has taken place with regard to the socialisation of the project, especially in view of the lack of any grassroots initiative.

As it has been stressed by numerous commentators, any socially grounded theory of the public sphere will have to take into account the social network structures which are in a position to sustain public spaces and public debate, and the communications systems that bind them (Friedland, 1996: 189). There is little doubt that Network Pericles has been informed by such an approach and has been geared towards mobilising civic resources with the objective of creating or resuscitating much-needed public spaces, not relying exclusively on CMC, but also through linking the latter with everyday public settings and practices. In an analysis of the impact of computer technology on large-scale social integration Calhoun remarks that one of the social changes that communications and information technologies are bringing about is the reduction of

> the place-centered functions of cities ... [which] challenges the realm of public life by limiting accidental contact among strangers. As it becomes possible to conduct economic and other affairs without entering into the company of strangers, we lose both cross-cutting ties and one of the bases of democratic public life.
> (Calhoun, 1986: 330)

Calhoun therefore identifies 'individualisation' of the citizen as one of the main processes that undermine the post-industrial public sphere, and effectively argues that democratic public life in contemporary societies presupposes and depends upon the existence of cross-cutting ties and a capacity for public discourse among relative strangers.

In a similar vein, Iris Marion Young refers to the condition of 'urbanity' and its democratic connotations as a model for the contemporary public sphere and transposes it over the civic landscape of contemporary societies. Young argues that 'urbanity is the horizon of the modern, not to mention the postmodern condition' (Young, 1990: 237). She claims that contemporary political theory must accept urbanity as a material given for those who live in advanced industrial societies. 'Urbanity' in her discourse does not necessarily refer to actual dwelling in the city but to a condition characteristic of modernity and

Back to the future of democracy? 55

a form of social relations that encompasses even the non-city-dwellers, namely, a condition of 'being together of strangers'. As she points out, city life is composed of a vast array of small communities. 'City dwellers frequently venture beyond such familiar enclaves, however, to the more open public of politics, commerce and festival where strangers meet and interact' (ibid.). Cities provide important public spaces – streets, parks and plazas – where people stand and sit together, interact and mingle, or simply witness one another, without becoming unified in a community of shared final ends. Politics depends on the existence of public spaces and fora to which everyone has access. In such public spaces, people encounter other people, meanings, expressions, issues, which they may not understand or with which they do not identify (ibid.). In fact, according to Young (1990) and Calhoun (1986), it is the mode of coexistence and of interaction which characterises the urban environment that is typical of democratic coexistence, comprising processes of encounter, exchange of views and deliberation, and the public spaces upon which these processes take place (see also Tsagarousianou, 1996).

Referring to the institutional level, Melucci (1989), also emphasises the need for the creation of public spaces for representation and negotiation independent from state institutions or the party system, as he recognises the rigidity of representative institutions. These new public spaces would allow conflicts and demands to be expressed in ways that the inflexible representative democratic institutional framework cannot allow. The expression of collective action through these soft-institutional settings, renders power visible and negotiable, and therefore demystifies power relations. Access to these public spaces would be open to social actors and would increase the ability of post-industrial democracy to hear (Melucci, 1989: 77). Such spaces might lead to the reinvigoration and democratisation of contemporary democracies by increasing the scope for autonomous public initiatives developing outside and independently of the state apparatus (Pakulski, 1991).

Synthesising these apparently distinct and unconnected attempts to link democracy to the development of new public spaces where 'strangers' interact with each other, deliberate, accept or reject each others' views, we can argue that contemporary democracy depends on the existence of a public realm quite different from the Habermasian public sphere, which appears to be devoid of social conflict and in fact mystifies social inequalities and the conflictual character of public encounters.

Clearly, whereas many CMC-based projects of local democracy are premised on individualistic conceptions of democracy which require neither the encounters of the sort that Calhoun and Young suggest nor the maintenance of the public spaces upon which these encounters and exchanges are taking place, the Network Pericles project places emphasis on the public character of processes of actualisation of citizenship and is premised on the principle of citizen initiatives. This it accomplishes in two ways. First, it offers citizens and citizens' networks the opportunity to present information directly to the public, safeguarding the public character of information provision. Second, the urban and civic landscapes the network is intending to create and sustain (in both the literal and metaphorical sense of these terms, actual and virtual) are characterised by a multitude of nodes of 'publicness' where encounters and exchanges might take place. In theory at least, the emphasis placed on the physical proximity of citizens during the deliberation and, especially, voting process, is expected to enable exchanges and encounters in a more general and abstract way.

It is not, however, certain whether Network Pericles's emphasis on the publicness of the political process it mediates will have any positive impact or whether it will remain a symbolic gesture in societies which reproduce individualism and private withdrawal. In addition, despite the advantages outlined above, the coexistence of electronic democracy with institutions and processes of representative democracy is not as straightforward as it might seem, or as presented by those involved in the project design. In fact, the addition of a direct/plebiscitary democratic element in a political process hitherto premised on representative liberal democratic institutions, entails the reification of two antagonistic modes of legitimisation and authority and can lead to permanent tension between the two. Indeed, it is difficult to see how such a tension can be avoided if the promised plebiscitary element inherent in Network Pericles is not relegated to a mere public opinion monitoring function.

At the moment of writing, the network operates on an experimental basis in a very small area and therefore has not been able to generate information regarding democratic participation. A number of questions remain unanswered: it is still unclear whether the network can encourage participation of inactive citizens or whether it will just offer a new avenue of political action to already politically active citizens. It is also unclear if the need for funding might strengthen processes of incorporation of the network to established political or financial interests. Network Pericles has not been the outcome of grassroots pressure; it has been designed as a top-down intervention which, alongside its direct democracy component, incorporates plans for civic education and social and spatial planning and intervention. Despite its noble objectives, it lacks 'content' while it offers a formal structure for the political process. This opens the network to the possibility of manipulation and of undermining its radical promise.

On the other hand, it is clear that such experiments can easily be misrecognised as a panacea for the decline of political participation and the disenfranchisement of a substantial proportion of contemporary citizenries. It is important to acknowledge that such experiments, however innovative they may be, contribute merely one more means of political action in contemporary hierarchical societies. The use of ICT in projects of direct democracy cannot by itself make up for the social inequalities that contribute to the disenfranchisement of large proportions of citizens, nor can it eliminate political cultures that may have fostered heteronomy and cynicism towards politics. One thing is quite clear: electronic democracy in its plebiscitary or deliberative permutations expressed in electronic democracy projects cannot by itself democratise the communities which it serves. The creation of public spaces, the articulation of views and demands, and the formation of active citizens requires much energy and commitment and grassroots involvement in public debate. Electronic democracy projects are not merely 'tools' devoid of any social content; social struggle is 'inscribed' into the very nature of the state and policy outcomes, and electronic democracy is no exception to this.

ACKNOWLEDGEMENTS

I would like to thank Dr Giorgos Kambourakis and Dr Marios Nottas at the Communication and Media Laboratory, National Technical University, Athens, and members of the Network Pericles team, the mayors of the municipalities of Argostoli, Mr Gerasimos Fortes, and Agioi Anargyroi, Mr Nikos Tambakidis for discussing aspects of Network Pericles with me. I would also like to thank colleagues at the Centre for Communication and Information Studies, University of Westminster for their comments at various stages of thinking and writing this paper.

NOTES

1 As illustrated in chapters 2, 4, 5, 6, 7, 8 of this volume, information provision has been seen as the main function of most ICT applications in local democracy.
2 Apart from Greek local authorities, participating in the network and co-operating with the NTUA-based team are the municipal authorities of Saint Brieuc (France) and Strovolou (Cyprus). In addition, the Athens municipality – the largest and one of the most enthusiastic participants in the network – is currently involved in negotiations with the EU to secure EU financing of 40 per cent to 60 per cent of the costs of inclusion in the network of interested EU local authorities.

3 The hopes that 'free radio' would bring an end to state monopoly of the airwaves in Greece did not really materialise, or rather did not take into account the effect of the intense lobbying by press magnates and other entrepreneurs who systematically conflated 'free' amd 'private' radio in their pursuit of their interests in the post state-monopoly era. At the time of writing, the Greek media, printed and electronic, are dominated by media magnates, with cross-ownership being the norm, with the exception of the state-owned broadcasting media sector.

REFERENCES

Abramson, J.B., C. Arterton and G. Orren (1988) *The Electronic Commonwealth: The Impact of New Technologies upon Democratic Politics*, New York: Basic Books.
Arterton, C. (1987) *Teledemocracy: Can Technology Protect Democracy?*, London: Sage.
Barber, B. (1984) *Strong Democracy: Participatory Politics for a New Age*, London: University of California Press.
Berelson, B. *et al.* (1954) *Voting*, Chicago: University of Chicago Press.
Calhoun, G. (1986) 'Computer Technology, Large-scale Social Integration and the Local Community', *Urban Affairs Quarterly*, 22 (2): 329–349.
Campbell, A. *et al.* (1960) *The American Voter*, New York: John Wiley.
Crozier, M. *et al.* (eds) (1975) *The Crisis of Democracy*, New York: New York University Press.
Dahlgren, P. and C. Sparks (eds) (1991) *Communication and Citizenship: Journalism and the Public Sphere*, London: Routledge.
Dahlgren, P. and C. Sparks (1993) *Communication and Citizenship: Journalism and the Public Sphere*, London: Routledge.
Dutton, W. and K. Guthrie (1991) 'An Ecology of Games: The Political Construction of Santa Monica's Public Electronic Network', *Informatization and the Public Sector*, 1: 279–301.
Eco, U. (1964) *Apocalittici e Integrati*, Milan: Fabbri.
Fraser, N. (1986) 'Towards a Discourse Ethic of Solidarity', *Praxis International*, 5 (4).
Fraser, N. and L. Gordon (1994) 'Civil Citizenship against Social Citizenship? On the Ideology of Contract-versus-Charity', in B. van Steenbergen (ed.) *The Condition of Citizenship*, London: Sage.
Friedland, L.A. (1996) 'Electronic Democracy and the New Citizenship', *Media, Culture and Society*, 18: 185–212.
Gandy, O. (1994) *The Panoptic Society*, Boulder, CO: Westview Press.
Garnham, N. (1990) 'The Media and the Public Sphere', pp. 104–114 in N. Garnham (ed.) *Capitalism and Communication: Global Culture and the Economics of Information*, London: Sage.
Guthrie, K. and W. Dutton (1992) 'The Politics of Citizen Access Technology', *Policy Studies Journal*, 20: 4.
Habermas, J. (1989) *The Structural Transformation of the Public Sphere*, Cambridge: Polity.
Held, D. (1987) *Models of Democracy*, Cambridge: Polity.
Kambourakis, G. (1995) Author interview with Giorgos Kambourakis (7 November).

Mavrogordatos, G. *et al.* (1988) 'Συγκριτικη Ερευνα Πολιτικης Κουλτουρας στις χωρες της Νοτιας Ευρωπης: Εισαγωγικες Παρατηρησεις', *The Greek Review of Social Research*, 96 A: 5–23.
Melucci, A. (1989) *Nomads of the Present*, London: Hutchinson.
Nottas, M. (1995) Author interview with Marios Nottas (9 November).
NTUA (n.d.) 'Direct Democracy Information Leaflet'.
Pakulski, J. (1991) *Social Movements: The Politics of Moral Protest*, Melbourne: Longman Cheshire.
Toffler, A. (1980) *The Third Wave*, New York: Pan.
Tsagarousianou, R. (1993) 'Mass Communications and Political Culture: Authoritarianism and Press Representations of Political Deviance in Greece', Ph.D. Thesis, University of Kent at Canterbury.
—— (1994) 'Πολιτικη Κουλτουρα και Μαζικη Επικοινωνια στη Συγχρονη Ελλαδα: Ο Αθηναικος Τυπος και οι Πολιτικες Μειονοτητες, in N. Demertzis (ed.) *Η Ελληνικη Πολιτικη Κουλτουρα Σημερα*, Athens: Odysseas.
—— (1996) 'Citizenship, Community and the Public Sphere: Communication and Democracy in Multicultural Societies', *Journal of Area Studies*, 8 (Spring): 31–50.
Young, I.M. (1990) *Justice and the Politics of Difference*, Princeton, NJ: Princeton University Press.

4 Berlin in the Net
Prospects for cyberdemocracy from above and from below

Oliver Schmidtke

INTRODUCTION

The development of computer-based communications technologies has given rise to challenging ambitions and projections. The German case is a good example of how hopes and projections about the new medium by far exceed what is technically or politically feasible in the medium term. Public discussion has indeed discovered the 'new media age' as a buzzword. Its implications and opportunities, however, for the democratic process have not yet caught wide attention. To be more comprehensively informed is a major issue, whereas the consideration of an active participation of the citizens has not been of major relevance for public discourse (Kleinsteuber, 1995). General notions such as the 'Informationszeitalter' (age of information) and the 'Information Superhighway' have been widely acknowledged as substantially changing our social environment. However, use of CCT is largely restricted to economic and technical elites or independent political groups. Considering that Germany is one of the most technologically advanced nations, Berlin, and the country as a whole, have been slow to appreciate the opportunities the new communications technologies provide, especially regarding official policy initiatives.

One of the key issues about which expectations and social reality do not meet is the debate on the impact of new communication techniques on the process of democratic decision-making. Many commentators celebrate the decentralised mode of communication as a step towards a virtual polis in which, be it on a national or local level, people could participate on equal terms in determining their public affairs. In public debates 'cyberspace'[1] is often assumed to be synonymous with the realisation of democratic ideals (Rheingold, 1994).

Central to the debate is the assumption that, given their decentralised and interactive nature, the new techniques will help to strengthen or even restore what Habermas (1989) has described as the 'universal communicative community'. The ideal is that communication, as the exchange of arguments, under conditions of equal access will be allowed to be the normative guide of democratic renewal. What is about to develop as the dominant structure of 'cyberdemocracy' does not, however, resemble this ideal. On the other hand, Habermas's idea of collective self-determination through individual participation may be better served by civic networking. As the following example from the German capital will show, it is more appropriate to speak about a highly diversified field of coexisting but not universally intertwined discourses and interactions. The communicative reality created in cyberspace is no 'global village'. There is nothing like a single polis constituted by computer-trained citizens, but rather different communities with their particular rules, aims and normative orientations. These diversified public spaces no longer constitute what has been labelled 'the public'. The new communications technologies will most likely intensify the process towards a diversified and fragmented field of coexisting communicative arenas instead of reinventing what could be considered as the universal public sphere.

This very general consideration has implications for the evaluation of the concrete political effects which the new communications media have, for instance, in an urban context. The different discursive arenas with distinct actors, which will be portrayed in the following, show how inappropriate it is to speak about the 'democratic' or 'anarchic' nature of the new techniques as such. Although they change the setting in which politics and the policy process occur, it is not clear whether this will necessarily mean a widening of the participatory qualities of the democratic system. In this respect, current public debate is characterised rather by a range of often speculative political projections than by an appropriate reflection of the actual tendencies and projects to be found in current social life. Media technologies do allow for more horizontal communication and interaction, although there is no automatic mechanism leading to a democratisation of public life.

Leaving aside the political dynamic generated by the new media themselves it is worth being aware of the technical and organisational distribution of the facilities allowing access to the cyberspace. This is relevant, first, as it helps to understand in which sectors of society computer-based projects have flourished. As Table 4.1 shows, most people who have access to the Internet in Germany use facilities either from the university or their workplace. Private accounts are still the exception. Second, such data give a first-hand indication why the ideal of a universally participating citizen in a model of cyberdemocracy is a long way off. In Germany the total number of people who have personal computers and access to the Internet is by international standards still relatively low. Only seven out of 100 interviewees randomly sampled used the Internet in Germany[2] in 1996 and, unlike other countries, there is little talk of guaranteeing access through libraries or public terminals. Based on the present distribution of access to the Net, an 'information society' with a digitalised process of political decision-making would discriminate against and/or exclude a large part of the population. This problem will not be discussed further, although one should be aware that these structural conditions in German society are unlikely to change as easily as enthusiasts of the information society predict.

Before turning to the actors shaping the new technologies in Berlin politics it is worth pointing out that the dynamic set free by the communications technologies substantially undermines the idea of fixed geographical entities. On the one hand, the world of cyberspace has legitimately been compared to the urban context, with its multitude of dynamic structures and interactions (Rötzer, 1995). Especially in its formative period computer-based communication has been built on the economic, social and political structure of urban centres, regarding both the production and the usage of the digitalised information (Kittlers, 1995). Furthermore, the city as a potential communicative community may become an important starting-point for a closer involvement of the citizens in the public decision-making process through the new technologies (Schieb, 1995).

Table 4.1 Means of access to the Internet

Route	No.
University	59
Employer	23
T-Online	14
Compu-serve	9
Private Mail-boxes	5
America Online	2
Microsoft Network	1

Source: Figures are based on a survey among 3,064 interviewees conducted by the Fraunhofer-Institut; published in *Der Spiegel*, November 1996.

On the other hand, however, these technologies simultaneously deprive the social space of its status as a clearly distinguished geographical location (Mitchell, 1995). The traditional concept of the polis is based on the people's interaction, which is bound to given locations in the city where one can actually meet and form a particular collective identity. Computer-based forms of interaction manifestly do not need this reference to a physical place. They delocate processes of public discourse. Cyberspace establishes a system of references and interaction only partly compatible with the traditional space of the city. Decentralisation and deterritorialisation are two tendencies endemic to the information communicated in cyberspace – and their effects on politics will be discussed in the next section. In this respect the city can no longer claim to be the place of an interaction exercised exclusively by the engagement and the resources of its citizens. Rather, as an exception, cyberspace is assimilated to an urban and spatially confined sphere and used as a means for administering the local. Even if information is primarily utilised and implemented within the urban context, by the very nature of the new media the communal context is closely connected with larger communicative networks. One can speak of an 'urbanisation' of the new media not yet as a social fact but it is clearly a possibility on the horizon. The central question I will deal with is how the geographically unrestricted virtual reality in the Net and the real geographical realm of the city interact and what impact this has on urban political life.

TOWARDS 'CYBERDEMOCRACY': THE RANGE OF EXISTING INITIATIVES IN BERLIN

In Berlin, compared to other cities, policy actors have been reluctant to make concrete plans beyond abstract hopes for the future. Citizen groups and political organisations, however, do not passively await proposals from above. What we find in Berlin is a network of diverse initiatives using the Internet for purposes of information exchange, different forms of interaction and political goals. The manifold, albeit segmented grassroot initiatives can be interpreted as an indirect reaction to the deficiencies from the administrative political level. Before describing some of the most important initiatives by non-governmental actors I will focus on the project advanced by the local administration.

The policy initiative: the 'City Information System' (CIS)[3]

It is only very recently that Berlin as an urban centre has been present in the Internet in form of a coordinated and policy-oriented project. In March 1996 the various initiatives in the urban context (such as online and btx services) were incorporated into a single project called 'city information system' (HTTP://www.berlin.de) and since then they have been coordinated by the Senat, the Berlin administration. Using the Amsterdam Digital City as a model, the major goals of the project were the improvement of the services for the citizens and, on this basis, a more direct interaction between the citizens and local government. As it says in the resolution of the Berlin Senat: the 'electronic information system' has the aim to aggregate information about the city and to make it available to the citizens and, as a second key group, to local businesses. The Berlin version of the 'digital city' offers a whole range of information on subjects from public or private services to information on Berlin-related political issues.

The homepage menu opens with a set of eight options out of which two entries ('Berlin: an overview' or 'tourism') give only very broad information about the city and its basic infrastructure. The other selections ('politics', 'culture', 'leisure time', 'science', 'economy') allow access to highly detailed information about services, projects and institutions. The political pages range from current news (with a national rather than local slant) and political debates to the structure and services of all levels of local government (mostly in the form of addresses and references to possible contact people). In terms of the number of users, the project 'City Information System' is in comparative terms already quite successful: the latest information speaks about 266,000 hits a month, almost 10,000 hits daily. (There are no figures that specify where these hits come from; they may come from Berlin and may come from elsewhere.)

Turning to the implications for the democratic process, the Berlin case clearly shows that the interactive and participatory potential of the new media is still far from being developed. The highly limited range of interaction with the agencies of local government and administration as well as the nature of the services presently provided show that on the city level it is more appropriate to speak about an information delivery system than a system of enhanced democratic practice. The online services have the character more of a computerised political manual than a medium of interactive communication.

This reveals a major problem in the development of the new computer-based media, which becomes pertinent in the urban context. Often the potentially interactive communication systems are utilised in a one-way manner. This means that these media are used in order to render public services more efficient or to provide the citizens with more comprehensive information on selective issues of communal concern without, however, allowing for an active participation of the citizens themselves. If the public is involved at all, it is asked to give suggestions or comments. There are simply no institutionalised ways of communication which, for instance, would involve the administrative staff. As was explained to me in an interview I conducted with a project coordinator (Ulrich, 1996): the messages and comments from citizens arrive in one single mail-box in the Senat (where the CIS is organised), are printed and then these print-outs are delivered in folders to the people in charge (who themselves are mostly 'computer-illiterate'). The chances for interactive and unbureaucratic communication are thus minimal within the current framework. Procedures to integrate citizens into the political decision-making process are virtually non-existent.

Beyond this official project, however, and organised in decentralised networks, are other initiatives that are more successful in terms of citizen participation. They are not directly related to discussing and settling local governmental concerns, but are directed towards collectively shared information on and discussion of specific topics. In this respect some professional groups are relatively strong in their presence in city projects. For instance, architects are highly willing to accept the new media to exchange information, debate new projects and communicate with local administration (within the context of the so-called Cybercity project). Again this is no surprise given that this occupational group belongs to those for whom it is quite normal to use the most advanced media. Another example is the department of the Humboldt University that has created a WWW-server on which Berlin-specific problems regarding city planning, big architectural projects or blueprints for reorganising urban traffic can be discussed.

The seeming inability of the Berlin administration to launch any projects actively involving its citizens sheds light on a structural problem: even if the new media provide the opportunity for participatory models, they are not by definition incompatible with a technocratic practice and top-down approach. The administrative procedures in particular can easily be deprived of the interactive and collective communication for which the medium allows (Lévy, 1994) (if interactive forms of communication are possible they are restricted to a local form of 'Internet Relay Chat'; see Seidler, 1994). In the case of Berlin there are only single initiatives which seek to establish concrete forms of direct interaction in terms of an ongoing computer-based contact between local government and citizens. Yet even these initiatives do not concern direct participation in the democratic process but focus almost exclusively on service delivery: access to libraries, ticket offices or services of the local administration (passports, taxes, etc.).

In the case of the CIS project in Berlin, there are not even any longterm plans to use the communications technology for democratic purposes. The chief coordinator of the project told me he personally, as well as those politically responsible, have major doubts whether any kind of direct democracy via the Internet is either practicable or normatively desirable. He said that it would be highly debateable whether decisions based on direct participation of the citizens would enhance the quality of a democratic system (Ulrichs, 1996). There is no single voice on this issue, but many attitudes seem to reflect a profound suspicion of direct forms of democracy which is deeply ingrained in the post-war political culture in Germany. The danger of populist strategies and an irrational decision-making process are presented as serious arguments against any form of 'direct democracy'.[4] In this respect the German debate on the political implications of the new communications technologies radically differs from the public discourse in the US: the overwhelming majority of politicians and administrative staff in Germany are more likely to be suspicious than hopeful regarding the impact the new technologies might have on the institutional set-up of the democratic system (Hagen, 1996). For some, any kind of direct involvement of the citizens into the political decision-making process is portrayed as a genuine threat to the democratic process and – at least implicitly – to their own power base.

Summarising the project's stand in the debate about the future of the new media, the coordinator of the project said that from the viewpoint of a policy actor, computer-based technologies could be used to render public services more efficient but not the representative system more democratic (Ulrichs, 1996). In this he is perfectly in tune with the official line of the Senat which he and his team were assigned to implement: the project is designed to improve the information provision and, in the near future, to allow for direct access to administrative services such as tax returns, identity card renewal, passports and so forth. The plan is to render usual practices in urban government and administration more efficient and easier without, however, changing qualitatively the status of the citizens in terms of an active political engagement.

Another serious drawback in this respect is the interest and conceptual orientation of those who in the future will run this Berlin information project in the Net. Until now the CIS in Berlin has been financed by a local government which, with the severe financial crisis it has to face, is no longer willing to provide the services in the current way. It is already agreed that exclusive rights to the network will be given to a private entrepreneur who will be entitled to complement this information package with additional commercial services. Even if the current organisers of the project say that, due to a legal agreement, there will be no change in the design of the present concept and the quality of the services, this step will without doubt change the set-up and the clientele of the system. The commercial aspect will probably become far more dominant, further diminishing the prospects for actively involving citizens in the political decision-making process. Administrative and commercial concerns are very likely to shape the further development of the project, whereas citizen participation in local politics is unlikely to be aspired to.

The example of the CIS in Berlin demonstrates that, in the German case, there is a huge discrepancy between the technical potential for enhancing the democratic quality of the political and administrative realm and the ways in which the network technology is employed. The new technologies can only develop a dynamic towards participatory models of decision-making if they are embedded in an organisational framework that allows for interactivity and citizens' involvement beyond the rigidity of traditional representative institutions. Those initiatives coming from local government, however, show a top-down approach that is oriented towards the rationalisation of the local policy rather than towards notions of active citizenship and democratic reform. A deep mistrust of forms of direct democracy have largely obstructed any policy initiatives to fund and regulate the use of new technologies in this regard.

Political parties and the Internet: lack of initiatives

The key agents who could counteract this development and become active in favour of advancing the 'democratic promise' of the new media are political parties or single politicians. However, for the political parties in Germany, both on a national and a local level, the new communications media have not yet been perceived as an opportunity, let alone seriously been used in daily practice. Irrespective of party affiliation, there are no serious projects considering and developing enterprises to employ these media for politics and the policy process. Issues such as the information infrastructure (for a discussion, see Canzler, Helmers and Hoffmann, 1995) or the other opportunities offered by the new communications media are discussed only very broadly with respect to jobs and future work structure, whereas their possible implications for the decision-making process in politics are rarely raised. The Internet specialist of the governing Christian Democratic Unionists said in an interview I conducted via the Internet that: 'Involving citizens directly might be a good idea for the future, right now it is simply not feasible' (Haas, 1996).

However, political parties do have a presence in the Net. Each of the major parties has a homepage in which the latest initiatives and policy discussions are presented. The design of this information is predominantly national, but there is some city-centred material on political issues in Berlin as well, especially major political issues that relate to Berlin, such as the proposed union between Berlin and Brandenburg or the future status of Berlin as the German capital, and these are given the chance to be discussed in the Net. A party functionary told me that the urban context is rarely considered in the WWW pages of the parties, because the clientele of the Net is still far too restricted to make it a politically worthwhile undertaking. Hence, only very limited resources are dedicated to communication via cyberspace, in particular regarding political issues in regional or communal contexts.

The layout of the existing parties' homepages has a distinct bias towards one-way information. Although there is, in principle, the possibility for the citizens actively to intervene and discursively interact with party representatives, this party service is clearly directed towards information and party advertisement. Where there are direct E-mail links to MPs, these are not necessarily read. I randomly picked two addresses of members of each of the five major parties asking for some information on a controversial current plan to build a road and rail tunnel in the centre of the city. Within four weeks I had received only two replies (out of ten) with the message that they would send me a party brochure on the topic.

A better turnout elicited in a test with a pilot project organised by the Freie Universität in Berlin entitled 'MPs in Internet' (http://www.fu-berlin.de/POLWISS/mdb-project). This service offers a whole range of information packages on different political questions and the opportunity to enter into an 'online discussion with MPs'. However, only one representative of every party in the Bundestag (the German parliament) is available and the entire project is restricted to the national level.

The current engagement of parties in the Net shows the same structural deficiencies as the main project of local government. Both are primarily directed towards a form of information and interaction that is designed to be a one-way process. Services are performed and packages of information provided in a more efficient way. However, the set-up of this communication system does not allow for (and is not planning to allow for) an active involvement of the citizens.

GRASSROOT INITIATIVES AND POLITICAL MOBILISATION WITH THE NEW COMMUNICATIONS TECHNOLOGIES

The lack of government initiative in Berlin leaves a vacuum that is exploited by the civic initiatives of grassroot actors. Rather than attempting to cover in detail the extent to which civil society organisations in Berlin and German politics are benefiting from the Net, I will show in general terms how such organisations can take advantage of the technology. I draw mainly on the recent social movements literature, which provides a general account of the problems people experience when they try to co-operate in collective political projects, in terms of individual motivations, organisations and so forth.

Focusing on the impact of the new technologies on collective action will allow us to substantiate Habermas's thesis about the political implications of decentralised communication processes. In a second step, the prospects for cyberdemocracy in an urban context will be examined by demonstrating the theoretical propositions in relation to grassroot actors who have adopted modern communications technologies. Two important examples of such grassroots initiatives in Berlin will be portrayed, with the aim of showing how the new media affect their mobilising efforts.

Computer-mediated communication, collective action and civic participation: five theses

Regardless of ideological orientation, the new communications technologies have structuring effects on political mobilisation. The central problem of collective action is the issue of why individuals should engage in actions directed towards collective goods in spite of the costs involved and in spite of the fact that the participants would benefit from its result even if they do not engage personally. The new communications technology, with its mode of transferring information and spurring mobilisation, significantly changes the environment in which this 'free-rider problem' becomes relevant. Five main aspects can be identified regarding the extent to which computer-based interaction facilitates the formation of collective action and structures those processes by means of which political mobilisation is inspired:

The new media reduce costs for collective actors

Approaches that work on the conceptual grounds of the resource mobilisation theory, in particular (Jenkins, 1983; McCarthy and Zald, 1977; Zald, 1991, 1992), have largely pointed to the role of organisational and institutional means for collective actors in spreading their ideas and in building up organisational competence and institutional structure (Garner and Zald, 1985). In this respect, the new technologies significantly reduce the costs of, for example, distributing such information as activist material, the communication of political ideas to the wider public and the coordination of protest actions. The American tradition in social movement research especially has looked at resources available to a collective actor in organising mobilisation. New communications techniques make more information more openly available, and in a more targeted way. They facilitate the coordination between geographically dispersed groups and hence change the opportunities for collective actors. As the example of the right-wing groups in Berlin shall demonstrate: Owing to Internet access even for small and formerly marginalised groups of activists, such groups are able to become politically relevant in public discourse. The existence of a powerful organisational apparatus no longer determines the likelihood of political mobilisation. Digitalised communication facilitates interaction with an enormous virtual community without presupposing that a group disposes of ways of communicating its ideas via face-to-face contacts or the heavily guarded mass media. Costs for distributing material, coordinating collective action and recruiting new members via the Internet are minimal.

The new media reduce individuals' costs for engagement and participation

Traditionally, it has been a major problem for collective actors to sustain a high level of activism because of the significant costs of actively participating in political campaigns (Friedman and McAdam, 1992). Time and money are scarce goods which are only rarely used extensively for communal and political purposes. With computer-based forms of interaction, however, these barriers to individuals wishing to engage in at least a basic form of collective action are significantly reduced. At a certain level of political mobilisation, to participate no longer means primarily to be physically present at a certain time and place, but rather to interact with and to support a collective actor via a medium that is not restricted by strict time schedules and precious resources. When basic interaction and networking is primarily conducted via the Net, time and space no longer restrain individual engagement. In this respect, the density of a movement's targeted social group (as for example the black population or students on big campuses) which has been portrayed as the major element in fabricating organised collective action (McAdam, McCarthy and Zald, 1988), has to be redefined. Cyberspace offers a medium in which people can interact and coordinate their actions without relying on face-to-face contact (Myers, 1994).

The new media reduce intra-organisational hierarchy and intensify the actors' sense of involvement

New media potentially lower the degree of hierarchical order in the communication process itself. Cyberspace does not initially appear to differentiate its users according standards of class, descent and power, as it seems to exclude none. The medium installs a system of interacting agents who are potentially equipped with the same rights and possibilities to take part in campaigns. The medium suggests that participants should be fully informed of what is going on within the group and be equally involved in the collective decision-making process.

Even if, as in the case of right-wing groups, these means can be used for purposes of sheer propaganda without any notion of democratic participation, the classless image of the media sets free strong motivational resources. In this respect, one has to take into account that, particularly in a state of institutionalisation, political groups have to fight against the problems created by bureaucratisation and organisational hierarchies (Kitschelt, 1990; Offe, 1985, 1990). One of the key elements of collective actors' attractiveness is that they avoid the image of a stratified organisation which operates similarly to established actors in politics. In contrast to the endemic tendency of established collective actors to lose their genuinely democratic character, the new communications technologies – at least potentially – provide effective means to set up an organisational framework for grassroots involvement.

The new media facilitate the formation of collective identity

The formation of a common sense of belonging and a collective identity can be identified as crucial for the mobilising efforts of collective actors (Melucci, 1985, 1988; Pizzorno, 1978, 1986). Traditionally, symbols, media presence or direct physical interaction have been the decisive means in creating such a common ground which supersedes single political conflicts and provides the critical resources for political protest (Cohen, 1985; Schmidtke, 1996). The interaction in the virtual space may change significantly the logic of fostering this 'pre-political' base for political mobilisation. Through interaction and computer-based discussions of ideas and interests, this commonality among individuals who do not even meet might be effectively fabricated. (In this respect, the new technologies might have an impact on political mobilisation similar to the one Gitlin (1980) described for the mass media in the 1970s.)

As the example of the right-wing groups will demonstrate, cyberspace is extremely productive in encouraging forms of collective identity where a certain degree of privacy and secretness is created by the medium. Private mail-boxes or a special coding system create feelings of belonging to an exclusive community and, as such, can provide emotional incentives for participation. In this case it is the mix of belonging to an elite group while simultaneously having the feeling of participating in this community on equal terms that constitutes much of the appeal of 'cyberspace politics' from below. Even if this form of interaction is not likely entirely to replace direct contacts as the crucial mode of generating a collective identity (McAdam, 1982), the new technologies will be a critical means in providing the link between face-to-face interactions and the broad media discourse as modes of identity construction.

The new media are effective in suggesting the strength and prospects of a collective actor

It is crucial for the mobilising efforts of collective actors credibly to suggest prospects for the successful realisation of their political goals. The likelihood of concrete achievements is a major motivational component of protest groups. In this respect, new communications technologies are productive in building the image of a resourceful and efficient agent. A group's wide network of participants and its interaction with other groups, both on the national and international level, is likely to attribute images of political power and influence to groups which normally are restricted to the limited communal sphere of influence. Even if it is used only by a limited number of people related to communal concerns, being present in the Net gives the impression to be part of a virtually global network of people. At least in this formative phase, the projection of the potency embedded in the new media itself is an important element in its mobilising capacities.

These five theses about the impact of the new media on collective actors' mobilising efforts, again, do not necessarily imply a dynamic towards more grassroots, democratic forms of political action. Although these technologies offer a whole range of procedures for diminishing hierarchical and bureaucratic modes of communication and transforming them into more democratic patterns, there is no 'natural', i.e., technically given drive towards participatory models of political mobilisation and decision-making. Enhancing the opportunity structure for these actors does not determine the concrete procedural mode or the political aims of the mobilisation.

The argument that the new communications technologies have, by their very nature, a somehow anarchistic, levelling effect on communication and political deliberation is doubtful. The new technologies, though opening the prospect for horizontal communication and 'disinhibiting effects' (Dutton, 1996), can easily be used in a highly hierarchical form. It is the social and political context that is decisive, not the medium as such, in determining the political prospects for cyberdemocracy. The new media can easily be used in such a way as to reproduce the hierarchical communications structures typical of an authoritarian approach to politics as the following example will show. The case of right-wing groups and student organisations will make clear how the new media change the environment and the organisational means for inspiring political mobilisation.

New opportunities for propaganda and mobilisation: right-wing groups

Extreme right-wing and racist groups have used the Internet in a highly efficient and publicly relevant way. Their activities and mobilisation have gained a new relevance due to the new communications media, even if the number of activists involved has remained low. This is particularly evident in Berlin, where formerly politically marginal groups have been successful in challenging some of the major obstacles right-wing mobilisation has to face in contemporary German society.

The central medium through which right-wing groups interact via the Internet is the so-called 'Thule-Netz' (Maegerel and Mletzko, 1994). It was inaugurated in 1993 and is based on a system of private mail-boxes. Its major goal is to distribute and discuss ideas and by this means to create a world-wide network of right-wing activists. At a European level it created an online 'data-bank with information for right-wing activists' (Schröder, 1996). The Thule-Net is highly efficient in terms of availability (it can be accessed with almost any PC) while at the same time offering a high degree of privacy for internal discussions and information (with the programme 'Pretty Good Privacy'[5]). Access is regulated with different degrees of 'exclusiveness': the broad public is provided with a highly limited selection of information, whereas the discussion forums are open only to the 'inner circle' of activists to which one gains access only after a long procedure of 'personality validation'.

Within these right-wing groups it becomes obvious that horizontal communication, for which the new technologies potentially offer the ideal infrastructure, does not necessarily lead to a democratisation of political processes. The Thule-Net has established a highly hierarchical mode of organising the communication among its participants which allows for control from above. The Net is created in such a way that all public messages first arrive in one single mail-box where they are examined, categorised and then distributed to the respective thematically specified mail-boxes. This, at least potentially, implies that all messages, the public as well as the encoded ones, can first be read and possibly manipulated by the organisers of the Net.[6] Regarding the impact the new media have on such right-wing groups' activities, I will briefly look at four aspects of how the cyberspace matters: 1) internal communication, 2) co-operation and mobilisation, 3) information and 4) engagement in public discourse.

1 One of the most important goals of using the new technologies in the case of right-wing groups is to establish a stable network of activists and supporters via processes of internal communication. The 'distorted' mobilisation of these groups – their weak popular base, lack of coordinated actions and the semi-clandestine way in which they operate – can be seen as the pivotal reason for which the new media have been adopted by this type of political actor: they are able substantially to reduce the costs for a more efficient integration and coordination of dispersed groups which formerly communicated, if at all, rather accidently via personal contacts.

   The sense of internal belonging is primarily created by a whole range of different mail-boxes and specialised 'boards' which are dedicated to themes relevant to right-wing discourse in Germany. Political issues such as the 'Holocaust lie', 'patriotic dissidents' or 'illegal immigrants' are 'discussed'. However, if one looks at what is publicly accessible and what has been documented by those who became 'insiders', it soon becomes obvious that the discussion forums are rarely used and are of a disgraceful quality (mostly slogans and racist statements riddled with spelling and grammatical mistakes indicating more than just the spontaneity of this form of communication). This is not primarily an open discussion between individuals, rather activists use these mail-boxes to spread propaganda material and coordinate protest actions.[7] Of particular interest for the participants is that they can inform others about the actions of significant political opponents (anti-fascist and anti-racist groups) and actions the police might take against them.

2 In the case of right-wing groups the facilities of the new technologies are most often used for purposes of political mobilisation. Behind the public façade which promises an 'open discussion among people of nationalist belief' the Thule-Net is used for the coordination of protest actions. Because of the endemic weakness of these groups'

grassroots organisations and networks, the computer-based communication has a crucial role in providing the medium through which protest actions can be coordinated and strategies planned. Recent police reports indicate that exchanges about forms and locations of illegal actions are increasingly conducted via clandestine computer networks. This also applies to an intensified international network among right-wing groups in Europe.[8] Formerly isolated and irrelevant organisations have thus gained new political weight through using the new technology, which has contributed to the integration of previously isolated groups into a larger network. By this means even local right-wing organisations gain access to resources and support which they traditionally lacked for their mobilising efforts. As I showed in the theoretical section, the new media are able to provide the organisational and even motivational resources by which means formerly excluded political opportunities become feasible for collective actors.

Last year the extremist Berlin group 'Bunker BBS-Mail-box' started to collect and electronically store data about political opponents. As anti-fascist groups in Berlin say, these data are used for actions designed to intimidate political adversaries from the Left and to organise single actions on a local level. This mail-box has become a kind of coordinating agency for the highly fragmented right-wing scene in Berlin.[9]

3 The highly hierarchical and semi-clandestine form of communication practice in the Thule-Net indicates that its benefit for right-wing groups is not that it permits authentic discursive interactions among its followers. What is more important is the almost cost-free distribution of information via the Net. Especially for those right-wing groups which often operate at the limits of legality, the new communications media have notably improved the opportunities for interaction and mobilisation. Two main obstacles have traditionally restrained right-wing mobilisation: first, the difficulty of gaining access and distributing propaganda material; and second, the fragmentation of isolated activist groups. To face these restrictions in the past, many right-wing groups had to spend many of their organisational resources in order to assure the communication of material and contacts in the face of police surveillance and the activism of anti-fascist groups.

Regarding the first point, cyberspace as a reality, beyond the principle of territoriality and hence national legal systems, has decisively altered the environment for these groups. Propaganda material that formerly had to be smuggled into Germany and distributed by a clandestine infrastructure can now be downloaded in minutes. Mostly from the US and Denmark, brochures or even entire books which in the past were officially not available are now commuted to German groups. If it does not provide information online, the Thule-Net does give its participants access to a list of addresses where relevant 'nationalist' publishers, parties or single activists can be contacted. The police acknowledge that national laws are incapable of implementing practical means to obstruct this illegal exchange (in Germany it is explicitly illegal to distribute any form of Nazi propaganda). Furthermore, the Internet allows right-wing groups to coordinate their actions on the national and international level, strategies that have become particularly relevant in bigger protest actions and cross-border political operations.

4 Beyond internal coordination, the new communications technologies have helped right-wing groups to engage in public discourse and to gain access to a new reservoir of potential adherents. Previously, recruitment was predominantly face-to-face, organised around football stadiums and bars (Stöss, 1989; for Berlin see Holthusen and Jänecke, 1994). It is the explicit aim of the Thule-Net to create a right-wing *Gegenöffentlichkeit* ('counter-public') designed to oppose what is perceived as the dominance of leftist ideologies. In this respect, it is remarkable that the information presented (to the wider public) clearly seeks to leave the intellectual ghetto in which extreme nationalist positions traditionally have found themselves in post-war German society. Topics such as the environment, music, philosophy and computers are presented in the form of 'discussion papers' or 'contributions of nationalist compatriots'. Regarding the propaganda campaigns, cyberspace further helps to coordinate the mobilising efforts of radical groups from the right-nationalist scene, groups which were formerly isolated. Many of the contributions one can find in the Thule-Net come from activists of the 'New Right' fighting for their political goals in distinguished intellectual journals rather than protests on the street.

It would be exaggerated to state that at this stage the new technologies provide an important public for right-wing groups. It is a rather 'specialized' and largely self-selected audience that is addressed by the Thule-Net in Germany. However, with the professional set-up of these programs and their explicit attempt to avoid openly racist positions, in the near future they might become a more important means for political mobilisation beyond their present primary role of internal coordination and information exchange.

Table 4.2 Internet users by education and occupation (percentage)

User group	%
Pupils	3.5
Students	48.2
Doctoral researchers	1.5
Civil servants	3.3
Employees	32.6
Self-employed	8.7
Non-employed	1.2
Other	1.0

Source: Survey by W3B Hamburg; 1,880 interviewees; published in *Der Spiegel*, November 1996.

New media and the student protest in Berlin

It is no surprise to note that those groups that become particularly active in cyberspace are those with a privileged access to the technical facilities. When considering the educational and occupational backgrounds of Internet users, the unequal distribution of those who can participate becomes obvious. Access to the Net is still a privilege of the educated and well-off, who are mostly able to use the facilities they have in their offices. Nearly half of all Internet users in Germany are students (see Table 4.2) and only a small minority of the users are female (according to the latest study only 7 to 9 per cent of Internet users are women). The most recent protests by students in Berlin against the financial restrictions for universities and their consequences for scholarly life are a good example of how the new media gain an increasingly important role in grassroots mobilisation.

With the help of the computer Net, the active groups in the three Berlin universities coordinated their protest actions, exchanged information and, at least in a rudimentary form, discussed initiatives and theoretical questions. Given that only a minority of Berlin students yet have free access to the Net, the communication network was used mainly by institutions and groups rather than individuals. As the coordinator of the network said in an interview:

> Being able to communicate among the groups involved in the protest was extremely important when it came to quickly informing the others what kinds of decisions had been taken for the strike and other protest action. By this it became possible to coordinate our actions and even to have 'organised' *ad-hoc* happenings.
> (Interview with H. Muller, September 1996)

Discussion groups were installed in which students could discuss political actions as well as debate strategies for their political campaigns. The 'strike offices' of the three universities involved in the protest communicated with each other via E-mail, exchanging information about forms of political actions, experiences and designs for coordinated protests (demonstrations, sit-ins, open letters to politicians, etc.). This helped to render their activities more efficient and to reduce organisational costs. Furthermore, and more significant in this case, on the organisational level a sense of community and identity was fostered by the communicative interaction between the groups from the different institutions.

The protest of the students was not only coordinated at an urban level with the help of the new technologies but the organisers also interacted with other university-based initiatives in Europe. Students from Paris, Vienna and Berlin, for instance, exchanged views and news about the present situation at their respective universities, possible protest actions to be taken and new ideas about the future shape of the academic systems. Thus, they simultaneously revealed the local and global reference-points of the technology.

It would clearly be an exaggeration to attribute a decisive role to new media in the formation of the student protest in Berlin. The communications technologies alone did not make possible what formerly was not practicable, but they were an important means in stimulating, organising and coordinating the protest. Of particular significance was the direct interaction between the activists which, by the very fact of establishing a communicative community, helped to encourage people to continue with their work and to orientate their ideas in exchange with other students.

The two examples of grassroots activities using the network technology show – beyond the impact the new media have on the formation of collective action – that the cultural environment is decisive in determining the political effects of the new communications technologies. The anarchical character of cyberspace does not necessarily lead to a democratisation of communication processes. Regarding the two cases dealt with here, the result is rather counter-intuitive: whereas for the students the new technologies provided only one means of communication in the contexts of a bottom-up, democratically structured group, they provided right-wing organisations with means for compensating for the lack of grassroots mobilisation. In right-wing groups the technology was not used to broaden and reinforce democratically organised interactive processes in civil society, rather it was turned into an effective tool of a highly authoritarian, closed organisational structure.

CONCLUSIONS

The low usage of the new communications technologies for democratic reform is a striking feature in German politics. As the example of Berlin shows, there are massive cultural and institutional obstacles to advancing and regulating the initiatives in the field of cyberdemocracy. Local administration and, more importantly, the overwhelming majority of the politicians, are highly sceptical about the supposed democratic promise of computer-based civic networks. Regarding both the CIS project in Berlin and political parties or administrative agencies on the national level, there is little enthusiasm about the prospects of an active involvement of the citizens in the political decision-making process. Political culture in Germany is still significantly shaped by an attitude which, after the experiences of the Weimar Republic, tends to equate democracy with institutional stability and thereby excludes reforms towards more participatory models as a genuine threat. Consequently, to employ the new technologies in this respect has never become a major issue in public discourse. Compared to the discussion in the US, policy actors and the major political parties in Germany largely refrain from perceiving the opportunities for innovative forms of civic participation as a chance for democratic renewal. This attitude is reflected in the fact that issues concerning censoring certain elements of computer-based communication (pornography and racist propaganda are seen as major problems) are high on the agenda of the public discourse on the new media in Germany. Political concerns about the right of free speech, in contrast, are rarely raised when it comes to dealing with the normative aspects of the new communications technologies.

As the implications of the computer technologies are still far from clear on the policy level, it is manifest that, regarding the social movement sector, the new medium will significantly change the conditions for political mobilisation in modern society. Computer-based forms of communication heavily impact on the way in which geographically dispersed people can interact with each other and engage in common political undertakings. New resources for involving and motivating people have become feasible, with a minimum of time and money needed by organisational networks. The exchange of information and the coordination of actions among ideologically aligned people has become much easier, substantially redefining the parameters of space and time within which collective action is generated. Regardless of the fact that political actors are just starting to engage in the new medium, the communications technologies will facilitate forms of political mobilisation beyond face-to-face interaction with a relatively small amount of organisational and material resources. Those political groups which are not structured into strong local networks in particular will gain new political opportunities for inspiring mobilisation by means of the new communications technologies.

In the German case, a variety of political agents have started to make use of the opportunities which the communicative market established by these new technologies offers. It is still too early to predict the manifold dynamics this development will provoke in the sphere of politics. However, the experiences in Berlin already make manifest the fact that the supposed new-media's drive toward a more democratic and participatory political life is only one feasible future scenario among many others. In particular, the example of the right-wing groups demonstrates that more horizontal communication by no means secures equal and democratic participation. We are faced with a technique in which a concrete mode of functioning is specified by genuine political decisions. A broadening of the participatory and hence democratic qualities is only one of the possible alternatives.

The crucial point in this respect is, along with the equal distribution of the technical facilities, the effort to assure active interaction between equal participants. As in more traditional media, computer-based communication can very well be used in a way which turns the mass of participants into passive consumers of information and services. This is true for both state agencies and businesses which seek to sell or distribute goods as well as for political actors who attempt to organise their constituency in an authoritarian way or to use the computer technology for the purposes of sheer propaganda. The decentralising and anarchic tendencies alive in cyberspace do not guarantee that economically and politically a more equal power distribution and a more democratic access to the political decision-making process is achieved. Cyberspace does not create a reality on its own, but it is closely linked to political and economic interests which will determine to what extent the democratic promise of these new media will be realised. In present German society the ideal of a universally accessible civic space providing the medium for the interaction of citizens in determining their communal concerns is far from being implemented in the political decision-making process.

The example of Berlin demonstrates that the still elitist technical access to the means of communication, a top-down approach by state agencies, commercial dominance and the authoritarian ambitions of some collective actors can be identified as the major threats to the vision of an interactive democratic community set forth by the new media. The current projects in Berlin give rise to the assumption that at present there are no practical policy initiatives on the horizon which would pave the way for a democratic involvement of the citizens via the new communications technologies. The only feasible way to free the democratic potential which is enclosed in the horizontal interaction of cyberspace is dependent upon the concrete engagement of independent citizen groups and hence the pressure from below. The optimistic images of cyberdemocracy too often forget that a democratic reform on the basis of the new communications technologies will become reality only as the result of intense political contests.

NOTES

1 I use the term 'cyberspace' in a general way to refer to a realm of computer-based communication processes that is completely decoupled from the need to meet physically.
2 These are unevenly distributed among the age cohorts. Whereas 14 per cent of the younger generation (those aged 14–29) use the Internet, among those older than 50 only 2 per cent do so. Figures come from a survey conducted by the EMNID institute in February 1996 and published in the weekly *Der Spiegel* (no. 11, March 1996).
3 Next to the main project organised by the Senat there are more agents offering (partly detailed) information on Berlin. For instance, some departments at the university give information about the city, cultural events or political key issues. The most successful among these is probably the http//www.city.net/ However, I will not consider these in detail because they are limited in terms of their clientele and do not have any ambition to change the policy process. An account of such initiatives in Berlin can be found under http:/www.is.in-berlin.de/users/mfz/public_html/citymetaphor
4 This is an argument taken from the broader debate on introducing elements of direct democracy into the parliamentary system. Often the experiences of the Weimar Republic are taken as a reference-point for basing accusations against such forms of direct democracy of providing the floor for populist if not demagogic political fights.
5 Furthermore, to gain access to the mail-box system beyond restricted 'guest' status it is necessary to become a member, which means providing the organisers of the Net with your personal data.
6 This is also important for another reason: the organisers of the Thule-Net are successful in omitting any message that too openly ignores laws that prohibit explicitly racist, Nazi or anti-semitic propaganda.
7 See the personal insights documented in Schröder (1995) and Steinmetz (1996), who penetrated into the digitalised network of the radical Right and gained detailed information about its form, content and political use.
8 In particular the links between German and American right-wing groups are strong (see *Frankfurter Allgemeine Zeitung*, March 1996).
9 Another example is the case of a right-wing pupils' group in Bavaria. Given their highly limited resources, they asked for help via the Thule-Net and received everything they needed – ranging from know-how and information material to money for printing (see Steinmetz, 1996).

REFERENCES

Canzler, W., S. Helmers and U. Hoffmann (1995) *Die Datenautobahn: Sinn und Unsinn einer populären Metapher*, Forschungspaper des WZB (FS II 95–101), Berlin.
Cohen, J.L. (1985) 'Strategy and Identity: New Theoretical Paradigms and Contemporary Social Movements', *Social Research*, 52: 663–716.
Dutton, W.H. (1996) 'Network Rules of Order: Regulating Speech in Public Electronic Fora', *Media, Culture, Society*, 18: 269–290.
Friedman, D. and D. McAdam (1992) 'Collective Identity and Activism: Networks, Choices, and the Life of a Social Movement', pp. 156–173 in A.D. Morris and C.M. Mueller (eds) *Frontiers in Social Movement Theory*, New Haven, CT and London: Yale University Press.
Garner, R. and M.N. Zald (1985) 'The Political Economy of the Social Movement Sector', in G.D. Suttles and M.N. Zald (eds) *The Challenge of Social Control: Citizenship and Institution Building in Modern Society*, Norwood, N.J.: Ablex.
Gitlin, T. (1980) *The Whole World is Watching: Mass Media in the Making and Unmaking of the New Left*, Berkeley, CA: University of California Press.
Haas, H. (1996) Author interview with Mr H. Haas, responsible for the WWW page for the CDU in Bonn (interview conducted via E-mail, September).
Habermas, J. (1989) *The Structural Transformation of the Public Sphere: An Inquiry into a Category of Bourgeois Society*, Cambridge, MA: MIT Press.
Hagen, M. (1996) 'American Concepts of Electronic Democracy and Their Significance for German Politics', paper presented at the EURICOM Colloquium on Virtual Democracy in Piran (Slovenia), 10–14 April.
Holthusen, B. and M. Jänecke (1994) *Rechtsextremismus in Berlin, Aktuelle Erscheinungsformen, Ursachen, Gegenmaßnahmen*, Marburg: Schüren.
Iglhaut, S., A. Medosch and F. Rötzer (1996) *Stadt am Netz: Ansichten von Telepolis*, Mannheim: Bollmann.
Jenkins, J.C. (1983) 'Resource Mobilization Theory and the Study of Social Movements', *Annual Review of Sociology*, 9: 527–553.
Kitschelt, H. (1990) 'New Social Movements and the Decline of Party Organization', pp. 179–208 in R.J. Dalton and M. Kuechler (eds) *Challenging the Political Order: New Social and Political Movements in Western Democracies*, Cambridge: Polity.
Kittlers, F.A. (1995) 'Die Stadt ist ein Medium', in: G. Fuchs and W. Prigge (eds) *Mythos Metropole*, Frankfurt am Main: Suhrkamp.
Kleinsteuber, H. (1995) '"Technologies of Freedom": Warum werden in den USA Medien so ganz Anders interpretiert?', *Amerikastudien*, 40: 183–297.
Lévy, P. (1994) *L'Intelligence Collective: Pour une Anthropologie du Cyberspace*, Paris: La Découverte.
McAdam, D. (1982) *Political Process and the Development of Black Insurgency*, Chicago: University of Chicago Press.
McAdam, D., J. McCarthy and M. Zald (1988) *Handbook of Sociology*, Newbury Park, CA: Sage.
McCarthy, J.D. and M.N. Zald (1977) 'Resource Mobilization and Social Movements: a Partial Theory', *American Journal of Sociology*, 82: 1212–1241.
Maegerel, A. and M. Mletzko (1994) '"Thule-Netz": Rechtsextremistischer Mail-boxen-Verbund', *Informationsdienst*, 5: 1–6.

Melucci, A. (1985) 'The Symbolic Challenge of Contemporary Movements', *Social Research*, 52: 789–816.
—— (1988) 'Getting Involved: Identity and Mobilization in Social Movements', pp. 329–348 in B. Klandermans, H. Kriesi and S. Tarrow (eds) *From Structure to Action: Comparing Social Movement Research Across Cultures*, Vol. 1, *International Social Movement Research*, Greenwich, CT: JAI Press.
Mitchell, W.J. (1995) *City of Bits: Space, Place, and the Infobahn*, Cambridge, MA: MIT Press (available online under: http://www.mit.edu,City_of_Bits)
Myers, D.J. (1994) 'Communication Technology and Social Movements: Contributions of Computer Networks to Activism', *Social Science Computer Review*, 12 (2): 250–260.
Offe, C. (1985) 'New Social Movements: Challenging the Boundaries of Institutional Politics', *Social Research*, 52: 817–856.
—— (1990) 'Reflections on the Institutional Self-transformation of Movement Politics: A Tentative Stage Model', pp. 232–250 in R.J. Dalton and M. Kuechler (eds), *Challenging the Political Order*, Cambridge: Polity Press.
Pizzorno, A. (1978) 'Political Exchange and Collective Identity in Industrial Conflict', pp. 277–298 in C. Crouch and A. Pizzorno (eds) *The Resurgence of Class Conflict in Western Europe since 1968* (2 vols), London: Macmillan.
—— (1986) 'Some Other Kind of Otherness: A Critique of Rational Choice Theories', pp. 355–373 in A. Foxley, M.S. McPherson and G. O'Donnell (eds) *Development, Democracy and the Art of Trespassing*, Notre Dame, IN: University of Notre Dame Press.
Rheingold, H. (1994) *The Virtual Community: Surfing the Internet*, London: Minerva.
Rötzer, F. (1995) *Die Telepolis: Urbanität im digitalen Zeitalter*, Mannheim: Bollmann.
Schieb, J. (1995) 'Stadt im Netz', *CHIP*, 5 May: 148–150.
Schmidtke, O. (1996) *Politics of Identity: Ethnicity, Territories, and the Political Opportunity Structure in Modern Italian Society*, Sinzheim: Pro Universitate Verlag.
Schröder, B. (1995) *Neonazis und Computernetz*, Hamburg: Rowohlt.
—— (1996) 'Neonazis auch Online in Österreich', *Der Standard*, 3 March 1996.
Seidler, K. (1994) *Computerfreaks like 2 Party: Relay Parties zwischen Virtualität und Realität*, Forschungspaper des WZB (FS II 94–104), Berlin.
Steinmetz, L. (1996) 'Verbreitung rechter Ideologien in Computernetzen', *Forschungsjournal Neue Soziale Bewegungen*, 1 March: 59–69.
Stöss, R. (1989) *Die extreme Rechte in der Bundesrepublik Deutschland: Entwicklung – Ursachen – Gegenmaßnahmen*, Opladen: Westdeutscher Verlag.
Ulrich, H. (1996) Author interview with H. Ulrich, Coordinator of the Project 'City Information System', Senatskanzlei, Berliner Rathaus (5 September).
Zald, M.N. (1991) 'The Continuing Vitality of Resource Mobilization Theory: Response to Herbert Kitschelt's Critique', pp. 323–347 in D. Rucht (ed.) *Research on Social Movements: The State of the Art in Western Europe and the USA*, Frankfurt: Campus; Boulder, CO: Westview Press.
—— (1992) 'Looking Backward to Look Forward: Reflections on the Past and Future of the Resource Mobilization Research Program', pp. 326–348 in A.D. Morris and C.M. Clurgh Mueller (eds) *Frontiers in Social Movement Theory*, New Haven, CT: Yale University Press.

5 Civic networking and universal rights to connectivity: Bologna

Damian Tambini

INTRODUCTION: THE RIGHT TO CONNECTIVITY – IDEAL AND REALITY

> The city of Bologna recognises that information is the essential condition to assure the participation of citizens in the social and political life of the city.
>
> (Article 8 of Bologna city statutes)
>
> All over the world a new dimension is evolving with unbridled momentum and making a major impact on democracy and development, stretching the horizons of citizenship: this is the world of new communication and information technologies, destined to revolutionise democracy and the economy.
>
> (Stefano Bonaga, Bologna's Officer for Innovation and Telematics, 1994a)

Bologna, Spring 1994. City officials suddenly begin speaking about the virtues of 'virtual democracy' and cyberdemocracy. *L'Unita*, the city's newspaper, runs a ten-part series on the computerised city; and journalists, local government officers and communications experts convene to discuss the possibilities of using the Internet to enhance local democracy. Bologna has found a new project, it seems, the construction of an electronic polis. The local authority named its civic networking scheme 'Internet for Bologna and Emilia' or 'IperBolE', which means 'hyperbole' in Italian. Service began in January 1995.

Behind this sudden flurry of activity was a two-pronged attempt to rejuvenate political citizenship in the age of new media. On one hand, city officials, arguing that the information society was coming into being, wanted to guarantee every citizen the right of access to the Internet, with the goal of empowering citizens, preventing the emergence of an uninformed underclass and creating a space for non-commodified communication about everyday local issues on the Net. On the other hand, the town won funds to conduct a series of experiments to develop software for civic networking and electronic democracy. The two sides of this new proposal in electronic democracy went together: by guaranteeing each individual – on paper at least – a 'right to connectivity' in the form of access to the Internet and the civic network, the city government rendered more feasible the experiments in electronic democracy. Only by giving all Bolognese residents access could they claim that their network was a public service that acted and deliberated in the name of the public and reflected the public will.

To guarantee rights to 'connectivity' is not, however, to ensure access in practice. The granting of the right to connect, if it is to be more than a slogan, requires a series of actions on the part of the local authority to guarantee not only access to the hardware, but also computer-literacy. The difficulties experienced in making access genuinely universal in turn impacted upon the development of the civic network. This review of the history of the IperBolE project in Bologna therefore reveals the relationship between active electronic citizenship and universal rights to connectivity, as it traces how the local authority attempted to enable citizens to exercise their rights to connectivity and participation.

Can a local authority grant a right of this kind? This question can only be answered in practice. A right exists when a situation emerges in which citizens can claim that right and authorities feel constrained to and are able to provide for it. Bologna has made a great deal of progress towards that situation. The Bolognese government has developed a commitment to the right to connectivity and explicitly refers to the Internet in the language of civil rights: 'The Internet is like a road system. Citizens should have the right to move freely through it' (Guidi, 1995). When formal rights language is not used, other similar formulations, such as universal service and universal access, are used instead. The basic aim is the same, however: creating the ideal, and thus the commitment to create the reality, of universal access. The degree to which this is achieved has farreaching consequences for the range of services, information and participation that can be provided in a civic network.

The rhetoric of 'cyberdemocracy' deployed in Bologna in 1993 and 1994 was thus to a great extent hyperbole indeed, used by some involved in the project to create political support for the scheme. Project Manager Leda Guidi reflected on the campaign behind the project:

[W]e had to load all these arguments with a lot of meanings, with ideologies, to make them pass. 'Electronic citizenship' 'teledemocracy'

and so on. We had to exaggerate. In Italy it is by no means clear that this space [CMC] will become a democratic space, because if nobody takes the initiative, the Net will become just the space of the market.
(Guidi, 1995)

Clearly, the rhetoric of virtual democracy was used to sell the wider political goal of a right to universal access to 'connectivity': access to communications networks and decommodification of its content.

The resulting set of initiatives are distinguished from the others in this book not only by this attempt to place civic networking in a context of universal rights to connection: Bologna's is more state-centred and one of the most Internet-oriented networks. These two features also have implications for the types of service, information and participation that can take place on the network.

A BRIEF HISTORY OF THE BOLOGNA PROJECT

The IperBolE project in Bologna developed very rapidly from 1993 to 1996. There were already a number of innovatory ICT projects in the city. The 'Cupcard', for example, was already held by every Bolognese, and by inserting it into cashpoint-type machines they could access medical services such as appointment making, and receive certificates on the spot, short-circuiting bureaucracy and queues. The success of the project (which had involved placing several cashpoint-type machines about the city) had created a special openness to the possibilities of using new technology in the city government, and there was much talk of extending the use of 'Cupcard' technology to other service areas. By 1996 a new initiative '*Dimmi*' (tell me) had been launched that allowed locals to conduct a variety of business with the city (e.g. payment of taxes and fines, information on various services). These initiatives reflect a tendency in Bologna to use CMC to deliver services, going beyond many other local authorities that merely use the technology to provide information.

Another input came from an initiative of the EU: the Citycard project under the Esprit project.[1] The aim of the 1.3m-Ecu project was to experiment with electronic solutions to problems of democracy, and Bologna became one of the pilot areas. This provided much-needed funding and a new focus that pushed Bologna towards the use of Internet technology. The EU's Citycard project started trialling 'teledemocracy and telegovernment' technologies in June 1994, in Bologna, Wansbeck (UK), Lisbon and Barcelona. Thus, Bologna became a test-site: some of the experimental solutions of the Citycard project were used immediately on the IperBolE network.

Bologna had long boasted a tradition of decentralised and open local government. This, together with the need to implement a 1990 law on Transparency in Public Services, led councillors to wonder if there was some potential to use the Citycard project to further open the town hall to its public.

In addition to the spread and popularity of the Internet[2] and the various projects of the local authority, Bologna had an edge in the development of these civic technologies for other more fortuitous reasons. The city is the home of CINECA, a universities computing consortium that in 1994 opened a new link with Paris and Geneva (Commune di Bologna, 1994a: 67). Since CINECA was on the local phone network, citizens could have access with relatively low phone tariffs.

THE CYBERDEMOCRACY DEBATE IN BOLOGNA

Debates on the general principle of electronic democracy

When it came to defending the project and asking for finance, the above factors were translated into arguments that the city of Bologna should take a pioneering role in the development of new forms of computer-mediated political participation. Cyberdemocracy, rather than the ideal of universal access, was the focus of debate. Existing traditions of government, close to the lives of the citizens and with a great concern for quality of life, found continuity in the project. So too did the radical traditions of Bologna. According to one IperBolE software consultant, 'the idea of the communal city is being transferred into the idea of the information city' (Mateuzzi, 1996). IperBolE was promoted by the long-ruling PdS (ex-Communist Party) group, which had a strong commitment to public information utilities: access to information as a right.

According to Stefano Bonaga, the IperBolE budget was passed relatively quickly and would have met more opposition had it been better understood. The arguments *against* the provision of Internet access were indeed few, since the project was relatively cheap, and promised to win Bologna prestige, in addition to providing for competitiveness of local industry, which is largely geared to export and thus dependent on cheap, fast communications.

Bolognese debates on IT in government paid little heed to civil liberties objections. Even the SIRIO project, a set of computerised cameras that recognise cars as they enter the city gates, and send fines to those not permitted to drive there, received little criticism along these lines. To the charge that putting politics online will simply exacerbate the division of society into the info-rich and the info-poor, the reply was to insist that it is necessary to make people computer-literate and to make the technology available to people precisely to avoid computer-illiteracy. Hence the fact that Bologna's project in cyberdemocracy, like democratisation historically, was based on an idea of universal suffrage. Plans were set down to train all on the staff and elected officers of the Comune (city government) to use the technology, and then to train the community. Public access terminals in libraries and social clubs would do the rest to make universal access a reality, they argued.

Some at the time complained that the discussion groups would be used for the exchange of erotic messages, but these fears were dispelled when it was pointed out that these could simply be routinely deleted. To the charge that E-mail contact with administrators was no different to paper mail, the reply was that interactive CMC enabled qualitatively different forms of administration–citizen communication, e.g. through discussion groups, and opportunities for automatic message-routing etc.

Lest it appear that the policy development behind the project was simple, it should be pointed out that it was not simply the expression of a utopian ideal, but the fortuitous coincidence of several different projects and policy games that led to the creation of the project.[3] It is further evident that the achievement of the longer-term goals of the project depends on a fragile synergy of other political projects within the Comune.

The following were outlined as the practical goals of computer-mediated democracy in Bologna, according to Comune documents and debates between 1993 and 1994:

- telereferenda;
- telepolls;
- full Internet access as a right for all;
- discussion groups;
- computer-literacy programmes;
- direct access to internal Comune information;
- E-mail links to representatives;
- local area 'civil society' network between administration, organisations and citizens.

The projects' PR literature was uncompromising:

> If the present initiative should finish simply with the installation of cables, computers and modems with a few semi-professional users of

the service, the project should consider itself as failed... We have the ambition that at the end of the project a new democratic fabric, a new space of working democracy will be formed in Bologna.

(Comune di Bologna, 1994b: 9)

Specific debates: Internet access; referenda and polls using CMC?

One key political problem concerned the proposal to offer Internet access to all Bolognese citizens free of charge. This led to protests within the Comune from those that argued that Internet access should be treated as a saleable service like any other, and thus the Comune did not have to take responsibility to provide it. (The chief opponents of Internet access, it was alleged, had connections with a company with an interest in Agora, a local Internet provider, and were simply protecting their own interests.) Support for IperBolE held in the Comune, however, and the funding for the project was passed. This was not the end of the problem, however, and a long legal battle between private Internet providers and the Comune, which they regarded as installing a state monopoly, ensued.

Referenda and surveys using CMC were the most problematic of the original suggestions. In Berlusconi's Italy the agenda-setting effects of polling and referenda were all too close to hand. Thus, Bologna sought other solutions:

> We have the plan to produce software that has the capability to perform opinion surveys. But we are trying to develop 'open surveys'. We want to do surveys that do not work by suggestion. We are a very long way from a referendum.

(Guidi, 1995)

This of course led to further technological problems: most computer applications that could serve as a model (e.g. banking networks) only offer very simple, menu-driven choices. It was asked why electronic polls have an advantage over old-fashioned paper and pen. The response was that, not only are they potentially an easy-to-use and permanent infrastructure, but they have the advantage of interactivity. An interactive poll, designed to avoid pre-setting an agenda, and 'capturing' the citizen (as the Bolognese literature puts it) would be qualitatively different to a paper-based one, where the agenda has been set by politicians and lobbies.

Given the fact that the EU Citycard project part-funded the initiative, and that Citycard's aims were fairly advanced uses of CMC for polling and referenda, there was some pressure to use these technologies in the

IperBolE network. Information Officer Bonaga, however, summarised the reasons why telereferenda and polls would not be instituted by outlining the conditions that would have to be met before they could be put into place:

- Consultation of citizens should be based on open interactivity. The citizen should be able to question the questions that she is asked, and ask for more information. So the question asked in any polls or referenda should not be closed.
- The citizen should have the opportunity to respond in a conditional way. E.g., if x occurs, then y should take place, but in the absence of x it shouldn't.
- The citizen should be able to respond in her own language, and respond in terms of matters of degree. Not just yes or no.
- It should be possible to annul the referendum if many citizens do not feel represented by the range of options, to avoid the possibility that the citizen feels captured by the poll.
- The Citycard initiative required that there should be kiosks around the city, to have access to the network. An online referendum assumes that all have access to vote.[4]

The right to connect is another way to express the last point, which is surely also the most important. Without universality of access, referenda and voting cannot be contemplated – a very simple fact which is none-the-less overlooked in many discussions of electronic democracy (Arterton, 1987). A further condition of the original Citycard initiative was that in its aim to develop interaction between administrations and citizens it should not limit the dialogue to menu-driven interaction. In the place of that closed, multiple-choice-type interaction should be a 'natural-language dialogue'. This would avoid agenda-setting. On the software side this led to the development of dialogue managers of various kinds. And further delays.

CYBERDEMOCRACY, BOLOGNA 1997: A COMPROMISE?

In 1997, a subscriber to IperBolE received a package of services:
- full Internet access;
- shareware to provide access to discussion groups and the Internet;
- limited technical assistance (to promote access for non-experts, mainly help in setting up the software);
- access to Comune-edited discussion groups, and E-mail between local organisations, citizens and administration;

- a hypertext data-base of civic information;
- international E-mail;
- international, local and national news groups.

Guidi summed up her short-term priorities for her use of Internet/WWW technologies. They were to:

- link up more of the offices of the Comune so that they can respond more effectively to enquiries;
- link all schools and libraries in Bologna;
- improve access and computer-literacy;
- have open access terminals in libraries and youth centres;
- develop the content of what people can access (information on the city);
- link up with other cities in Italy and with Barcelona, Amsterdam, Helsinki and Manchester, on the 'Digital Cities' project in Europe.

By November 1996, six terminals were open to the public in libraries, by appointment and with technical assistance. Dozens more were semi-public, however, being housed in schools, clubs and the offices of political and cultural organisations.

Software

The home-user software was the standard programs that are used by any World Wide Web or Internet user (Netscape, Mosaic, etc.). Old versions of these programs were provided free by the city.

In developing the other software for the project, the city government had a close relationship with their technological partners Omega Generation, a small local software design firm, and CINECA, the university computing centre. They were provided with a UNIX operating system and ample current CMC software, such as ftp, gopher, WWW, WAIS and mail. Further, a list server, a news distribution server, a WWW server and a mailer were put in to operation. The software for the project was developed with EU financing. The R & D work which the long-term goals require (especially the Comune–Internet interface, kiosks, polls and referenda) is still underway and will require further funding if it is to reach its stated goals.

Funding

The project cost between 500 and 700 million lire per year (about US$0.5m) from its beginning in 1994 until the end of 1996. Of this, 50

92 *Damian Tambini*

per cent came from outside grants, mainly from the EU, and the remainder was from the Comune's own budget, which is renewed annually.

System architecture:

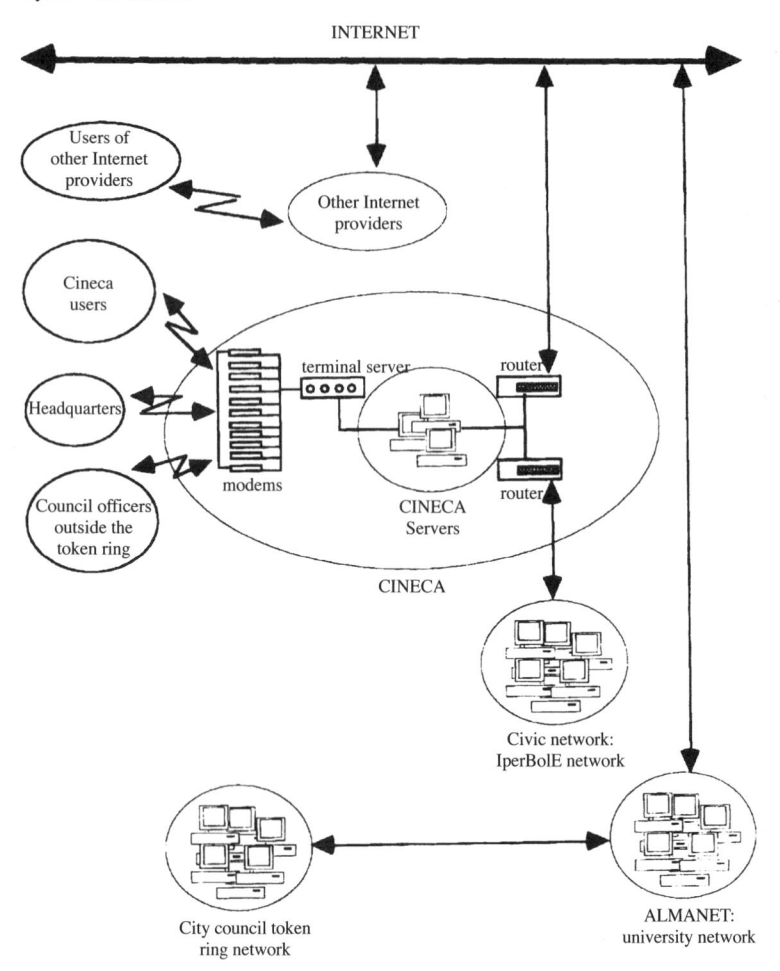

Figure 5.1 City council connections

Civic networking and rights to connectivity: Bologna 93

Hardware

Figure 5.1 shows the system architecture. The network is split into two, with the CINECA machine serving as a mirroring system, updated daily, and as a back-up to the machine based in City Hall. It is also IperBolE's link to the outside world. It is via the CINECA server that Bolognese citizens exercise their right to access the Internet, and through which external users can read (in certain periods they have been able to contribute to) the city's discussion groups and hypertext pages. The CINECA machine is linked via a 64-kb cable to the Hewlett Packard/UNIX machine based in the offices of Leda Guidi, officer for citizen–administration relations. Citizen access to the network is via a terminal server which is attached to sixteen modems. Also in Guidi's charge are links to an Apple Aws 95, a Mac 6150/7.5 and the WWW server. It is this WWW server on which the Comune posts information on the city, events, current issues, etc. Other government-related institutions, such as the police station and the Ministry of the Interior, have access via a second WWW server.

Server: There are two main servers: Accursio (the HP9000 Comune server) and Nettuno (the HP9000 CINECA server).

Modems: In addition to the sixteen modems located in the council offices, there are sixty-four at CINECA.

Protocols: Users may connect to Nettuno or to Accursio. Accursio allows only SLIP connections while Nettuno allows only PPP connections (faster and more reliable).

News server: Nettuno is the only news server.

Web server: There are two web servers (at CINECA and at City Hall) and the city information is daily mirrored on the CINECA server.

Mail server: Mail messages are managed as follows: A pop3 server runs on Accursio, and users read mail from this server. When users send mails, a SMTP server on the CINECA server is used. This solution balances the weight of mail processes.

Access control: The mail access control (XTACACS) is performed by the Accursio server. There is a secondary server at CINECA, to serve the sixty-four modems, that is updated by the main one at intervals.

Proxy server: The proxy server will be soon moved to a machine at CINECA.

The use of the network: universal?

By the end of 1996, over 5,000 private citizens had subscribed to the IperBolE project for use on PCs in the home. So had 200 local organisations, which we can assume have multiple users. These organisations generally had a homepage with links from the Bologna local government homepage. The list of associations included professional groups, lobbies and pressure groups such as Amnesty International, non-governmental organisations, cultural organisations and businesses. In addition to these, thirty schools, seven trade unions, the police stations, several hospitals and several nearby local government offices were registered. Leaving aside the tiny Emilia Nationalist Party, only two political parties had subscribed (the two parts of the old Communist Party – Rifondazione Comunista and the Pds). Local small- and medium-sized businesses can get full Internet access at a discount price from IperBolE.

Given that the Comune offers Internet access through the same accounts as those that offer access to the civic information and discussion groups, however, counting subscriptions is not a good measure of the scheme's success in fostering democratic participation. The IperBolE organisers reported 5,000–10,000 'hits' per day at the close of 1996 (ten times the figure for a year previously), but were unable to distinguish those made by Bologna citizens from those of external netsurfers who 'visited' the Bologna site. By November of 1996, IperBolE reported that a total of 15,000 E-mails had been sent to the city administration via the system and a total of 12,000 replies returned. According to a survey of users carried out by the projects organisers, three-quarters of them reported using the newsgroups, slightly less than reported using the E-mail service. Although the data, as an online survey, probably overrepresent heavy users, the findings were as shown in Tables 5.1 and 5.2.

Table 5.1 Use of E-mail by IperBolE users

I use the E-mail service...	no.	%
always	104	42.6
very often	62	25.4
often	39	16.0
little	18	7.4
never	10	4.1
no reply	11	4.5

Source: Comune di Bologna, Servizio IperBolE, Online User Survey, 1996

Civic networking and rights to connectivity: Bologna   95

Table 5.2 Use of discussion groups by IperBolE users

I use the Newsgroups...	no.	%
always	29	12.0
very often	56	23
often	58	23.8
little	57	23.4
never	30	12.3
no reply	14	5.7

Source: Comune di Bologna, Servizio IperBolE, Online User Survey, 1996

SURFING BOLOGNA: READING CIVIC COMMUNICATIONS IN BOLOGNA

(See at http://www.comune.bologna.it)

What is posted by the Comune?

The city's read-only information data-base aims to provide citizens with the information and contacts that they need, broadly, in order to participate in local civil society. Netsurfers will find that the format is a standard hypertext menu, usually with one or two layers of links for each option. The homepage menu includes around thirty options, including maps, information on the departments of the Comune and the services offered (see the list on p. 104). This WWW server boasted 6,000 pages of information at the end of 1996, with 763 links to external pages. There is a 'Guide to Public Administration and Organised Civil Society' containing links to lists of voluntary associations, the police, hospitals and schools. Indeed, there are many lists. There are, however, few direct E-mail links from these pages, even when the organisation concerned has an IperBolE account. What you have in the guide to civil society is an equivalent to the Yellow Pages, with lists of telephone numbers and street addresses rather than genuine attempts to exploit the interactivity of the technology. Elsewhere, the home pages offer minitel-type benefits, such as train and bus timetables, but again, interactivity is lacking here. There is no booking service available, so electronic citizens have to queue at the station like everyone else.

If not seen as a Yellow Pages, the Bologna data-base might read a little like a state propaganda organ, since the pages are all put together by the staff of the Comune, and they are not shy about self-promotion. They tend to promote the local authority itself. A link to a small, out-of-town Comune's information pages led me to the slogan 'Granorolo Town Hall: We are Working For You'.

What are the citizens talking about with one another?
A cynic might say that when they are not talking about sport and showbiz they are talking about what they have been told to talk about. In the discussion groups, as with the information pages, the Comune retains a strong agenda-setting role. They designed the original list of discussion topics, the rules for setting them up, and retain the right to censor discussions, removing party political propaganda, publicity and erotic messages. The news discussion groups have one- or two-page introductions to their topics, which will clearly be the most constant and influential reference-points in the discussions. There are three types of discussion groups: free, moderated and restricted ('restricted' having a powerful chairperson, and access limited to subscribing members; 'moderated' groups have a less powerful chair; 'free groups' might be a misnomer, given that the topic of discussion has been chosen by the Comune and the agenda firmly set with an introductory passage).

The right to set the agenda is clearly currently in the hands of the designers of the project (in practice Leda Guidi). There have been no discussions about whether to elect discussion moderators. Guidi chose the subjects of the discussion groups, and as in the case of erotic and party political messages, reserves the right to censor discussion groups. Citizens can, if they are seconded by twenty others, set up their own discussion groups, so there is the potential for more spontaneously organised discussion groups to replace those initially set up by the Comune.

The more popular groups are often concerned with leisure interests (e.g. motorbike riding) and parenting groups. Of more directly policy-oriented discussions, the busiest by far was that given over to traffic. The popularity of rather apolitical, leisure interests rather than civic political ones is reflected in the new citizen-selected discussion groups, marked in the list below with a star.

Bologna discussion groups

Bologna by night*
environment
swap shop*
Charta 94 (council initiative)
Citycard (council initiative)
computers
cooking*

culture
cinema
books
music
future
Project IperBolE
work
Metropolis (space to debate the hot topics of the metropolitan area)
 metropolis.communication
 metropolis.railways
 metropolis.ATC programmes
 metropolis.tourism
multiethnic Bologna
navigator?
new groups (discussion group to discuss the addition of new groups)
polemics*
politics*
technical problems
health
unions
showbiz
sport*
test
traffic
university*
travel*
jokes exchange*

IPERBOLE: KEY ISSUES

In the first years of the project, some revealing problems arose. I will deal with these under the headings of: take-up, selectivity, 'netiquette' and content regulation, translation, legal problems, privacy, and user identity. Each of these, as I will note, is affected in a different way by the varying degrees to which the Comune manages to deliver on its promised right to connectivity.

1 Take-up

Whereas the administration explains slow or low take-up in terms of a lack of hardware and/or of computer-literacy, the lack of take-up by the town hall's own staff is less easily explained. Training courses have been offered free to staff, they have the hardware, and still they rarely respond to E-mails that concern their department. Even the founder and chief defender of the project, Stefano Bonaga (1995), admits that his colleagues 'respond very little at the moment'. Bonaga and the project's defenders say that it is just a matter of time: that computer-literacy, like all forms of literacy, will have to be carefully fostered and taught. But the project itself does not have the resources to take responsibility for education on this scale. None the less, this assumes that education programmes will be taken up if offered, and that is by no means a given. The campaign for universal access and computer-literacy has therefore become fundamental to the project's success. In January 1997 the first city-wide computer-literacy project focused energies on the long term: setting up courses on the culture and techniques of the Internet in the city's high schools.

2 Selectivity

This raises the question of the selectivity of electronic citizenship. Athens excluded women and slaves. Does electronic Bologna systematically exclude any group? In Bologna, users are more likely to be in their 20s or 30s, male (86 per cent), and occupied either as a student, a manager or a professional. Not only are cyber citizens only a fraction of the population of Bologna, therefore, they are a very distorted sample. It has been said about the Santa Monica experiment that the user of PEN was likely to post quite reactionary, right-wing opinions, judging from comments in the discussion groups (Varney, 1991; Dutton, 1991). In Bologna, however, the political profile of the user, judging from the discussion groups is less right-wing, which suggests that it is not the technology *per se* that imposes any kind of bias on debate; political norms on the Net may simply reinforce local political hegemony.

Table 5.3 IperBolE users by age

Age	Percentage	Total from first 5,000 users
under 20	2	100
20–30	35	1,750
30–40	37	1,850
40–50	18	900
60–70	6	300
over 70	3	150
	1	50

Source: IperBolE user survey, 31 October 1996

Civic networking and rights to connectivity: Bologna 99

Table 5.4 IperBolE users by gender

Sex	Percentage	Total
women	14	742
men	86	4,558
	total	5,000

Source: IperBolE user survey, 31 October 1996

Table 5.5 IperBolE users by profession

Profession	Percentage	Per 5,000
student	19.0	950
housewife	0.51	26
soldier	0.3	26
pensioner	0.3	7
company director	1.0	89
manager (*impiegato*)	41.0	2,034
unskilled worker	0.6	27
small business owner	1.0	70
private sector professional	18.0	906
self-employed	1.0	52
other	12.59	630

Source: IperBolE user survey, 31 October 1996

Selectivity of users is likely to result from inequalities of access and of computer-literacy levels. According to Leda Guidi, the Comune is behind in its programmes to link each city quarter with the network and provide open access terminals in public places. One hindrance is that, because most initial users are novices, each terminal requires a member of staff to teach the uninitiated how to use the system. Therefore, all public access terminals are in schools, clubs or libraries, where staff can be on hand to assist the public.

3 'Netiquette' and content regulation

Insults, 'flaming' and rudeness were not a problem in Bologna's civic network in its first two years. Any *risqué* comments, for example in the new joke exchange discussion group, were simply removed by an operator. One fracas that did give system administrators a headache involved a customer of a local pizzeria criticising the establishment online for not providing a receipt (a sure sign of tax-dodging in Italy) – and for making bad pizza. The owner of the pizzeria hired a lawyer when he heard of this, and only dropped the proceedings when he had an apology from the Comune and all concerned. In general, however, such events were isolated, easily dealt with by informal E-mailed warnings. It has never been necessary to exclude users. Although there is no reassuring precedent to govern such occurrences, the IperBolE organisers were more worried about commercial and propagandistic use of the network than online manners.

Electoral propaganda posted on the IperBolE bulletin boards does get 'flamed' by users. The real problem for the Comune, however, is its legal status during election campaigns. Although there has never been a prosecution for online propaganda, it would appear to be an offence under the new anti-Berlusconi *Par Condicio* laws.[5] At the same time, the Comune did not want to make the network politically irrelevant by excluding the parties. For the present, a compromise position has been found: political parties can post information that is defined as '*generale*' (contact numbers, names of representatives, addresses, etc.) but not that defined as '*ideologico*', such as manifestos and speeches. Therefore, the situation arises where individuals, but not parties, can post political messages. Here IperBolE faces similar problems to public broadcasters – of balance in representation – and will not include party political ideological content until this problem is resolved and a way of ensuring balanced coverage in interactive media is agreed. The distinction between ideological and general information is, however, harder to draw regarding information on Web pages than it would be on TV; there is more information and it is generally provided by political actors themselves, not 'impartial' presenters. Further, if a BBC-type quota system were introduced, it would be more difficult to regulate equality of coverage, because links render space infinite in this medium which is not governed by time-scarcity as is broadcasting. The anomalous – but somehow very 1990s – situation of encouraging political participation while discouraging parties and ideology is therefore an unstable compromise.

4 Translation: the authority-citizenry interface

The key technological problem was the interface between the existing IT systems that are used in the local authority and the communications protocols used on the Internet. Given the broader aim of rendering the local administration transparent, the ideal would be to permit citizens access to all information that is stored on the Comune's own databases: to open the intraNet to the Internet. According to the Comune, technological problems prevent this.

Bologna's technical consultants hope eventually to give access via the Web to internal Comune information in the most simple and direct way, rather than via hypertext. 'I should be able to enter a keyword, e.g., tourism, music or travel, and the interface should be able to find me all the documents that match with that word' (Guidi, 1995). The aim has been to automate response to standard enquiries. For example, the program could tell you where your planning permission application is, when it will be complete, whether there are any problems with it, etc.

Ideally, according to Bonaga, the Internet should therefore serve as an instrument through which the Comune can communicate with itself and with its citizens. Thus far, however, short of manually re-entering all town hall records in an Internet-compatible format, it has become clear that there was no simple way to do this and thus the interface would be unfeasible in the short term. It became the subject of longer-term research. Thus, a revised plan was outlined for the administration–citizens interface, effectively a compromise.

Message routing was more successful. It was agreed that citizens did not know sufficiently well how the city bureaucracy worked. Therefore they did not know to whom to address their various comments or complaints, or indeed how to go about making suggestions or starting citizens initiatives. As part of the Citycard initiative, software was designed that would recognise the subject of E-mail messages by keywords, and re-E-mail them to the appropriate offices. The system, trialled as part of the Bologna civic network from October 1996 onwards, required each local government office to list about twenty keywords that describe their competencies and to give each one a score from 0–15 reflecting its importance to that office. The message goes to the office where it scores most points after all the words in it are analysed by the programme. In the first month of the trial, the system was able to send 80 per cent of messages sent to the general postbox on to the correct offices. Those messages that the system is unable to send on are sent to a default mail-box and forwarded by an operator. On the basis of these manual operations the keyword systems are refined.

5 Legal problems

By offering Internet access as a free service, the Bologna local authority has challenged the *status quo* by making public provision in this largely privately operated medium. As a result, the city authorities became involved in a legal battle as private Internet providers attempted to protect their markets from what appears to them to amount to a state-owned monopolistic takeover.

There may also be legal difficulties with the provision of free software. The city government has to take care not to take actions that would be interpreted as piracy, while at the same time promoting the use of the civic network through keeping it as cheap as possible in order to support universal access.

6 Privacy

As the services available over the network expand, so too do the potential problems with privacy: it would be beneficial to put some information – e.g. personal health records – out of reach of the network, and there may in the future be the need to create a password system, or have some form of decoder in the home. Whether there will also be attempts by the state to limit encryption (and thus permit better surveillance of content) remains to be seen. There is no evidence that users of the IperBolE services exchange encoded messages.

7 User identity

Privacy and legality come together when decisions are made on how to identify users. According to Guidi, 'we have a system that does not identify the user until the Comune, according to an agreed process, decides to identify her, with judicial involvement. The name and surname remains in a closed envelope' (Guidi, 1995). The citizen gives messages anonymously, so that no one in the Comune can legally be identified, even by those within the Comune. Subscribers to discussion groups do, however, more often than not sign with their own names, and occasionally list additional information such as street address. This contrasts with solutions in other cities, such as Santa Monica, where the citizen is automatically named online. User identity is one aspect that might become crucial in the event that the technology does become more important in the future. For example, if any attempt is made to use the technology to conduct referenda or elections, it will become necessary to link identities of users with those of real citizens/legal subjects, in order to prevent duplication of identities. Conversely, there is the prospect that, as with experiments with interactive TV (Arterton, 1987: chapter 6) there will effectively be one voice per household, as many users (conventionally a family) will share an appliance and a single account. The gender and social implications could be far-reaching. This aspect of design could therefore potentially limit the degree to which the technology could be used as an instrument of conventional, representative democracy.

If any form of electronic voting came into being, of course, having voters identified by name would compromise secrecy of the ballot. In the case of voting and referenda, therefore, 'we might need two separate systems, one for voting and another for other services' (Mateuzzi, 1996).

CONCLUSIONS. UNIVERSAL VERSUS NON-UNIVERSAL CYBERCITIZENSHIP

There are two basic responses to the problem of information-poverty in the era of converging media and the Internet: a conservative one and a radical one. The conservative one is to keep the key transactions of democracy offline, to ensure that those who do not have access to new media will not be disadvantaged. This is difficult, but referenda, voting and even polls can as we have seen, be kept off, due to the non-representativeness/non-universality of connectivity. There remains, however, the problem of a growing inequality of access to political information. Alternatively, you can opt for the radical solution and try to put everything and everyone online; this was the response chosen by the city of Bologna. The inevitable compromise – of attempting to guarantee universal citizenship rights of connectivity, but succeeding only in part – is the structure of the drama of cyberdemocratisation, and the reason why so many of the democratic hopes associated with this technology are not to be realised for some time.

T.H. Marshall has been a silent companion throughout this chapter. It is precisely his schema of citizenship theory that inspired this approach. He traced the emergence of civic, political and social rights in the history of England, and I have used a similar framework to analyse the emergence of 'rights to connectivity' in Bologna. For Marshall, there was a progressive dynamic begun by the granting of civil rights in the seventeenth century that led necessarily to the political and then social rights necessary for their provision in practice. (Universal political rights, for example, are impracticable without the education and welfare rights that make it possible to act politically.) For the case of Bologna, in contrast, I have examined the extent to which a progressive dynamic in citizenship practices can be created around issues of connectivity. Just as the granting of political rights ultimately led to the provision of social rights to education, the granting of rights to connectivity in Bologna were seen as necessary for the practical exercise of political rights, and this led to the commitment to rights to education in computer-literacy. Like Marshall, I traced how a right was given as though it was really attainable, and showed how the dynamic of citizen involvement depends on the process whereby actors try to turn right-as-ideal into right-as-reality.

104 Damian Tambini

Table 5.6 Planned and current services in Bologna's IperBolE project

Services originally suggested	State of play of these services
Telereferenda	R&D (very long-term goal)
Telepolls	R&D (very long-term goal)
Full Internet access as a right	Granted spring 1996; growing use
Discussion groups	Up and running; mainly entertainment (non-political) use
Computer literacy programmes	Some provision to Comune staff, funding problem
Direct access to internal Comune information	Large technological problems and delays; long-term goals; some selected information is available
E-mail links to representatives	They do not read their E-mail
Local area network between administration, organisations and citizens	Many have suscribed; difficult to say how much this network is being used, and what for

Table 5.7 Universal versus partial cyber citizenship

Service	Civic networking without universal access/rights to connectivity	Civic networking with universal access/rights to connectivity
Discussion groups	Free but irrelevant	Potentially binding or advisory role (like parliamentary committees)
Polling	Unfeasible due to selectivity of sample	Possible in long term
Voting referenda	Unfeasible due to selectivity of sample	Possible in long term
Service delivery	Unfair as it promotes inegalitarian access to services	Possible in long term
Information provision	Leads to politically disenfranchised underclass of uninformed	Many possible applications
Civil society networks	Possible	Useful: provides individual actors with better ways of finding those who serve their interests, and provides civil society organisations with cheap communications

Given that by the end of 1996 only a very unrepresentative minority – around 5,500 of Bologna's 390,000 people – had subscribed as individuals to IperBolE, it may seem a trifle early to speak of universal cybercitizenship in Bologna. But grant that, after only three years, IperBolE terminals were in more than one home in thirty, and many more citizens accessed the network than that, from their work-places, clubs or from public places. (This compares favourably with the early provision of libraries, television and telephone services.) But the city's excursion into cyberdemocracy had always been a two-pronged one. On one hand, the project's backers wanted, for political reasons, to institute a 'right to connectivity' for the citizens of the town. On the other hand, spurred by their role in trialling technologies for an EU research project, they wanted to demonstrate what could be done with these technologies – given universal access.

For civic networking with and without universal access are two entirely different things. Leaving aside the merits of rights to information in the broader national and supranational context, IperBolE shows how civic networking could be transformed by universality of access. Bologna, as the only case in this book that attempted to base a civic networking project on the foundation of universal access, and as one that has attempted to make that ideal a reality, illustrates the implications of such a decision on several levels. Thus, the degree to which universality of access is granted can transform:

The range of services that can be contemplated: voting and polls, as we saw, were entertained only as experiments in the Citycard project, although in the original debates and documents they had been seen as a key target of IperBolE. The principal reason that they were not instituted in the first three years of the project was that universal access could not realistically be granted, and therefore referenda or polls, whatever the advantages of interactivity, would not be legitimate.

The weight of services such as discussion groups in the broader political context: without a convincing principle of universal access, we cannot assume that anyone interested in a topic, or affected by a political discussion on it, can contribute to discussions about it. Indeed, it could be argued that, due to the selectivity of the 'sample' of civic networkers as compared to the total population, there is a strong argument not to listen to online discussion groups. Until universal access is a reality, such groups can have no more importance than conversations in a local bar. If, however, in ideal and practice the discussion group is open to all citizens who want to participate, its role may be similar to a council committee, and it could potentially carry some weight in an advisory capacity.

The efficiency and legitimisation of communications provided: it is a commonplace to complain about the level of culture on the Net – discussion groups are unedited, and the advantages of free access are often outweighed by the disadvantages of wading through byte after byte of dross, or worse, 'flame wars' and online insults. In other media, such problems are avoided through the presence of editors, and this is the role of the system administrators on IperBolE who, in some documents indeed refer to themselves as the 'editorial board'. I have at various points touched upon the disadvantages of this powerful role (bias and agenda-setting) but it also has its advantages: for example, ensuring to a certain extent a minimum of content quality. Only by ensuring a reasonable level of content can operators hope to break the vicious circle of low-content quality which leads to low participation, which compounds problems of low quality, and so forth.

The aim of universal service in Bologna also permitted centralised infrastructure investment, which, together with the larger numbers involved, reduces the overall cost of services to the citizen/consumer.

The details, for example, regarding what constitutes universal access or service, and when we could realistically say that a population enjoys the right to connectivity remain to be seen. (Do we need a terminal in every home, or in every library, for example? How is a degree of computer-literacy to be defined?) Even in Bologna such rights as a reality are still in the distant future. The recent initiatives in Bologna do, however, demonstrate what a difference commitment to rights as ideal can make to a project in civic networking.

IperBolE also shows how the hype surrounding civic networking can be useful to those who seek to promote rights issues. The ideals of rights to information and the idea of public information utilities are not new, but originated in the 1960s. In Bologna, however, these abstract ideals were given a solid and attractive rationale by linking them to the hopes currently held in civic networking. The policy process showed that cyberdemocracy arguments are a newsworthy and palatable sweetener for the more dense and stale rights to connectivity arguments.

IperBolE: the BBC of the Internet?

The project also reveals the problems that any centralised attempt to carve out a 'public space' on the Net is likely to face: apart from the legal problems and monopoly criticisms raised by profit-oriented

Internet providers, the public provider is likely to face accusations of bias and selectivity along the same lines as public broadcasters did in the 1970s and 1980s.

Problems of bias diminish, to a certain extent, with time as the network incorporates citizens' own initiatives and interactivity becomes more important, as the changing lists of newsgroups illustrate, but further research into agenda-setting on the Net would be necessary to understand better these forms of bias. Hidden forms of agenda-setting, such as FAQs (frequently asked questions) are a common feature of discussion groups, but it is the more obvious ones, such as censorship and automated censorship, and encryption as a response, that are getting more attention.

Whether there is a body capable of deciding between radical and conservative responses to information poverty, however, remains to be seen. Net culture has developed a strange allergy to any form of state intervention, but Bologna demonstrates that some intervention may be necessary for the useful application of CMCs in democratic processes. This case further demonstrates that the possibilities for civic networks are completely altered when the right to connectivity (as an ideal, but especially as a reality) comes into play.

The key question remains, however, whether access to the Net is indeed comparable to civil, political and social rights of citizenship in the past. Just how important is computer-literacy and connectivity likely to be in the exercise of political citizenship? The answer, of course, is that it is circular: computer-literacy will be as important as we decide it will be. Where progressive authorities gamble that they can reach more through the radical route they will do so, but many will see a more egalitarian future of political participation through the conservative strategy.

ACKNOWLEDGEMENTS

I would like to thank the following people in Bologna for interviews: Stefano Bonaga, Giovanna Dore, Leda Guidi, Matteo Mateuzzi and the staff of Sportello IperBolE. I would like to thank the following people for commenting on this paper in the various stages of its development: Cathy Bryan, Klaus Eder, Nicholas Garnham and Yasemin Soysal.

NOTES

1 Esprit project number P8123.
2 *La Repubblica*, the national daily ran twenty-one stories on the previously obscure technology between September 1994 and April 1995.

3 The project's development, like that in Santa Monica thus depended on an 'ecology of games' (Dutton, 1991). The expansionist ambitions of the office for relations with the citizens, together with local software companies' aims to get their hands of EU money, the ideas of public information utilities and the desire to make the Internet public were only part of the concatenation of motivations.
4 From Bonaga (1995) and Comune di Bologna (1994b).
5 These laws were passed to prevent Berlusconi using his newspapers and TV stations to promote his new political party, Forza Italia.

REFERENCES

Arterton, F.C. (1987) *Teledemocracy: Can Technology Protect Democracy?* London and New York: Sage.
—— (1989) 'Teledemocracy Reconsidered', pp. 438–450 in T. Forrester (ed.) *Computers in the Human Context: Information Technology, Productivity and People*, Oxford: Basil Blackwell.
Baker, T. (1981) 'Teledemocracy: Bringing Power Back to the People', *Futurist*, December: 6–9.
Bellamy, C., I. Horrocks and J. Webb (1995) 'Exchanging Information with the Public: From One-stop Shops to Community Information Systems', *Local Government Studies*, 21 (1) Spring: 11–30.
Bonaga, S. (1994) 'Servizio di Comunicazione e Relazioni con i Cittadini' (speech) Comune di Bologna.
—— (1995) Author interview with Stefano Bonaga, founder of HyperBolE project, at Comune di Bologna, Piazza Maggiore, Bologna (3 November).
Comune di Bologna (1994a) *Democrazia Virtuale* (local authority booklet).
—— (1994b) *Internet Per Bologna e l'Emilia-Romagna. Ampliamenti del Progetto Esprit Citycard. La società civile in Rete a Bologna* (local authority PR document).
Dutton, W.H. (1991) 'An Ecology of Games: The Political Construction of Santa Monica's Public Electronic Network', *Informatisation and the Public Sector*, 1: 279–301.
Etzioni, A. (1972) 'Minerva: An Electronic Town Hall', *Policy Sciences*, 3: 457–474.
Fishkin, J. (1991) *Democracy and Deliberation: New Directions for Democratic Reform*, New Haven, CT: Yale University Press.
Garnham, N. (1986) 'The Media and the Public Sphere', pp. 37–53 in P. Golding (ed.) *Communicating Politics: Mass Communications and the Political Process*, New York: Holmes and Meier.
Guidi, L. (1995) Author interview with Leda Guidi, Manager, HyperBolE, at Comune di Bologna, Piazza Maggiore, Bologna (23 May).
Habermas, J. (1989) *The Structural Transformation of the Public Sphere: An Inquiry into a Category of Bourgeois Society*, Cambridge, MA: MIT Press.
Hacker, K. (1996) 'Missing Links in the Evolution of Electronic Democratization', *Media, Culture and Society*, 18: 213–232.
McLean, I. (1986) 'Mechanisms for Democracy', pp. 135–157 in D. Held and C. Pollit (eds) *New Forms of Democracy*, London: Sage.
Mateuzzi, M. (1996) Author interview with M. Mateuzzi, Omega Software, Bologna (3 November).

Myers, D.J. (1994) 'Communication Technology and Social Movements: Contributions of Computer Networks to Activism', *Social Science Computer Review*, 12 (2): 250–260.

Piercy-Smith, J. (1995) *Digital Democracy: Information and Communications Technologies in Local Politics*, Commission for Local Democracy, Report No. 14, May.

Rheingold, H. (1994) *The Virtual Community: Surfing the Internet*, London: Minerva.

Sparks, C. (1991) 'Goodbye, Hildy Johnson: The Vanishing "Serious Press"', pp. 58–74 in P. Dahlgren and C. Sparks (eds) *Communication and Citizenship: Journalism and the Public Sphere*, London: Routledge.

Toffler, A. (1980) *The Third Wave*, New York: Bantam.

Valaskakis, K. and P. Arnopoulis (1982) *Telecommunitary Democracy: Utopian Vision or Probable Future?*, Montreal: McGill and Montreal Universities, Gamma Research Service.

Van Dijk, J. (1996) 'Models of Democracy: Behind the Design and Use of New Media in Politics', *Javnost/The Public*, 3 (1): 43–57.

Varney, P. (1991) 'What's Really Happening in Santa Monica?', *Technology Review*, November/December: 43–51.

Williams, F. (1982) *The Communications Revolution*, New York: New American Library.

6 An Internet resource for neighbourhoods

Ed Schwartz

Neighborhoods Online is an Internet resource centre established by the Institute for the Study of Civic Values in Philadelphia, in co-operation with a local community network known as 'LibertyNet', to assist groups both within the city and around the country that are working to improve conditions in the neighbourhoods and communities where we live.

On the surface, this would appear to be an improbable project. Organised nationally – even internationally – its primary goal is to assist organisations operating at the local level, as distinct from local community networks examined elsewhere in this volume, whose primary goal is to extend online access and develop resources for individuals.

By contrast, those of us who are building Neighborhoods Online are concentrating on *groups* working in inner-city neighbourhoods in the United States, where Internet access is still largely out of reach. The E-mail lists and Websites associated with the project are designed to help staff and leadership of these organisations connect with one another, gain quick access to information related to neighbourhood problems, and keep track of legislation and public policy decisions that will affect them.

The activists and policy-makers who now use Neighborhoods Online don't know one another, but a long-term goal of the project is to bring them together around common issues and goals. Where the mass media and corporations are now trying to configure the Internet as a new centre for broadcasting and marketing, Neighborhoods Online is exploring its potential for political empowerment.

To explain how Neighborhoods Online is evolving, I want first to describe the community-based organisations and broad-based neighbourhoods' movement that it is intended to serve. From there, I will outline the basic steps that we are taking to meet their needs. Finally, I will discuss the challenges that we face as we seek to build the programme in the years ahead.

THE NEIGHBOURHOODS' MOVEMENT

While there is a rich tradition of civic and political associations in the United States going back to the country's founding, the modern neighbourhoods' movement can be said to have emerged in the 1960s. Both the War on Poverty and the federal Model Cities programme focused primarily on helping the poor fight their way into the political system through building grassroots organisations at the local level. These were effective enough to have prompted a backlash from big-city mayors, making it easy for Richard Nixon to kill the programmes almost as soon as he took office.

Yet what the Nixon administration did, ended up contributing to the process that it was supposed to shut down. By turning more than $4bn directly over to cities and smaller communities in the form of a Community Development Block Grant (CDBG) – and insisting upon 'citizen participation' in the implementation of local plans – Washington was creating a local pot of federal money in cities throughout the United States around which citizen groups could organise. In Philadelphia, as an example, more than 100 organisations stormed the city council in 1974 – the first year of CDBG – to protest a plan advanced by the Mayor, Frank Rizzo, to demolish 10,000 vacant houses in the inner city that residents felt ought to be rehabilitated. By 1976, at a city-wide convention, 1,000 neighbourhood activists coalesced around what became known as the Philadelphia Council of Neighborhood Organizations, to advance their demands for better housing and broad-based improvements in neighbourhoods throughout the city. Similar coalitions were emerging in cities all over the United States.

By the 1990s, neighbourhood empowerment had become a central theme in the politics of urban America. Now politicians run campaigns for mayor and city council on platforms that included support for one or more of the following:

Community development corporations – These are non-profit organisations created to undertake housing rehabilitation and business development within the inner city. CDCs, as they are known, now receive significant support from foundations at every level and have become primarily instruments for implementing the local housing rehabilitation programmes that neighbourhood activists used to fight.

Neighbourhood town watch organisations – These are organisations created to involve citizens in partnerships with local police in fighting crime and drugs. 'Community policing', whereby a Police Department establishes strong relationships with people in the neighbourhoods – has become the law-enforcement method of choice in most cities. As a result, inner city residents are now working *with* the police as often as groups in the 1960s used to protest against them.

Adult literacy groups – These are organisations created within inner city neighbourhoods to help adults improve basic literacy. As the job market becomes increasingly competitive, programmes of this kind are starting to compete with CDCs and town watch as important neighbourhood activities.

Neighbourhood planning councils – These are councils established under direct auspices of the mayor's office to involve local residents in the development and implementation of comprehensive plans for the neighbourhoods. While these do not exist everywhere, a number of cities – Boston, Massachusetts; Cincinnati, Ohio; Minneapolis, Minnesota; Portland, Oregon, as examples – have integrated them directly into the structure of local government.

In short, while people who move to the suburbs often assume that they must solve problems on their own, for those who remain in cities, co-operation among residents and with City Hall has become a prerequisite to survival. At this point, neighbourhood activism is not simply an aspect of urban life, it is the centrepiece of local politics, with remarkably similar programmes and strategies in cities around the country.

Yet for all the similarities in these efforts, there is little direct connection between them. The obstacles are considerable. They reflect many of the same problems that face individuals in disparate sections of the country who try to work together.

Community groups remain isolated from one another. Unlike churches or unions or chapters of a single national group like the National Association for the Advancement of Colored People (NAACP), no structure ties them together. Empowering such groups involves building coalitions, as happened with the Philadelphia Council of Neighborhood Organizations (PCNO) in the 1970s. This wasn't easy then, and it still isn't. PCNO itself, as an example, no longer exists.

It's not easy to get good information about government programmes operating within neighbourhoods. These don't get media coverage unless they are obviously failing or someone is stealing money from them. As an example, I spent four years directing Philadelphia's Office of Housing and Community Development that administers our federal Community Development Block Grant. Even though we oversaw the rehabilitation of more than 4,000 houses and apartments, conducted hearings every year around our annual plans, and I personally received decent coverage in the press, I doubt that to this day most Philadelphia residents could identify what the 'Community Development Block Grant' is. The press rarely makes a clear connection between specific governmental activities and the programmes that support them, so how could the broader public be expected to understand it. The result is that few citizens have any idea at all what the federal government is doing within our communities.

Most serious, even though thousands of local civic groups and various national neighbourhood coalitions have emerged over the past twenty-five years, they play no role in electoral politics. Even in the United States, few people have even heard of National Peoples' Action or the National Association of Neighborhoods or the Industrial Areas Foundation – national coalitions involving hundreds of locally based organisational alliances to advance public policy relevant to their concerns. Between these groups, they represent at least 3,000 neighbourhood associations all over the United States. Yet, unlike the Christian Coalition or environmental groups like the Sierra Club, when politicians start running for office these groups disappear. They were all but invisible in the Presidential and Congressional campaigns of 1996. If community and civic organisations refuse to get involved in politics, how do they expect to have an impact on the political system?

These are significant problems. In fact, I left my own position with the City of Philadelphia in 1992 to concentrate on them full-time as President of the Institute for the Study of Civic Values, the think-tank that I had created in Philadelphia in the 1970s to promote civic and community participation.

It was clear that the neighbourhoods' movement itself had to be revived and redefined. The economic decline of urban America was accelerating, while community groups were focusing most of their energies on housing rehabilitation. Drugs and AIDS were becoming pervasive in the neighbourhoods, while the homeless were lying all over the streets. It was clear that a new neighbourhood agenda had to concentrate on job training, adult literacy and improving the schools, but most civic associations were not prepared to deal with them. Moreover, even if organisations in one city began to undertake new initiatives, there was nothing tying any of our efforts together.

As I started learning how to use the Internet in 1994, I conceived of Neighborhoods Online as a way of overcoming the political obstacles that had prevented locally based organisations from exerting effective national pressure. That became our explicit objective in establishing the service the following year.

Neighborhoods Online has come a long way toward meeting its basic objective. By using the Internet, local groups within a city and throughout the country can connect with one another in ways that have never been possible before. With Congress and federal departments and even state and local governments starting to go online, the Internet now gives us quick access to information about programmes and legislation that we can use ourselves and share with one another. Most important, the Internet offers even grassroots groups a new way of conveying our own views to our fellow citizens, and to the people in power.

In short, by using the Internet, we are working to overcome the sense of isolation, ignorance and impotence that prevents organisations and individual activists at the local level from becoming a strong force in national politics. Our major Internet tools – E-mail and the World Wide Web – are tailor-made to deal with these problems. As Neighborhoods Online has evolved over the past two years, we are beginning to find solutions.

NEIGHBORHOODS ONLINE

There are three basic elements to what we're doing through Neighborhoods Online. First, we're building a Website, with the aim of making it easy for groups and concerned citizens to access information about programmes, issues, and political developments that are relevant to neighbourhood empowerment. Second, in Philadelphia we're pursuing a systematic strategy to help civic organisations and human service agencies access the Internet and learn how to use E-mail and the World Wide Web in their work. Third, we're developing E-mail lists for Philadelphia (neigonline@libertynet.org), the Commonwealth of Pennsylvania (penn-neighbor@civic.net), and the United States (civic-values@civic.net and build-com@libertynet.org) with the aim of creating networks of neighbourhood activists who are prepared to work together to build a national movement around the economic, social and political goals that bring us together.

Our platform has been LibertyNet – a regional community network serving the nine-county Philadelphia metropolitan area. Its sponsors include a Pennsylvania economic development agency known as the Benjamin Franklin Partnership; the University of Pennsylvania;

Philadelphia's major public radio station – WHYY; the Free Library of Philadelphia; and the Philadelphia School District. Especially since there was no one in this planning group with a full understanding of the grassroots organisations that I most wanted to bring online, I thought there might be a basis for collaboration.

In the spring of 1994, I started exploring with LibertyNet's director, Chris Higgins, how we might work together. As I saw it, LibertyNet was a TV station; we were a TV programme. How, then, could our specific project fit into the broad array of services that LibertyNet hoped to provide?

Gradually, the basic elements of the project took shape – the Website, the recruitment and training strategy, and a system of local networks. That summer, the William Penn Foundation – a local foundation with a long-standing commitment to neighbourhood empowerment – provided a start-up grant of $50,000. We unveiled Neighborhoods Online in February of 1995 to a packed audience of community activists who now wanted to access the Internet as well.

Today, Neighborhoods Online is among the leading Internet resource centres promoting neighbourhood activism throughout the United States. Our E-mail lists involve more than 1,000 subscribers – locally and nationally – in ongoing discussions of issues related to neighbourhood empowerment. There have been over 50,000 'hits' on our Websites since August 1995 – federal agencies, non-profit organisations, and university-based urban studies programmes all link to them on the web. Even though our focus is distinctly American, we have attracted interest from the United Kingdom, Ireland, Australia, and Hong Kong. At this point, in fact, hundreds of people are connecting with us every day. They include organisers, staff members of non-profit organisations, elected officials, journalists, college faculty and students, and just average citizens looking for new ways to solve neighbourhood problems. Not only do they access our Website, many are participating in our E-mail lists as well. Moreover, each of the services offered by Neighborhoods Online stands on its own; they reinforce one another. Together, they represent a comprehensive support system for neighbourhood activism that, we believe, will grow in scope and significance in the months and years ahead.

Neighborhoods Online – The Website

The Website involves ongoing collaboration between the Institute for the Study of Civic Values and LibertyNet. Initially, I provided the content; LibertyNet produced the web pages. Then a programer at

LibertyNet showed me how easy it was to learn HTML. Now I provide both the content and the pages, but I still need LibertyNet to supply scripts for more complex operations.

There are, in fact, two distinct web pages associated with Neighborhoods Online. The basic site at http://libertynet.org/community/phila focuses on Philadelphia. This menu accesses web pages created by civic groups, human service agencies, and state and city agencies that operate within Philadelphia. It includes federal agencies and national organisations related to neighbourhood empowerment, but our primary emphasis is on local programmes and groups. We've even developed separate menus for each of our twelve Neighborhood Planning Districts, comparable neighbourhood menus are being developed in Minneapolis, in Boulder, Colorado and on a number of other local community networks.

We maintain a separate menu for neighbourhood activists around the country at http://libertynet.org/community/phila/natl.html. We added Neighborhoods Online: National to the site in August 1995. Here, we access only the federal agencies and national organisations, without the Philadelphia programmes and groups, as a service to neighbourhood activists throughout the country. As a result, Neighborhoods Online: National has developed a life of its own. You can find it on Web pages managed by the Department of Housing and Urban Development, the National Civic League, National Public Radio, the Community Development Society and local community networks from Tempe, Arizona to Ireland. We're now being accessed more than 500 times a week. Clearly, we're meeting a need.

What makes these menus unique is not simply the information that we provide – which is largely retrieved from other sites – but the way in which we organise it. The people who live in a neighbourhood want it to be clean, safe, economically viable and a decent place to raise their children. As a result, the primary concerns of community organisations have been housing and community development, neighbourhood safety, economic opportunity and security, and education. We divide Neighborhoods Online into Web pages that reflect these concerns, while providing a specific menu devoted to neighborhood empowerment itself.

What programmes and services do we include? In each area, we offer links to the following resources:

Current news: This might include press releases from the White House or a federal agency, selections from a pertinent source within the media, or 'alerts' from an online service covering issues relevant to neighbourhoods. A housing activist can access HUD's daily focus message from the community development menu. An educational reformer can get quickly to the Office of Education's 'Daily Report Card' from the education menu. A person concerned about welfare reform and poverty can read 'alerts' distributed by HandsNet, an online service aimed at people working with the disadvantaged. Of course, it is possible to access any of one of these using their respective universal resource locators (URLs). Neighborhoods Online makes it easy, however, by consolidating them in one place.

Data-neighborhood: Activists frequently need data to include in proposals or articles on the problems that they are trying to solve. Each menu in Neighborhoods Online now enables users to access data relevant to their needs. Most important is a link to demographic files maintained by the Census Bureau. A search engine at this site makes it possible for users to retrieve comprehensive information about any census tract, zip code or community in the country. Here, again, it is possible to link to the Census Bureau directly, but most neighbourhood groups don't even know that this resource exists. By accessing Neighborhoods Online, they are quickly made aware of it.

Federal agencies: Since most programmes dealing with economic and community development depend upon federal funds, quick access to agencies like the Department of Housing and Urban Development or the Small Business Administration is an enormous asset. In the past year, every federal agency has established its own Website. Many of them include detailed information on how their programmes are being used by states and cities throughout the country. This sort of information has not been available in the past, and it is difficult to retrieve in any other form to this day. Neighborhoods Online links to the relevant sections of each federal agency directly.

Comprehensive resource sites: In each area relevant to neighbourhood revitalisation, there are now groups managing Websites that provide access to a wide range of Internet resources. The Community Development Society supports a homepage of special interest to housing activists. There are wide ranges of web pages relevant to small business development. EnviroLink and the EcoNet menu supported by IGC are of invaluable service for environmentalists. Neighborhoods Online takes advantage of all these services, linking them to the appropriate menu in our own system.

Advocacy groups: There are important advocacy groups operating in each area. Here, too, Neighborhoods Online makes it easy to find them. Welfare activists gain immediate access to the Children's Defence

Fund – which is taking the lead in trying to protect poor children from the national assault against public assistance now characterised in the United States as welfare 'reform'. Environmentalists can find the League of Conservation Voters and the Sierra Club on Neighborhoods Online. Groups like the NAACP and the Urban League representing African-Americans are on the menus as well. When the service began, few such organisations maintained their own Websites. At this point, we add new groups almost every week.

Legislators and legislative committees: The 'Empowerment' menu on Neighborhoods Online enables a user to find any Congressperson and Senator, read his or her ratings from a wide range of interest groups (courtesy of Project VoteSmart), identify their leading sources of campaign contributions (from the Center for Responsive Politics) and save their E-mail addresses for future correspondence. Every menu devoted to a particular problem – community development, economic development, education, etc. – includes the House and Senate Committees with legislative responsibility. Few sites related to public issues include this information, even though it is easily obtained through CapWeb, an online system with links to the US Congress. Neighborhoods Online makes it possible for users to access specific Congressional committees directly.

The casual Internet browser or the political voyeur may have little use for Neighborhoods Online. The information that we provide is structured to benefit people and groups working to solve problems where we live. Given that community activism has yet to find an appropriate niche in national politics, conventional political sites like the 'Jefferson Project' or 'Politics Now' ignore us. Yet, as word of the service continues to spread, we are hearing from new grassroots organisations almost every day.

NEIGHBORHOODS ONLINE – RECRUITMENT AND TRAINING

The Institute for the Study of Civic Values is also working with LibertyNet in Philadelphia to help non-profit groups in Philadelphia gain access to the Internet. After all, why design an elaborate Website like Neighborhoods Online if people can't use it? Unfortunately, as one organiser put it at conference on community networking, non-profits operate on two sets of priorities: critical and urgent. Going online rarely gets beyond urgent. This was certainly true in 1995, when we launched Neighborhoods Online. Most groups were enthusiastic about the service, but unable to take advantage of it. It is less true now – as it is for much of the country – but there are still significant obstacles that we have to overcome:

- an organisation's staff and board has to be convinced that the Internet can benefit them;
- the organisation needs to be able to secure an Internet account without a lot of hassle and at reasonable cost;
- the organisation's staff needs to be trained and given technical support in using the Internet;
- the organisation needs to see a way to reach its members through the Internet, even if this can't happen right away.

Fortunately, over the course of the first year of the project, the Institute and LibertyNet found ways to address these problems. Moreover, similar projects are developing in other cities as well.

The main selling-point for the Internet has been Neighborhoods Online itself. We were careful to wait until there were enough organisations and agencies on the Website before even unveiling it to the non-profit community. Now we can display the wide range of federal agencies, national organisations and even local groups that have emerged on the Net since we started. Every city department in Philadelphia had its own Website by the summer of 1996 – a fact which was of special interest to local groups – providing quick access to information about programmes and services that is not easy to obtain otherwise.

In the beginning, the Internet was a hard sell. Now, all it takes is a few minutes to demonstrate what's available through Neighborhoods Online and non-profit directors want to sign up. In the first year, we enrolled seventy-five groups. Since then, the number has more than doubled.

Thanks to the Philadelphia-based William Penn Foundation and other local support, LibertyNet was been able to offer one free account to each non-profit organisation – at least for the first year. Even after this period, subscriptions are less than $20 for twenty hours a month. Organisations are not only given the opportunity to develop their own web pages, they are expected to do so, since the whole idea is to build LibertyNet into the premiere Internet resource centre for the entire Delaware Valley. This does take time, but since the cost is less than $100 and LibertyNet offers HTML training workshops, gradually groups are taking advantage of the offer.

The Institute and LibertyNet collaborate in providing training and support to groups that subscribe through Neighborhoods Online.

During our first year, much of the Institute's training took place at the Computing Resource Center (CRC) at the University of Pennsylvania in one of the best labs in the city. There, a gifted trainer – Caroline Ferguson – worked directly with us to offer workshops in E-mail, the Web and Neighborhoods Online itself. Following the introductory workshop, LibertyNet staff members – in this case, AmeriCorps volunteers – were available to give hands-on support to non-profits experiencing difficulty in installing the Internet software (Eudora and Netscape) or in maintaining their accounts. Today, LibertyNet itself has built a strong enough training staff to assume complete responsibility for this aspect of the project themselves.

Our most ambitious project, however, is a long-term effort to help organisations to connect with their own members through LibertyNet and Neighborhoods Online. Again, however, what good does it do to provide information if no one has access to it? Here, a partnership with the Free Library of Philadelphia provides the solution. Thanks to a $1.2 million grant from the William Penn Foundation, each branch library in Philadelphia is now receiving twelve computers linked to the Internet, LibertyNet and Neighborhoods Online. These will all be in place by the end of 1997 – with staff trained to show people how to use them.

LibertyNet has been aggressive in its efforts to extend Internet access to individual residents in low-income neighbourhoods as well. In 1995, for example, it was one of a handful of organisations nationally to win a coveted National Telecommunications Information and Assistance (NTIA) grant from the Commerce Department to provide broad Internet access to residents of three of the most economically distressed areas of North and West Philadelphia now designated a federal Empowerment Zone.

The Bridge Project, as it is called, is offering Internet access not only through the libraries, but community centres and even a 'truck with a tale' provided by the Free Library to run Internet demonstrations at neighbourhood events. The Institute's own role in the project has been to develop and maintain an 'Empowerment Zone Online', menu as part of Neighborhoods Online, with links to agencies and organisations that can assist both organisations and individuals in meeting the substantive goals set for the Empowerment Zone itself. Here again, we all work together as a partnership in these efforts – even using an E-mail list ourselves to share ideas and information as the project unfolds.

In effect, then, helping community organisations learn how to use the Internet has turned into an organising project in itself in Philadelphia, managed largely by LibertyNet and the Institute, but now involving a number of other groups. From a modest beginning – I used to say that putting our Website together at first felt like building a hotel on Venus – we have reached the point where virtually every community development corporation, neighbourhood advisory committee, adult literacy programme, job training agency, and human service provider is either already online or trying to figure out how to get there.

Eventually, we even intend to help block captains gain access to the Internet. There are 6,000 block associations in Philadelphia that constitute the back-bone of clean-up, recycling and town watch programmes in neigbourhoods throughout the city. We believe that being able to communicate with these groups via the World Wide Web and E-mail – and to help them connect with one another – would provide an enormous boost to civic participation in Philadelphia generally. The Police Department has been supplying CB Radios to town watch groups for years on this basis. In this case, we believe that we can work with the libraries to build the network. Does this sound far-fetched? Remember when no one had fax machines? As far as we're concerned, it's just a matter of time.

NEIGHBORHOODS ONLINE – NETWORKING

Our ultimate goal, in fact, is not merely to help individual neighbourhood groups secure Internet accounts, but to help them start functioning as part of a network. Even the Neighborhoods Online Website is more an electronic resource centre than an instrument of empowerment in itself. The greatest tool for political organising on the Net, in my judgment, is the E-mail list, where people can share information with one another and develop strategies for change. We are now managing four separate lists related to neighbourhood activism – each with its own subscribers, but all moving in the same direction. Over time, we believe that these will emerge as the major vehicles for change.

We've created two lists related to Pennsylvania – 'neighbors-online', for groups in Philadelphia; and 'penn-neighbor', for activists throughout the state. There are only 250 subscribers between the two lists, but the groups that they represent involve thousands of people within their respective communities.

Our own aim here is to strengthen relationships between neighbourhood organisations that may know about one another but do not work together. The groups working on housing rehabilitation, anti-drug campaigns and educational reform are often quite different, even within the same neighbourhood. We include them all in 'neighbors-online' and 'penn-neighbor'. Now, we're at least describing our programmes to one another and sharing announcements of upcoming events. Most important, when legislation that affects all of us is about to be debated – like proposals to throw people off welfare even when there are no jobs – we're in a much stronger position to give it our undivided response.

We also support two national lists – 'civic-values' and 'build-com'. 'Civic-values' is a list that involves more than 400 community and political activists – mostly in the United States, but with representation from Canada, the United Kingdom, Australia and Hong Kong as well – who enjoy discussing issues and ideas. It's not narrowly focused on neighbourhoods, but we do explore how problems such as corporate downsizing and programmes such as welfare reform affect us in our own communities. Indeed, if any of our lists do end up producing a 'neighborhood agenda' for America, it will be 'civic-values', given the keen interest in public policy manifested by the list's active subscribers and their willingness to tackle knotty issues in depth.

'Build-com' is an even more complex E-mail list to manage. Over the past three years, we have been experimenting with a new approach to community planning, whereby we use principles in the Preamble to the Constitution (like 'secure the blessings of liberty to ourselves and posterity' and 'promote the general welfare') to help civic groups and government to develop explicit social contracts for neighbourhood improvement.

We have had considerable success with this process in Philadelphia, where we have tested it in a number of different neighbourhoods. We have even developed a discussion guide describing the process – which we now call, 'Building Community in the American Tradition' – for use by groups around the country as part of the National Endowment for the Humanities 'National Conversation on What it Means to be An American'.

Now, however, we're helping activists in other cities learn how to use our process via an E-mail list – 'build-com' – thanks to a grant from the Surdna Foundation. We have brought representatives from more than twenty cities and rural communities together online to explore how they are organising within their own areas and how the materials that we have developed might be helpful to them. The process has been difficult, given that the participants here maintain busy schedules in their own communities. Yet, when we can find a way to help organisers use this sort of E-mail as a resource for themselves and as a way of building broader coalitions, we will have made a major contribution to the broader goal of making the Internet work to strengthen democracy.

It is important to note, moreover, that while each of our lists has an identity and a purpose of its own, they all reinforce one another. The Website provides visibility. The E-mail lists encourage us to work together. Together, they constitute an online system for neighbourhood empowerment that will simply grow stronger as more groups start using the Internet in the years ahead.

FROM NEIGHBORHOODS ONLINE TO EMPOWERMENT

Civic participation within an individual neighbourhood empowers people in two ways. First, they can take direct action to deal with situations that they can handle by themselves. They can sponsor block clean-ups and recycle trash. They can join a town watch and look out for one another's homes. They can solicit volunteers to help kids with their homework. Some people can even learn how to run GED classes for adults who don't have high school diplomas. These are simple steps that people can take in their own behalf, once they start working together.

Second, people who organise within a neighbourhood are in an ideal position to pressure elected representatives to deal with problems, since we vote where we live. They might be able to clean a block by themselves, but somebody has to pick up the trash. They can watch out for one another's homes, but they still need the police and the courts to catch and prosecute criminals. They can help children do their homework, but they need to fight for schools that provide quality education. They can encourage high school drop-outs in the neighbourhood to get their high school diplomas, but they also need to fight for public programmes that will make this financially possible. Even much of what we now characterise as 'voluntarism' in America still depends upon an active partnership between government and citizens to make it work.

Neighborhoods Online aims at helping citizens use the Internet to strengthen all of these efforts:

- by building a Website that accesses public agencies directly, we enable activists to retrieve invaluable information on problems and possible solutions that has been inaccessible to them up to now;
- by establishing E-mail lists for neighbourhood activists at the local, state, and national level, we are creating organisational networks and coalitions that start to work together within the political process;
- by using both the Website and our E-mail lists to show people how to send messages to their own elected officials and to the local and national media, we are turning grassroots activism into a movement that can affect every level of American politics.

In short, we are building Neighborhoods Online to demonstrate to people working in communities and neighbourhoods all over the

United States that the Internet represents a powerful vehicle for change. Even if most individual citizens in America are still not able to go online, most citizen organisations certainly can – and through them, individuals will gain a powerful voice. I have no doubt that thousands of community organisations will be building their own E-mail lists and Websites over the next several years, as an integral part of their programmes. The benefits are becoming obvious to everyone.

Moreover, the timing is exactly right. The 'citizens' movement' – as many in the American press are now calling it – is not some new invention of the 1990s. It is, in fact, an attempt to recover an ethic that we nearly lost – namely, that we all ought to help one another and participate in community affairs. Once again, this spirit is bringing all segments of this society back to civic and political life. Whether through the 'Million Man March' or the 'Stand for Children' sponsored by the Children's Defence Fund or just through hundreds of grassroots groups operating at the local level, Americans are no longer rallying around leaders. We are rallying around ourselves. Now – through the Neighborhoods Online – we are starting to talk to one another.

7 The First Amendment online
Santa Monica's Public Electronic Network

Sharon Docter and William H. Dutton

American state and local governments have moved towards the use of information and communications technologies to provide an increasing array of public services. Paralleling developments in other parts of the world, American public agencies – from the White House to hundreds of cities and town halls – are emulating the private sector; trying to increase the speed, accuracy and efficiency of public services; and talking about bringing government closer to the public (Taylor *et al.*, 1996).

Since the 1960s, scholars, politicians and journalists have championed the use of electronic communications systems, like interactive cable television, to improve the responsiveness of political institutions and allow for more direct citizen participation in public affairs (Becker and Scarce, 1984; Sackman and Boehm, 1972; Sackman and Nie, 1970; Williams, 1982). Teledemocracy experiments provided some limited support for claims that these projects could generate greater levels of political participation, enable citizens to better understand complex issues, allow legislators to become better informed of problems and issues, and increase the accountability of elected representatives as citizens become more politically sophisticated (Arterton, 1987; Slaton, 1992). They also generated concern over the risks of direct, push-button democracy (Abramson *et al.*, 1988; Laudon, 1977).

In the 1980s, US governments began to use information and communications technologies (ICTs) for electronic service delivery. Most governments had limited ambitions for providing easier access to public information over the telephone and via electronic kiosks – emulating innovations in electronic banking like the automated teller machine. However, a few local experiments were guided by visions of electronic democracy that harkened back to earlier debates over teledemocracy generated by innovations in remote computing, audience response systems, telephone conferencing and interactive cable television (Arterton, 1987; Laudon, 1977; Raab *et al.*, 1996). In the 1990s, it was the Internet that generated renewed enthusiasm for electronic democracy. By 1996, for example, over 1,000 US cities had established a 'homepage' on the World Wide Web.

The rapid growth of the Internet and electronic service delivery has created a sense of optimism among academics, policy-makers, and the general public concerning the power of these technologies to transform government. All of the hopes outlined in the introduction to this book are much in evidence across the US, where electronic service delivery is expected to empower citizens who are less politically active, encourage collective political action through the formation of subject-specific discussion groups, and remove intermediaries, whether political parties or the mass media, in favour of more direct forms of democratic representation. In fact, much of the advocacy of electronic democracy emanates from the US.

This chapter is based on a case study of one of the longest-running and most innovative US experiments in electronic democracy, the City of Santa Monica's Public Electronic Network (PEN). The PEN system is a particularly valuable case study because Santa Monica was one of the first cities to offer its citizens access to an interactive public electronic network. PEN was designed to facilitate access to public information, government departments and agencies, and public officials by the city's residents as well as to create a forum for public discussion.[1] In operation for over seven years, this case provides a unique opportunity to examine key legal and design issues concerning local governments' implementation of electronic democracy within the US context.

A HISTORY OF THE PEN SYSTEM[2]

The PEN system went online in February 1989. It is an electronic mail and computer conferencing system owned by the City of Santa Monica, California (see Figure 7.2 (Appendix)). PEN is operated by the city's Information Systems Department (ISD), which played a primary role in its development. It runs on a minicomputer and public terminal equipment donated by Hewlett-Packard, the city's major equipment vendor, using conferencing software and consulting support from MetaSystems, a software and management consulting firm (Dutton and Guthrie, 1991).

The setting of an innovation in electronic participation

Two factors help explain Santa Monica's early interest in this system. One is that the city has had a political culture supportive of participation in local politics (Guthrie and Dutton, 1992; Kann, 1986). For

The First Amendment online   127

example, there was considerable support within the city for a local and interactive cable television system in the early 1980s as a means for supporting increased political participation (CCTF, 1984). Another factor was the city's early implementation of an electronic mail network for city personnel, which put Santa Monica technically ahead of many other cities and created an understanding and acceptance of E-mail. Electronic mail was an important mode of communication at all levels of the city's administration (Barrette, 1994; Mayell, 1994). In 1984, for example, the city was one of the first in the nation to introduce the use of portable laptop computers by top managers and the city council so that they could access the city's electronic mail system from their homes as well as their offices.

Ｔhe city's use of E-mail and remote access from laptop computers was routine in late 1986 when a resident asked the city council if he and other residents could use their personal computers and modems to access documents on the city's computer system, such as council agendas, minutes and staff reports. Initially, top managers, including the Director of Information Systems, questioned why anyone would want to dial into a computer for such information. However, discussions several years earlier on the potential for an interactive cable TV system to link citizens and the council had interested some citizen activists, council members and staff in the idea of electronic participation in local government. While the city judged interactive cable TV to be premature, given costs and existing technology, computer access seemed like a far less costly approach to some of the same objectives. The cable TV discussions had convinced council members and the City Manager's office to avoid a system for voting and polling citizens from their homes, in favour of one that focused on allowing citizens to gain electronic access to public information.

In line with this history, the city perceived broad public support for electronic access. The city council supported a survey of residents by the Information Systems Department to determine if there was sufficient interest in such a system. Also, the City Manager's office brought in an outside consultant to help the city explore various options. The survey lent support to the project, indicating that nearly one-third of households in the city had a personal computer and that many were interested in electronic access to city services.

Another driving force was an interest in keeping information services centralised within the Department of Information Systems. The director of the department had centralised computing services within the city. Some proposals raised the possibility of placing responsibility for a citizen-oriented system outside the control of Information

Systems. While initially concerned about the security of a publicly accessible system, this bureaucratic threat along with his own growing vision of an 'electronic city hall' helped the director secure outside support. Financial hurdles were overcome when the Director of Information Systems was able to attract hardware donations from Hewlett-Packard, the city's major equipment vendor. The city also received a donation of conferencing software from MetaSystems. With this support, the director convinced the city to place responsibility of its development and implementation within his department.

The role and design of an electronic network

The City Manager's office and some department heads, such as the Police Chief and Librarian, envisaged the system primarily as an additional means for broadcasting information to residents. The City Manager's office and other staff also recognised that the creation of an electronic network accessible by citizens could achieve other public policy objectives which would benefit the citizens of Santa Monica. Traffic and parking, for example, could be reduced if routine transactions could be completed electronically, thereby reducing trips to city hall. Service to citizens might be improved if citizens could communicate with city representatives electronically.

The Director of Information Systems and other city staff broadened their vision of electronic access to incorporate the idea of what they called an 'electronic city hall' that would facilitate debate and discussion of public issues and local activities. Some in the city wished to restrict the system to supporting vertical communication between the residents and the city. Others, who supported the electronic democracy component, used a technical argument – that the donated software could not be modified easily to prevent citizens from sending messages to one another – to convince the city that the system should also support horizontal communication among the public.

Advocates of PEN made analogies between electronic conferencing and participation in a town hall or public meeting. For example, it was determined early on in the development of the system that users must register using their real names. Just as people appearing at a city council meeting would identify themselves, so also the identity of PEN users should be known to others within the electronic community.

When PEN went online, it included three components:

- a read-only link that allowed citizens to dial up a menu of over 250 categories of information, ranging from the council's agenda to information on how to obtain city services;

The First Amendment online 129

- a 'mail room', which allowed citizens to send messages to all city departments, to consumer affairs, to quick reference (for short answers to library reference questions) and, eventually, to individual registered users, including public officials and residents;
- a conference feature that allowed groups of users to participate in a wide variety of electronic meetings – users could read all the entries to-date on a selected conference topic and enter their own comments for others to see (Table 7.1).

PEN was later expanded to include:

- online forms, such as applications;
- data-bases, including archives for the city council and planning commission (Table 7.1).

The utilisation of PEN

PEN's launch generated a steady stream of newspaper articles and publicity, including a lead article in the region's major daily, the *Los Angeles Times*. Usage was free to all Santa Monica residents who registered with the city's Information Systems Department. In later years, the city allowed non-residents who worked in Santa Monica to register for PEN use. The city installed public terminals in libraries and other public facilities and offered free training so that people who did not have a computer and modem in their home could gain access to PEN. Approximately 20 per cent of PEN accesses were from these public terminals. Those citizens who registered to use PEN were required to sign a User Agreement, where they, for example, promised to display common courtesy and to avoid libellous or obscene remarks.

During its first year, 1,800 residents registered to use the PEN system. By its third anniversary, PEN had 4,505 registered users, including sixty-six city staff. Less than 5 per cent of Santa Monica's 86,905 residents ever registered to use the system, but this represented about 10 per cent of the 44,860 households in Santa Monica and a far greater number than even proponents might have expected in light of the earlier market failures of videotext systems in the US. Moreover, PEN was able to sustain 400 to 600 active users in any given month in its first years (see Figure 7.1).

During these early years, the public's use of PEN was focused more on communication with others than on retrieving specific information. PEN services accessed most frequently were computer conferences on local and national issues, followed by the use of electronic mail.

Despite the early popularity of mail and conferencing, about four

130 Sharon Docter and William H. Dutton

Table 7.1 PEN's menu of information and communication services

Menu item	Function	Examples of selections
City hall	Information retrieval	Information desk; agendas, schedules, notices and reports; city government; public works; planning and building; city attorney; public safety; transportation; rent control; environmental programmes; parking and traffic
Community centre	Information retrieval	Recreation and parks; library; neighbourhood groups; office of the disabled; senior citizen centre; city supported community services; schools; cultural arts; convention and visitors bureau
Mailroom	E-mail to and from city, departments, other users	Read new E-mail; send; delete; read; list E-mail; list city hall E-mail-boxes; PEN participants' menu
Conferences	Computer conferencing	Selections include moderated city conference (on topics such as rent control, the environment, PEN) or unmoderated free-form conferences (on topics such as movies, youth, restaurants)
Online forms	Transactions	Library registration; business licence renewal; filing of a consumer complaint; petty theft report; request for removal of graffiti
Current events	Information retrieval	Browse complete calendar of events for upcoming week
Data-bases	Information retrieval	Municipal code; maximum allowable rents; city services guide; city council archive; planning commission archive; business directory

years after its inception, participation in PEN conferences and mail systems began to decline and shift to the Internet. From the autumn of 1992, when many users expressed concern about the lack of civility on PEN,[3] there appears to have been a slow but marked decline in the use of PEN (see Figure 7.1).

PEN conferences were unable to sustain the participation of key opinion leaders within the community. During its first year, for example, several elected and appointed officials were active users of PEN and participated in PEN conferences. At least three city council members,

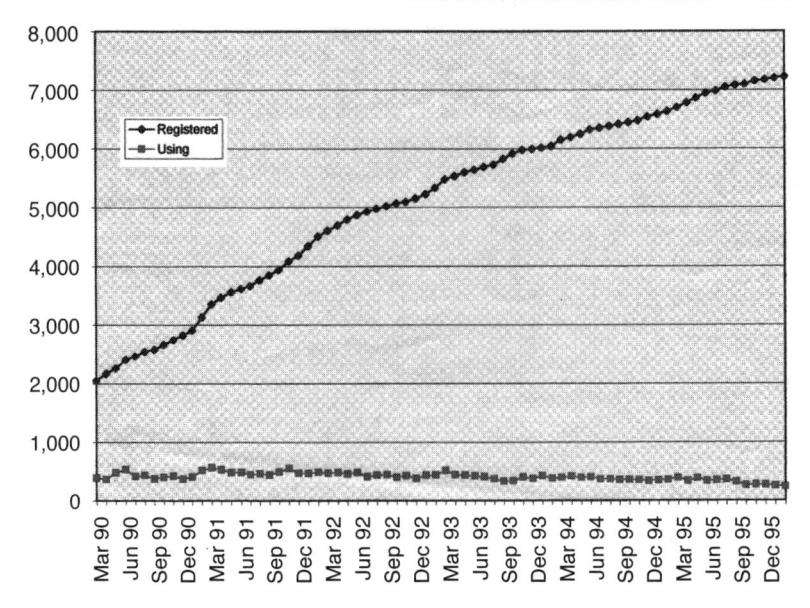

Figure 7.1 Registration and use of PEN (1990–96)

the City Attorney and members of the city's Planning Department were active PEN users (Guthrie *et al*, 1990). Six years after PEN's inception, no elected officials participated on the conferences (Holbrook, 1994). Moreover, while the number of users and public accesses to the system increased during PEN's first three years, since 1991 the number of users and public accesses has declined. By its seventh year, PEN sustained an average of 313 users per month.

However, while fewer Santa Monica residents logged directly onto PEN, dialling into city hall and using their name and password, thousands from around the world began to access PEN over the Internet. The net consequences of this growth of Internet access and decline of local dial-in access has been viewed as positive by the city, and overall has led to greater utilisation of the system. It also supports a shift in priorities of the city, away from discussion and towards the provision of information and electronic public services.

THE LIMITED DIFFUSION OF PEN

A variety of factors led to a decline in the use of PEN for local forums and a shift in focus towards providing information, increasingly over the Internet. One major factor was conflict within the PEN community itself over the appropriate norms governing interpersonal communication. Personal attacks and 'abusive' behaviours caused some to abandon participation on the PEN system (Holbrook, 1994; Kurtz, 1994; Mayell, 1993; Wolf, 1995). Many perceived the network to have been dominated by a group of about thirty or forty heavy users who often 'flamed' other users (Mayell, 1993; Kurtz, 1994). One frequent user, for example, wrote messages which appeared to be delusional. He would write pages and pages of text concerning 'Satan' and 'Jesus Christ', often referring to the city as 'Satan Monica'. He also appeared to have a vendetta against a particular social service agency within the city and would write pages of text criticising the agency and its director. Another PEN user became notorious within this virtual community for his frequent attacks on almost all other users that he encountered, including children and the homeless.

A closely related issue was dissatisfaction over the quality of debate and communication. Over time, people who had participated on PEN, including city council members, staff persons and community leaders, found participation in the conferences too cumbersome (Holbrook, 1994; Mayell, 1993). The perception grew that conferences often lacked substance and that they frequently became 'unruly' (Holbrook, 1994; Kurtz, 1994; Lawrence, 1993; Mayell, 1993; Wolf, 1995). City staff would have to wade through long postings that would often be 'off-thread' or not relevant to the subject matter of the discussion. There was a sense that the conferences were out of control (Wolf, 1995).

The Internet seemed to be another major factor limiting the development of PEN along its initial design path. While the civility, composition and quality of conferences might have driven some residents and opinion leaders off the system, others seem to have been attracted to the Internet. The explosion of interest in the Internet also contributed to a decline in the local network's use, along with demands from residents for PEN to become accessible via the Internet. In late 1994, the city began exploring ways to provide access to PEN over the Internet, which it soon implemented. The PEN computer was able to double as an Internet server so that anyone with Internet access could view information available on the system, although they could not participate in conferences or use the PEN E-mail system unless they dialled directly into the city's computer (Wythe, 1996).

The city is also discussing the possibility of emulating many not-for-profit community networks and providing free or low-cost access to the Internet for PEN-ners. Allowing access to the Internet from PEN would transform the entire nature of the system from a local and interactive bulletin board service and forum to a gateway which provides

The First Amendment online 133

access to a vast array of information from all over the world. Some assume that once the system is opened up to the world via the Internet, the larger base of new participants will overwhelm and discourage those few users who have disrupted the conferences (Wolf, 1995). When PEN was introduced in 1989, it was a novelty. Many early and heavy users were computer enthusiasts (Guthrie *et al.*, 1990). With the growing sophistication and popularity of the Internet, PEN has had to compete with numerous Internet discussion groups around the world as well as with all the colour and graphics of WWW pages. PEN was always plain old text in order to minimise problems with standards. Individuals initially intrigued by the novelty of PEN might well have moved on to other channels for electronic communication.

THE FIRST AMENDMENT ONLINE

Despite the fact that a minority of users engaged in disruptive behaviour, staff within the Information Systems Department, along with city management, did not take steps to remove or censor users. Consistent with the advice of the city's legal advisers, PEN was a government-owned system to which the First Amendment would strictly apply. The Assistant City Manager, for example, noted that the city construed the First Amendment 'absolutely as liberally as possible' and discontinued or suspended the services of only a handful of users for behaviour, such as making personal threats or harassing other users (in violation of a restraining order) or using PEN for commercial purposes (Barrette, 1994; Wolf, 1995). This view was shared by PEN staff, who noted that the city took a very strict interpretation of the First Amendment, and that this strict interpretation may have been a factor which led to the demise of successful conferences.

The establishment of a First Amendment guideline

Private, for-profit information services, such as Prodigy or America Online, face very few constraints in creating rules of conduct that are designed to appeal to the greatest number of users. The City of Santa Monica, on the other hand, perceived itself to be bound by legislative and constitutional constraints which prevented the city from interfering with citizens' speech or discontinuing access for disruptive behaviour (Barrette, 1994; Mayell, 1993; Wolf, 1995).

The City Attorney at the time of PEN's launch and his legal advisers influenced how the city perceived its First Amendment obligations. The City Attorney took a strong stance with regard to the First

Amendment's application to PEN. Legal advisers within the city noted that punishing users for the content of their expression by removing them from the system would be a fundamental violation of the First Amendment of the US Constitution (Lawrence, 1993; Myers, 1993).

Because PEN was viewed as a public forum, legal advisers noted that access should be easily available and that the government should not in any way regulate the content of citizens' speech, despite complaints by users that the speech of some was offensive.

Case law regarding the legal status of publicly owned electronic networks is not substantial. However, the point of view of the city's advisers was consistent with case law concerning the First Amendment's application to government-owned property used for expressive purposes, such as streets and parks.

The First Amendment precludes the government from interfering with the content of citizens' speech. While, historically, the only media to receive First Amendment protection was the written word, as new communications technologies have developed, First Amendment protection has gradually been extended to these newer media. The degree of protection afforded the various media has varied depending upon the unique characteristics of the given media. Thus, the print media, the broadcasting media and telecommunications have carved out separate and distinct legal niches with the regulation of each medium based on very different legal assumptions.[4]

The former City Attorney of Santa Monica appears to have correctly predicted that the First Amendment would be strictly applied to electronic communications, as lower court decisions in the mid-1990s have extended broad First Amendment protection to the Internet.[5] A 1996 district court opinion, for example, contrasted the Internet with other communications industries. While the economics of the print, broadcasting and cable industries have led to a few wealthy voices dominating the marketplace of ideas and thereby shaping public opinion, the Internet has had a 'democratising effect' which has created a parity among speakers and listeners, and increased the diversity of content available to citizens:

> It is no exaggeration to conclude that the Internet has achieved, and continues to achieve, the most participatory marketplace of mass speech that this country – and indeed the world – has yet seen . . . [I]ndividual citizens of limited means can speak to a worldwide audience on issues of concern to them.
> (*American Civil Liberties Union v. Reno*)

Moreover, the constitutional status accorded computer-mediated communication is equally important, regardless of whether or not the speech at issue is of a political or non-political nature:

> Federalists and Anti-Federalists may debate the structure of their government nightly, but these debates occur in newsgroups or chat rooms rather than in pamphlets... More mundane (but from a constitutional perspective, equally important) dialogue occurs between aspiring artists, or French cooks, or dog lovers, or fly fishermen.
> (*American Civil Liberties Union v. Reno*)

Thus, when the speech of a PEN user became an issue because of violation of the User Agreement or because it was offensive, legal advisers within the city were consulted and users' access to PEN were suspended or terminated in only a few extreme cases (Kurtz, 1994; Mayell, 1993; Wolf, 1995). Early and later PEN Project Managers have noted that they were influenced by the City Attorney's point of view and, to some extent, by their own beliefs about the importance of the First Amendment (Kurtz, 1994; Mayell 1993).

Interpersonal influence

Within this context, both users and the city tried more informal mechanisms to regulate content. First, users often appointed themselves to criticise other users for abusing the system. Users castigating others for going off the topic of a conference – breaking the thread of the conversation – became known as 'Thread Police'. The criticism of some users, however, actually added to the sense of incivility, such as when users critiqued others' spelling, grammar and rationality.

When users became disruptive or abusive to others, one PEN Project Manager (Sharon Mayell, who preceded Keith Kurtz) used informal means to encourage more civil discussion rather than formal sanctions. She would send out messages which she called 'Den Mother Notes'. They were designed positively to encourage users to change their behaviour:

> I would have people, residents, occasionally call me up and say 'why wasn't I doing something about this profanity,' that there were young kids reading it. And I would basically say it's a speech medium and so I would send what somebody had termed a 'Den Mother' note to people. Y'know: 'You're a very articulate person. I don't see why you have to use that kind of language. This is a community resource and we would appreciate it if you would contribute to the discussion...' That was my Den Mother letter.
> (Mayell, 1993: 15)

The next PEN Project Manager would also informally chastise those users who offended standards of common courtesy. However, while the informal notes were initially effective, instances of abusive, rude or indecent language became so frequent that the PEN staff did not have time to respond in this way to all instances.

Balancing administrative and free speech concerns

In this way, a conflict between legal, free speech and administrative concerns arose. On the one hand, city management and the Information Systems Department had a strong interest in bringing as many citizens onto the system as possible so that the system would function more efficiently and the cost of the system to the city would be justified. On the other hand, if the city drafted and enforced a strict set of rules which were designed to appeal to the broadest possible audience, like the private information service companies, then this would run counter to a strict First Amendment interpretation of the medium, as the First Amendment specifically functions to protect speech that the majority may find offensive or marginal.

The city was faced with a paradox in terms of finding ways to preserve civil libertarian values. On the one hand, the First Amendment was enacted to ensure that many diverse voices will contribute to the marketplace of ideas. First Amendment values are arguably jeopardised when a few people begin to dominate debate on political issues and intimidate other people to such a degree that they are shut out of the marketplace and refuse to participate on electronic conferences. On the other hand, policies or technologies designed to regulate speech may chill constitutionally protected speech, and have been judged counter to constitutional principles in the US.

Moderated conferences

Members of the Information Systems Department struggled with ways to resolve this problem and examined various technical and policy alternatives which could keep discussion civil while preserving First Amendment values. One of the first alternatives suggested was shutting down all of the free-form conferences and allowing only moderated conferences. In a moderated conference, instead of citizens being able to freely talk to one another, a designated 'moderator' would review all postings to the conference before they would be allowed to appear. The moderator (either a city staff person or a citizen) could rule some comments out of order. This idea has been used in managing computer conferences since the invention of the medium in the 1970s (Hiltz and Turoff, 1978).

The initial suggestion to shut down all the free-form conferences came from Ken Phillips, the former Head of the Information Systems Department. Phillips had envisioned an 'electronic city hall' and thus advocated the creation of conferences at PEN's inception. He was an important proponent of extending the city's concept of E-mail so that PEN would include citizen-to-citizen interaction rather than only permitting citizens to E-mail the city. However, four years after the creation of PEN, he believed that the free-form conferences had become so unruly that the city should consider ways of shutting them down. Other staff within the Information Systems Department favoured leaving the free-form conferences in place, but advocated implementing other policies which would increase civil discussion and debate.

When users became aware of the plan to shut down the free-form conferences, a group of users vehemently protested to the City Manager. By this time, Phillips had left the City of Santa Monica for a new position. Information Systems Department staff agreed, in response to user complaints, to leave most free-form conferences in place. However, they also established plans to develop a moderated, structured conference which was intended both to provide a space for more civil discussion and to allow city staff to use the PEN system more efficiently. The hope was that the moderated conference would bring people back onto the PEN system. The moderated conference was called the 'City Conference' and replaced the free-form conferences that dealt specifically with city government issues. The City Conference listed seventeen issue items that directly pertained to local matters, such as homelessness and rent control. Users participating in the moderated City Conference were restricted to two postings per issue item per day and each posting or message could not be longer than thirty lines. The posting was also required to be directly relevant to the topic – 'on thread'.

Staff within the Information Systems Department acted as moderators. Rather than sending messages directly to one another or to city officials, messages concerning the City Conference were directed to the moderator. The moderator reviewed each message and determined to which issue area it was most appropriate. The moderator then posted the message under the appropriate issue area. If a posting was not on thread, then it was put into a miscellaneous category entitled 'Extra! Extra! From the City Desk!' The City Conference was designed to make city staff use of PEN more efficient both because postings would be shorter in length and because the moderator would forward postings relevant to particular city departments to the appropriate city staff as E-mail. It was a city policy that appropriate staff must respond to E-mail messages, just as they must respond to letters received via the US mail.

Shortly before implementation of the City Conference, approximately 10–12 users participated in a meeting with the Head of the Information Systems Division and PEN staff. During the meeting, the users angrily expressed concern that the city would close the free-form conferences. Users were assured that the free-form conferences would continue (though they were not assured that conferences would continue indefinitely). Information Systems Department staff explained, however, that the moderated 'City Conference' would allow for more structured interactions, but that other less structured areas within PEN would also remain available.

While the users were generally not opposed to including a moderated conference, some favoured approaches whereby individual users rather than city staff would be the moderators. Two suggestions were raised which would allow for user-moderated conferences to supplement the free-form and City conferences. One user proposed that a User Committee of five individuals be elected online. The Committee would establish rules of conduct for PEN. If a user violated the rules, then the Committee could sanction the user either through a warning, through moving the response to the free-form conference or through making the user read-only, so that the user could still read the discussion, but could no longer offer comment.

Another user proposed that citizen moderators be established for particular discussions. The moderator would initiate the discussion and establish the rules. If comments were not germane to the discussion, then the moderator could move the posting or make the user 'read-only' in that discussion. Citizens, then, could have clear expectations about rules of conduct for particular discussions. For example, the user who had initially proposed this alternative noted that if users wanted to go to the 'biker bar', they could go to the biker bar and be aware of what the rules of conduct would be in that forum; if users wanted to have a more civil discussion, then they could go to the salon. In this manner, users would be aware that the rules of conduct for the biker bar would be different from the rules of conduct for the salon.

The city ultimately rejected the user-moderated approach in favour of the city-moderated approach. While members of the Information Systems Department and the City Attorney liked the idea of having users moderate their own conferences, modifying the software to institute user-moderated conferences was more costly and difficult to set up than the city-moderated conference. Initial technology design decisions, then, were an important factor that influenced later design choices.

Institution of the moderated format arguably raised First Amendment issues, as the line between moderation and censorship is not always clear. The former City Attorney, for example, believed that the implementation of the moderator format constituted censorship. He believed that a governmental representative's pre-screening of citizens' speech was a prior restraint of speech, which is presumptively unconstitutional (Myers, 1993). On the other hand, the acting City Attorney at the time that the moderated City Conference was implemented took the position that the City Conference did not constitute censorship of speech, but instead was a valid regulation of the time, place and manner of speech.

According to US case law, the government may regulate the time, place and manner of speech if the regulation is content-neutral, if the regulation is necessary to serve a significant government interest and if there are reasonable alternative channels available for the communication of the information (*Frisby v. Schultz*, 487 U.S. 474 (1988); *Clark v. Community for Creative Non-Violence*, 468 U.S. 288 (1984)). The implementation of the City Conference arguably served a significant government interest in that it made discussion more efficient and allowed more people to participate in debate. Moreover, alternative channels were available for the communication of information, because postings which were not relevant to particular discussion items were posted to the miscellaneous area. It was the view of the acting City Attorney that, if comments which were not relevant were deleted from the system, then this could constitute a prior restraint in violation of the First Amendment. However, because alternative channels were available via the miscellaneous area, then the moderated conference did not violate the First Amendment (Lawrence, 1993).

As it turned out, the City Conference was not entirely effective either in reducing incidents of 'flaming' or in keeping discussions on topic. The delays caused by moderators frustrated many users. The moderated City Conference cut down on the speed of communication because all postings had to be reviewed and then sent to the appropriate issue area. Therefore, many users circumvented the City Conference by creating discussion items in the free-form conferences which were identical to the moderated conference.

PROSPECTS

By late 1995, many cities had begun to institute electronic networks. However, no other US city had instituted a highly interactive network such as PEN, which allows for extensive citizen-to-citizen communication. In recent years, the city has made some strategic choices to focus its attention on marketing the public information utility aspects of the PEN system. No changes have been made with regard to the computer conferences. In fact, after experimenting with moderators, the city decided to leave the computer conferences alone.

However, the city is in the process of re-engineering the information retrieval (broadcasting one to many) and service delivery components of the PEN system. The PEN system is referred to as a public information utility (PIU) and efforts have been instituted to expand the range of electronic transactions that citizens may complete. The city is also expanding the range of available information. In 1994, for example, the city began making the Municipal Code available to residents via PEN. The library catalogue, which was formerly a separate system, is also available and this has become a frequently used component of the system.

Decisions to emphasise the utilitarian aspects of PEN appear to be driven by economic concerns rather than free speech concerns. The annual operating budget for the PEN system is $110,000 (Barrette, 1994; Wolf, 1995). City council members and City Managers have revisited questions raised at the launch of PEN. For example, what should be the role of a tax-supported system? During budget discussions, members of the city council asked whether government should be in the business of providing free electronic mail services for citizens within the city. Questions were raised about the value this brings to the city and whether this is the appropriate role for government.

In response, the city prioritised the features of PEN which it believed to be most important to government and began to concentrate staff resources on those elements. At the same time, the city is seeking to maintain its role as an innovator, exploring ways in which the emergence of inexpensive multimedia kiosks and the growth of the Internet can be used to support and extend key functions of PEN.

THEMES OF ELECTRONIC DEMOCRACY IN THE CONTEXT OF THE PEN PROJECT

With over seven years of experience with electronic participation in government, Santa Monica, California offers a unique vantage-point on key questions raised about teledemocracy and posed in this volume (see Chapter 1).

Access to public information: a new channel

Did PEN provide citizens with easy and efficient access to public information? If viewed as a substitute for existing mass media, it would be difficult to argue that PEN is either easier to use or more efficient. For example, local newspapers, radio broadcasts and mailings reach far more local residents and more frequently and reliably than PEN. Even within the context of PEN, the information retrieval features of the system were less intensively used than were features permitting communication between people.

However, PEN complemented rather than substituted for other media and provided some advantages over them. For example, it did permit the city to reach the public directly, as opposed to depending on journalists. Immediately following a major earthquake north of Santa Monica in 1994 (the 'Northridge' earthquake), there was a flurry of activity on PEN, with citizens seeking emergency information. Nearly all personnel reported that PEN had virtually no effect on their use of the mails, telephone or face-to-face communication (Dutton, Wyer and O'Connell, 1993). City personnel have used PEN in ways that complement existing media – adding another channel within which they must manage citizen communications.

In the case of Santa Monica, and increasingly with other cities, the marginal costs of offering online access to public information has been low and declining. The city was already generating and distributing information in electronic form over its in-house electronic mail network to city personnel and council members when a citizen asked if he and other residents could have access to the same information. Then, with electronic information available for PEN users, it has taken a small investment of time and expertise to make this information available around the world over the Internet.

Top managers in the city found the information retrieval components of the system to have been efficient and successful. Sharing this evaluation, the City Council chose to develop the broadcasting component of the system further and has made additional information available to residents over PEN. Since 1995, for example, additional read-only information was added, such as rent control guidelines, a guide to city services, archives of the city council and planning commission, and a directory of local businesses. Internet access has led the city to add information of interest to tourists and non-residents, such as information on Santa Monica hotels, restaurants and attractions, that are a service to local business.

Electronic service delivery: expanding promise

Electronic service delivery (ESD) overlaps but moves beyond the provision of public information (Taylor *et al.*, 1996). In offering citizens direct access to public services, such as in processing routine requests, like licence applications and permits, ESD can allow some routine services to be handled electronically, which increases the efficiency of staff and enables around-the-clock access from the home and public locations. It holds the promise of decreasing costs, while improving service delivery in ways that the private sector has done with, for example, the automatic teller machine.

A census survey of city staff who used PEN confirmed that the city's personnel believe PEN enhanced service delivery. Most managers and staff believed that PEN was 'useful' to their work and also made their work more interesting (Dutton, Wyer and O'Connell, 1993). While staff viewed PEN as useful, most also believed that the system increased their workload. Most respondents (82 per cent) reported that use of the network increased requests for services. Of all respondents, 46 per cent believed it had increased the number of complaints the city received. Thus, PEN improved service delivery, but also placed more time pressures on city staff, who were required to respond in a timely way to requests and complaints.

Santa Monica managers have viewed the service delivery component of PEN as important and, as with the broadcasting function, have turned their attention to marketing service provision and developing it more fully (Barrette, 1994; Wolf, 1995). City management, for example, has chosen to make the read-only and service delivery components of the system available to Santa Monica residents via the World Wide Web, so that more Santa Monica residents can access them. These services include registering for a library card, requesting removal of graffiti, filing consumer complaints and applying for a local commission, board, or task force.

The importance attached to this service delivery component by the city is not simply driven by improvements in efficiency. It also enables the city to pursue other policy objectives, such as reducing traffic and parking problems by making even a small reduction in trips to city hall.

Empowering marginal groups

The PEN system was successful early in its existence in attracting the involvement of a sizeable number of Santa Monica residents. Each month, 400–600 residents used PEN. This number was substantial if compared to the number participating in local public affairs, such as attending a council meeting. Moreover, the computer conferences generated lively and substantive discussions of public affairs issues and quickly became the most frequently used component of the PEN system. A large proportion of accesses (nearly 50 per cent) was to computer conferences on local and national public affairs issues, such as the homeless (Guthrie *et al.*, 1990).

PEN did not bring a whole new set of participants into the political process. Television viewers were not pulled away from their sets to lead active roles in local politics. Most users were already interested in local public affairs and many were actively involved before PEN's launch. Compared to other residents of Santa Monica, PEN users were more likely to be active and interested in politics (ibid.). PEN offered another channel of communication to citizens already interested in politics – citizens who may attend council meetings and call or write their local representative anyway.

Nevertheless, at the margins, PEN permitted some individuals to become involved in local politics and public affairs who might not otherwise participate. In a survey of Santa Monica personnel, for instance, those familiar with PEN reported that PEN offered the opportunity for a new set of people to become involved in local government, such as those whose schedules or commitments would not otherwise permit them to participate (Dutton, Wyer and O'Connell, 1993; Mayell, 1993; Wolf, 1995). One case in point was a lone parent with work and child care responsibilities that prevented her attendance at council meetings. PEN permitted her to follow public affairs after her children were in bed and to participate in debates and discussion of public issues. Another example was a homeless man, who wrote:

> [Being homeless] makes 'normal' contact with other humans almost impossible . . . This is why Santa Monica's PEN system is so special to me. No one on PEN knew that I was homeless until I told them. PEN is also special to me because after I told them, I was still treated like a human being. To me, the most remarkable thing about the PEN community is that a City Council member and a pauper can coexist, albeit not always in perfect harmony, but on an equal basis.
> (quoted in Schmitz *et al.*, 1993: 17)

At the margin then, PEN has been able to give some voice to individuals interested in politics who might not otherwise be able to participate.

In other cases, there are some examples that suggest PEN drew some individuals into public affairs. For example, some residents who used PEN initially to access the library's catalogue found themselves browsing through other read-only information, such as agendas and minutes of the city council (Barrette, 1994).

Virtual political organisations

PEN fostered horizontal as well as vertical communication networks. The computer conferences and E-mail on the PEN system were designed to encourage citizen-to-citizen interaction about issues of local importance. Proponents of the conferences argued that pluralist democratic systems are best supported by a design which facilitates the expression of citizen opinions to leaders and encourages public discussion of issues thereby expanding the formation and marketplace of ideas. Citizen-to-citizen links were viewed as an important mechanism to nourish community organising and as a tool to facilitate political participation.

The city council also considered adding voting and polling capabilities to the PEN system, but ultimately rejected this idea because it conflicted with their conception of the role of citizens in decision-making. They feared that polling would encourage residents to make snap judgements, which would nevertheless carry a great deal of legitimacy, making it difficult for the council to dismiss them.

Early promoters of the system were surprised at the proportion of horizontal communication among citizens as opposed to the more vertical communication between citizens and city staff. The conferences came to be viewed as the core of PEN, what a PEN manager called 'the personality of the system' (Mayell, 1993).

The PEN conferences, at least initially, were successful at qualitatively improving political participation. In-depth interviews of members of city government along with surveys of PEN users and city staff suggest that the PEN conferences stimulated discussion about local political issues, aired more sides of issues, and helped involve key opinion leaders in discussions (Dutton, Wyer and O'Connell, 1993; Mayell, 1993; Wolf, 1995).

Supporting and generating collective action

Santa Monica's network, while not transforming the nature of collective action, supported a number of group political activities and actually led on several occasions to the formation of citizen groups (Rogers, Collins-Jarvis and Schmitz, 1994). Within six months from the inception of PEN, for example, an online discussion group was formed to generate dialogue and initiate political action which would enhance services for the homeless. Homeless individuals were among the discussion participants. Eventually, the group formulated a proposal to provide a shower facility, laundry room and storage lockers for homeless people (Schmitz *et al.*, 1993). A similar kind of discussion group was formed among PEN users concerned with feminist issues (Collins-Jarvis, 1993).

Emerging dilemmas for representative democracies

Santa Monica's experience indicates that the Internet and the multimedia revolution will not short-circuit such major dilemmas of democratic participation as public apathy. Most of the public in Santa Monica and other American cities are not very interested in local politics and are not interested in either real or virtual participation. Nevertheless, technological change in the household and government, illustrated by burgeoning interest in the Internet, suggests that electronic participation is likely further to be developed by governments throughout the US. As it is, new dilemmas of equity and content regulation are likely to emerge around electronic forms of participation – dilemmas foreshadowed but unresolved by Santa Monica's electronic city hall.

Unlike private information service companies, access to PEN is free to all Santa Monica residents. The city also has offered free training so that individuals who are not computer-literate may gain access. Moreover, ownership of a computer is not necessary, as twenty public terminals have been placed in sixteen locations around the city. A sizeable proportion of all accesses (about 20 per cent) have been from these public terminals.

The use of public terminals and the important role played by an interest in politics helped the city to create a community of users that was more diverse than the population of home computer users. For example, the PEN community included the unemployed as well as managers and professionals, the homeless as well as home owners and renters. In addition, an unusually high number of early PEN users were women, although PEN is still used mainly by men and boys (Collins-Jarvis, 1993).

In part, because computer-mediated communication often lacks social presence or cues about the social context, interpersonal communication can be more stark and less civil online (Kiesler, Siegel and McGuire, 1984; Short, Williams and Christie, 1976; Sproull and Kiesler, 1991). People are less likely to fear the social consequences of their rude or uncivil remarks in electronic communications as opposed to face-to-face communication because electronic communications are perceived to be more impersonal and ephemeral.

One city council member who initially was a heavy user of the PEN system reported that he no longer participated on the conferences because of the excessive 'flaming' (Holbrook, 1994). A survey of Santa Monica personnel involved in the PEN system also found that PEN seemed to encourage some users to send rude messages over the system. Of the city's staff involved with PEN, 47 per cent said that mail messages on this system were 'more often' rude than other messages, while 42 per cent said 'no more often', and 10 per cent said 'less often' (Dutton, Wyer and O'Connell, 1993). Moreover, a recent online survey of PEN users' perceptions of their rights and responsibilities indicated that users were more concerned about questions of taste, decency, civility, offensive language, personal attacks and threats than any other category of issues (Dutton, 1996a).

Concerns over civility, then, appear to have been a key factor which prevented more widespread participation in the computer conferences. As noted above, the city saw few policy alternatives available to decrease instances of 'flaming' because the First Amendment was read to preclude the regulation of citizens' speech. Some policy or technical alternatives, such as the institution of citizen moderators for conferences or the introduction of user-controlled filtering mechanisms to filter out abusive language or comments from particular users, would, in all likelihood have been constitutionally acceptable. However, once it had already been established that the conferences would be free-form, it was difficult later to introduce the structure of the moderated conferences. Users had grown accustomed to the speed of communication offered by the free-form conferences and were not willing to lose this advantage of the system. In fact, as soon as the moderated conference was introduced, many active users circumvented the moderated conference entirely by creating free-form conferences which were identical to the discussion items on the moderated conference.

By the summer of 1996, the PEN Project Manager noted that user complaints about rude or uncivil behaviour had dropped dramatically. This might signal the maturing of more civil norms governing speech within the PEN community. Some of the more offensive users might have left the system, but also the system might have lost those most offended by the lack of civility. Whether there has been a decline in abusive comments or users are growing more accustomed to the First Amendment online, the management of electronic forums seems to be a new dilemma for democratic systems.

OPPORTUNITY LOST OR REGAINED?

From the city's perspective, the most promising components of PEN are the broadcasting and transactions component of the system, not the interactive elements designed to foster electronic democracy, and the city is interested in building on these components. Many other cities have emulated aspects of PEN, particularly its use for broadcasting and conducting simple transactions, some of which involve E-mail. Local government enthusiasm for the Internet, as with most other organisations, is focused on the World Wide Web and its potential for broadcasting.

PEN was inspired by some of the same hopes that spawned experiments with local and interactive cable television in the 1970s. Perhaps it should not be surprising to see the transformation of PEN from the main focus being on providing a local and interactive public information utility to a more one-way medium accessible from anywhere in the world. Such was the evolution of cable television.

Not surprising, but disappointing given PEN's early history. In several respects, particularly early on, PEN conferences were successful. Key opinion leaders participated. Many other users – 'lurkers' – surveyed discussion. Groups formed. Policies were influenced. Electronic mail supported networking among residents interested in local politics. Over time, however, both residents and the city became less committed to the forums as they became a source of problems and complaints with no clear remedy. The Internet could be used to reinforce the movement of PEN towards the provision of information and services and could actually undermine its value as a forum for local debate and activity. Alternatively, the Internet might breathe new life into PEN by bringing a critical mass of residents into the nation's first public electronic network.

APPENDIX

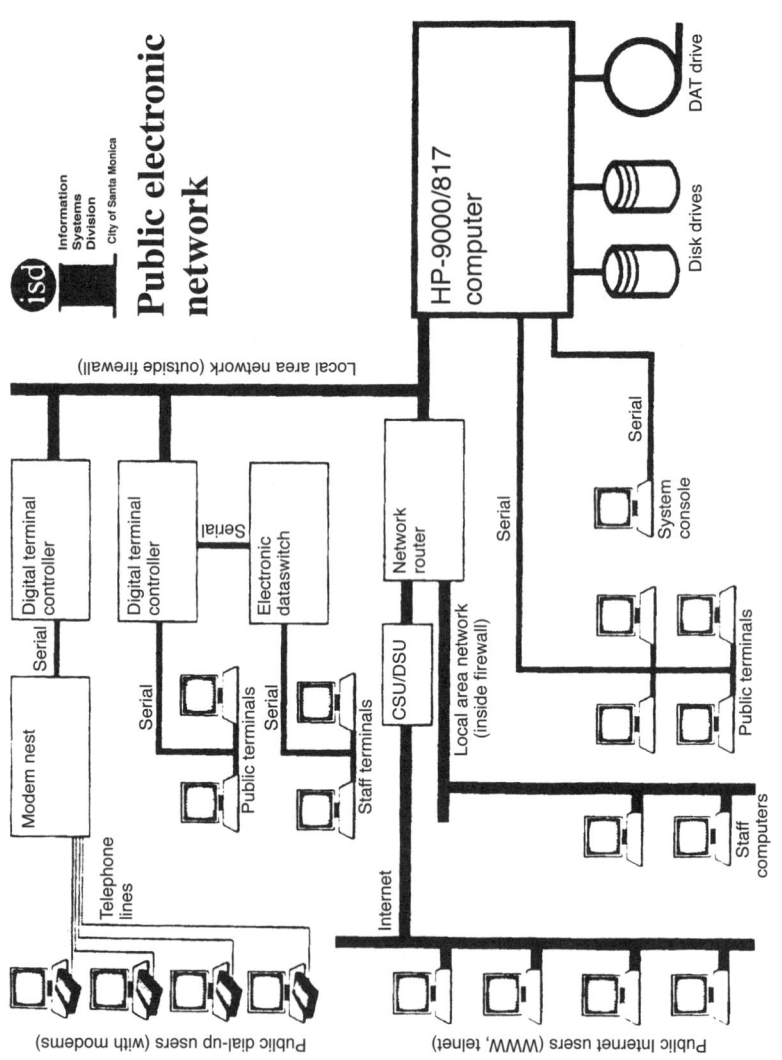

Figure 7.2 Diagram of the Public Electronic Network (PEN), City of Santa Monica

NOTES

1 Earlier overviews of the design and implementation of the PEN system, on which this study builds, are provided by Dutton and Guthrie (1991) and Guthrie and Dutton (1992).
2 This section draws on and extends earlier work by Dutton (1996b), Dutton and Guthrie (1991), Dutton, Wyer and O'Connell (1993), Guthrie and Dutton (1992).
3 See Dutton (1996a).
4 See Pool (1983) for an overview of these legal traditions.
5 See *ACLU v. Reno*, 929 F. Supp. 824 (E.D. Pa. 1996), *cert. granted*, 65 U.S.L.W. 3411 (1996) (striking down as unconstitutional the Communications Decency Act which prohibited the communication of indecency over the Internet. In December 1996, the US Supreme Court agreed to review the case.) See also *Shea v. Reno*, 930 F. Supp. 916 (S.D.N.Y. 1996), *petition for cert. filed*, 65 U.S.L.W. 3323 (1996).

REFERENCES

Abramson, J.B., F.C. Arterton and G.R. Orren (1988) *The Electronic Commonwealth*, New York: Basic Books.
American Civil Liberties Union v. Reno, 929 F. Supp. 824, 881 (E.D. Pa.1996) (Dalzell, J.), *cert. granted*, 65 U.S.L.W. 3411 (1996).
Arterton, F.C. (1987) *Teledemocracy: Can Technology Protect Democracy?*, Newbury Park, CA: Sage.
Banker, R.D., R.J. Kauffman and M.A. Mahmood (1993) (eds) *Strategic Information Technology Management: Perspectives on Organization Growth and Competitive Advantage*, Harrisburg, PA: Idea Group Publishing.
Barrette, L. (1994) Author interview with L. Barrette, Assistant City Manager, City of Santa Monica, California (June).
Becker, T. and R. Scarce (1984) 'Teledemocracy Emergent: The State of the Art and the Science', paper presented at the annual meeting of the American Political Science Association, Washington, DC.
CCTF, Cable Communications Task Force (1984) *Cable Communications in Santa Monica*, Santa Monica: CCTF.
City, L. and S. Kiesler (1992) *Connections: New Ways of Working in the Networked Organization*, Cambridge, MA: MIT Press.
Clark v. Community for Creative Non-Violence, 468 U.S. 288 (1984).
Collins-Jarvis, L. (1993) 'Gender Representation in an Electronic City Hall: Female Adoption of Santa Monica's PEN System', *Journal of Broadcasting and Electronic Media*, 37 (1): 49–63.
Dutton, W.H. (1996a) 'Network Rules of Order: Regulating Speech in Public Electronic Fora', *Media Culture and Society*, 18: 269–290.
—— (1996b) (ed.) *Information and Communication Technologies: Visions and Realities*, Oxford: Oxford University Press.
Dutton, W.H. and K.K. Guthrie (1991) 'An Ecology of Games: The Political Construction of Santa Monica's Public Electronic Network', *Informatization and the Public Sector*, 1: 279–301.
Dutton,W.H., K.K. Guthrie, J. O'Connell and J. Wyer (1991) 'State and Local Government Innovations in Electronic Services', unpublished report for the

Office of Technology Assessment, U.S. Congress. Annenberg School for Communication, University of Southern California.

Dutton, W.H., J. Wyer and J. O'Connell (1993) 'The Governmental Impacts of Information Technology: A Case Study of Santa Monica's Public Electronic Network', pp. 265–296 in R.D. Banker, R.J. Kaufman and M.A. Mahmood (eds) *Strategic Information Technology Management: Perspectives on Organization Growth and Competitive Advantage,* Newbury Park, CA: Sage.

Frisby v. Schultz, 487 U.S. 474 (1988).

Guthrie, K.K. and W.H. Dutton (1992) 'The Politics of Citizen Access Technology: The Development of Public Information Utilities in Four Cities', *Policy Studies Journal,* 20(4): 574–597.

Guthrie, K., J. Schmitz, D. Ryu, J. Harris, E.M. Rogers and W.H. Dutton (1990) 'Communication Technology and Democratic Participation: The PEN System in Santa Monica', paper presented at the Association for Computing Machinery's Conference on Computers and the Quality of Life, Washington, DC, 13–19 September 1990.

Hiltz, R. and M. Turoff (1978) *The Network Nation: Human Communication via Computer,* Reading, MA: Addison-Wesley.

Holbrook, R. (1994) Author interview with R. Holbrook, Member, Santa Monica City Council, City of Santa Monica, California (August).

Kann, M. (1986) *Middle Class Radicalism in Santa Monica,* Philadelphia, PA: Temple University Press.

Kiesler, S., J. Siegel and T.W. McGuire (1984) 'Social Psychological Aspects of Computer-Mediated Communication', *American Psychologist,* 39 (10): 1123–1134.

Kurtz, K. (1994) Author interview with K. Kurtz, PEN Project Manager, City of Santa Monica, California (March).

Laudon, K. (1977) *Communications Technology and Democratic Participation,* New York and London: Praeger.

Lawrence, J. (1993) Author interview with Joe Lawrence, Acting City Attorney (April).

Mayell, S. (1993) Author interview with S. Mayell, former PEN Project Manager, City of Santa Monica, California (June).

Myers. R. (1993) Author interview with R. Myers, former City Attorney, City of Santa Monica, California (April).

Pool, I. de Sola (1983) *Technologies of Freedom,* Cambridge, MA: Harvard University Press.

Raab, C., C. Bellamy, J. Taylor, W.H. Dutton and M. Peltu (1996) 'The Information Polity: Electronic Democracy, Privacy, and Surveillance', pp. 283–299 in W.H. Dutton (ed.) *Information and Communication Technologies: Visions and Realities,* Oxford: Oxford University Press.

Rogers, E.M., L. Collins-Jarvis and J. Schmitz (1994) 'The PEN Project in Santa Monica: Interactive Communication, Equality, and Political Action', *Journal of the American Society for Information Science,* 45 (6): 401–410.

Sackman, H. and B. Boehm (1972) (eds) *Planning Community Information Utilities,* Montvale, NJ: AFIPS Press.

Sackman, H. and N. Nie (1970) (eds) *The Information Utility and Social Choice,* Montvale, NJ: AFIPS Press.

Schmitz, J., E.M. Rogers, K. Phillips and D. Pascal (1993) 'The Public Electronic Network (PEN) and the Homeless in Santa Monica', paper presented at the annual meeting of the International Communication Association, Washington, DC, May 1993.

Shea v. Reno, 930 F. Supp. 916 (S.D.N.Y. 1996), petition for cert. filed, 65 U.S.L.W. 3323 (1996).

Short, J., E. Williams and B. Christie (1976) *The Social Psychology of Telecommunications*, London: Wiley.

Slaton, C.D. (1992) *Televote: Expanding Citizen Participation in the Quantum Age*, New York: Praeger.

Sproull, L. and S. Kiesler (1991) *Connections: New Ways of Working in the Networked Organization*, Cambridge, MA: The MIT Press.

Taylor, J., C. Bellamy, C. Raab, W.H. Dutton and M. Peltu (1996) 'Innovation in Public Service Delivery', pp. 265–282 in W.H. Dutton (ed.) *Information and Communication Technologies: Visions and Realities*, Oxford: Oxford University Press.

Williams, F. (1982) *The Communications Revolution*, Beverly Hills, CA: Sage.

Wolf, J. (1995) Author interview with J. Wolf, Director, Information Systems Department, City of Santa Monica, California (October).

Wythe, R. (1996) Author interview with Roslyn Wythe, Department of Information Systems, City of Santa Monica, California (July).

8 Manchester
Democratic implications of an economic initiative?

Cathy Bryan

INTRODUCTION

There are currently a number of local authorities throughout the UK which are using information and communication technologies (ICTs) to supply information to and receive it from citizens and which, to varying degrees, embody the principles of the civic networking movement. The first attempt in the UK to bring this technology within the control of a city-wide, publicly initiated project took place in Manchester. This chapter sets out to examine the origins of Manchester City Council's (MCC's) Information City initiative and the factors which have influenced the direction it has taken since inception.

BACKGROUND AND HISTORY OF THE MANCHESTER HOST

In the UK, debates regarding the civic uses of ICTs have historically been confined to urban studies and local government departments, and this approach has focused on the viability of the city in the face of a set of economic changes such as industrial decline and ecological deterioration. This set of issues has been identified as one of the major problems facing local government in the 1990s (O'Connel and O'Tuama, 1995). A number of academics have sought to address these problems within the locus of the development and use of ICTs at the city level (Bellamy and Taylor, 1994; Castells, 1989). Manchester City Council drew heavily upon these models of urban regeneration and built its plans for the Information City initiative upon the premiss that new information and communications technologies

> are playing an increasingly important role . . . in providing the dynamic for the emerging 'information economy', or 'information society' where multimedia based teleservices . . . and teleworking

represent a major economic change comparable to a new industrial revolution.

(Carter, 1991: 1)

What national debate there has been about the use of ICTs in the public sector in the UK has focused on issues of efficiency in the management and delivery of services (Horrocks and Webb, 1994). These narrow foci correspond to the Thatcherite emphasis on public spending cuts and the general climate of the 1980s in which civil society was subordinated to the official language of citizen as consumer and sustained by the Major government's Citizens' Charters, which outline minimum levels of service and opportunities for redress. Local government in the UK has less scope for the development of local projects as it has both less autonomy and less resources than equivalent bodies in the US (ibid.: 29). It is in the face of these obstacles that Manchester's Information City initiative has evolved and it is, I would argue, as a result of the stringent control exerted on local finances that the focus of the Manchester initiative has been directed towards the community benefits of group access to ICTs and their economic benefits rather than the participatory agenda of other city initiatives featured in *Cyberdemocracy*. These concerns are reflected in the origins of the Manchester Information City initiative in the Centre for Economic Research (CER) at Manchester Metropolitan University and in the Economic Development Department of Manchester City Council. In order to win the initial £300,000 Urban Programme grant from the Department of the Environment, a series of face-to-face negotiations between the City Council Development Department and civil servants at the Department of the Environment took place over a twelve-month period, and during this time the civil servants were gradually convinced of the relevancy of ICTs to economic development (Carter, 1995b). The first feasibility study was undertaken by the CER and a co-operative telematics provider called Soft Solution (Leach *et al.*, 1990) to consider the possibility of transporting rural telecottages to an urban environment in the form of Electronic Village Halls. In 1990 the Manchester initiative was launched, explicitly to help develop local regional development strategies by facilitating access to ICTs for small-to-medium-sized enterprises (SMEs). This historical origin goes some way to explaining the lack of explicit reference to democratic aims of the project and the lack of political dimension generally to what was, at the time, considered to be a purely economic initiative. Before going on to consider how the scope of the Information City has broadened since outset, some understanding of the basic geography of the initiative is helpful. The main hardware component of the initiative is the HOST, the mainframe computer which provides both the intra-city communication facilities and access to other networks via the Internet.

THE MANCHESTER HOST

The Manchester HOST is a proprietary information resource which was established by MCC and Manchester Metropolitan University in 1991. At this time the Internet had not yet developed into a consumer entity and the plethora of Internet access providers that have sprung up in recent years were nowhere to be seen. The user-friendly graphic-rich and hypertext-linked World Wide Web was still in its infancy and hence the HOST was developed as a proprietary service which required membership for access. Compared to today's Web-based technology, the HOST was not easy to use and it was envisaged that individuals would access the HOST through organisations rather than from the home. The penetration of PCs to the home, while still only 18–25 per cent of all households in the UK (compared to an estimated 30 per cent in the US) was practically zero at the beginning of the decade and, with the exception of professional computer users, home computer use was confined to wordprocessing and game-playing. Technical support for the Manchester HOST services has been provided since its launch in February 1991 by co-operative company, Soft Solution. The Manchester HOST consists of a minicomputer which is linked to the international GeoNet system, and through this to the Internet. Local personal computers are able to access the HOST via the telephone line and a modem through which they are able to receive communication services such as E-mail, conferencing, computer file transfer and information services. What follows is a brief synopsis of the services relevant to this discussion.

1 Bulletin boards

These function as public notice-boards and are only available to subscribers to the GeoNet network. The bulletin boards are broken down into three distinct types, namely: information boards, which provide details of public services such as the addresses and opening times of Citizens' Advice Bureaux across Manchester; public discussion boards, including boards relating to disability, human rights and the Internet; and private boards, such as those maintained on behalf of the Labour Party and a number of trade unions.

2 Public information

This includes connections to public information providers such as the Citizens Advice Bureau (CAB). All neighbourhood offices and housing offices are now online and a local advice workers network is being set up by MCC. The service, called Manchester Advice Network, will include all welfare rights officers, money advisers, housing aid advisers, as well as the voluntary sector advice agencies.

3 E-mail

This communication facility is generally regarded as one of the most useful aspects of computer-mediated communication (CMC), allowing quick and inexpensive exchange of information between networked individuals. However, its practical benefit to the citizens of Manchester, either as a communication tool between each other or as a means of accessing public information, is limited by the lack of any public access points. In the words of one of the training staff at Chorlton Electronic Village Hall, 'E-mail suffers from the first telephone thing – where you can only really use it when everyone else uses it' (Robinson, 1995).

4 Internet/World Wide Web

When the Manchester initiative first began the Internet was not seen to offer a likely route to the attainment of the project goals. However, the rapid growth of this particular communications technology led POPTEL to establish a series of a homepages on the WWW for themselves and a number of the city's information providers (Manchester Housing, CAB, MIND) in 1995. Initially, these sites were simply billboards, alerting individuals who had not subscribed to the HOST to its presence, and providing a taste of what was on offer. The site has expanded over the last twelve months and now offers extensive information of MCC services, CAB contact points and opening hours and the ability to contact service operators directly from the Website using E-mail. Similar sites are under development for the two sister HOSTs in Kirklees and London.

5 The Electronic Village Halls (EVHs)

The EVHs are central to the Manchester initiative. The concept of the EVH had its origins in Scandinavia in the mid-1980s, as an attempt to overcome some of the employment problems generated by the geographical dispersion of the population, and as such EVHs are generally oriented to the provision of training in the use of ICTs and the extension of skills to previously marginalised sections of the community.

The development of the EVHs in Manchester is particularly pertinent to the discussion of the democratic implications of the Manchester initiative because of their role in broadening the demographic spread of the HOST's potential user base. Initially, a number of existing community-based organisations were invited to take part in a tendering process to win funding for a period of two years. It was decided by the MCC that existing community-based organisations should be encouraged to take part in the tendering process as well as organisations which had been constructed specifically for the EVH tendering process. Of the three EVHs currently in existence, two – Chorlton Workshop and the Greater Manchester Bangladesh Association and Community Centre – were existing community-based organisations and as such they continue to have their own distinct identities above and beyond their work as an EVH, and this is manifest in the individual perspective each has on the role they perceive for themselves in relation to the wider aspirations of the city initiative. The Women's EVH was developed specifically for the initiative and it is for this reason that it emphasises its telematics function to a greater extent than the others.

Chorlton Workshop EVH, which characterises itself as a small independent voluntary organisation 'which prioritises black people, women with children under five, people with disabilities and people without further or higher education qualifications' (Chorlton EVH, 1995: 3) runs a range of courses which reflect its origins as a community workshop. These include instruction in knitting and sewing, basic computer-literacy courses, and maths and English tuition. The role of Chorlton Workshop as a provider of telematics services, and its relationship with the other EVHs, has been influenced by both its independence and its ongoing struggle for funding. Since the core funding for the development of the EVH finished at the end of 1994, Chorlton EVH has received funding from a plurality of sources, including the Further Education Funding Council (FEFC), Europe/Manchester City Council, charitable grants and some income generation.

The necessity of looking beyond the HOST project for funding has led to Chorlton EVH trying to juggle the services it provides to fall within the different requirements imposed by different funding bodies and, while its 1994 annual report acknowledges the increased interest in the Internet which has been generated by the national policy debate surrounding the Information Superhighway, resources are limited and the lack of phone lines renders provision of E-mail facilities and access to the WWW problematic. The Women's EVH and the Bangladesh Association are organised on similar principles, undertaking outreach work among marginalised members of their target communities and encouraging them to take advantage of their courses in basic computer-literacy skills. While nominally linked by their involvement with the Information City initiative, only limited emphasis has been placed on encouraging networking between the three EVHs, and Chorlton Workshop acknowledges that it has both 'the strength of being self-directed and the weakness of not having the support available through being part of a larger structure' (Chorlton EVH, 1995: 11). Similarly, there has between no real attempt to provide a single forum in which the EVHs and the community information providers can talk about the development of the project as a single, unitary entity. The extension of valuable computer skills to enable access to employment for women and ethnic minorities and the unemployed or previously unskilled is the priority of all those involved in the EVHs and there has been no formal attempt to encourage the utilisation of these skills in the discussion of public affairs or the translation of these skills into civic action. One study in particular, that of East Manchester's failed bid to win funding to become an EVH (Ducatel and Halfpenny, 1993), highlights some of the difficulties that imposing a concept, which had originally been developed to combat the problems of extending telecommunications services and related skills in rural Scandinavia, to urban Manchester has involved. While any problems of credibility and the related fear that the EVHs might be a political fad which merely diverts scarce funds from other community projects seem not to have hindered the development of the three EVHs, it would be unrealistic to expect the EVHs to translate the extension of skills into a wider sense of civic participation. As Ducatel and Halfpenny point out:

> [M]otivation of local participation in solving [these] long-term problems is likely to require more than a superficial engagement between a technically trained EVH officer and the community. If the Scandinavian experience applies to the British context, the EVH needs a local product champion who is enthusiastic, socially skilled, and knowledgeable about the area; initial technical skills are less important. The EVH will succeed as a community initiative only to the extent that it is seen by locals to be relevant to their own perceptions of needs and aspirations. It needs to be issue

based, not necessarily technology based, with a language that is accessible.

(ibid.: 377)

TELECITIES

An important part of Manchester's activity as an information city is its participation in and co-ordination of the Telecities Network, a lobbying and information-sharing organisation, born out of the broader Eurocities organisation and co-funded by DGXIII. Telecities,[1] now run from the Brussels-based Telecities Co-ordination Office, was launched in 1993 as a result of a workshop in Manchester which had been convened to discuss the strategic issues relating to developments in ICTs and specifically their implications for urban areas. Initially, at a working group of the Technological Co-operation Committee of Eurocities, the founding members'[2] stated objectives were to 'promote the exchanges of experience' and 'examine the issues related to the development of harmonised info-structures or telematics networks and services across Europe which will serve both the development of local industrial and service sectors, local society and citizens'.[3] Since its inception Telecities has initiated a number of projects, such as the Barcelona-led DALI, which aims at implementing new Delivery Access to Local Information Services as well as providing a forum for debate and information sharing.

DEVELOPMENT OF THE INFORMATION CITY

An 'ecology of games' approach (Dutton and Guthrie, 1991) provides a useful model through which to trace the evolution of the Manchester initiative and to expose the ways in which Manchester's Information City initiative is conceptually different from similar city-based initiatives using ICTs in other parts of Europe and the US. Dutton and Guthrie's ecology of games analysis examined the influence of competing and co-operative decision-making among the players' within the Santa Monican public information utility and assessed the overall outcome as the cumulative effect of a series of incremental decisions. It is useful with regard to the Manchester initiative because an ecology of games approach tolerates a degree of fluidity in the way in which concepts such as democracy have been employed as the project has evolved. One of the factors which is brought into view with such an analysis is the political affiliations of the players in the Manchester initiative. The company which has been providing telematics services for the

Manchester initiative since its launch in February 1991 is a co-operative called Soft Solution which, with its sister company POPTEL, provides telematics services to the Labour Party and much of the trade union movement. One could speculate that it was due to the political principles of the Labour-run City Council that they rejected a proposal for a privately run teleport aimed at servicing the business community (Walker, 1996) in favour of a system which was part funded by public grants, in order that the principle of equal access to ICTs might be fundamental to any system which might evolve. However, while it has been argued that

> the left has . . . tended to fall back either on idealist formulations of free communications with no organisational substance or material support or on technical utopianism that sees the expansion of channels of communication as inherently desirable because pluralistic
> (Garnham, 1993: 364)

the left-wing orientation of Soft Solution and of MCC, did not hinder the decision to seek private funds in order to construct a private–public partnership which would ensure the development of telematics services within the city that have a community-directed approach to the provision and pricing of services while not relying on a unilateral, public source of income. While the feasibility studies commissioned by MCC prior to launching the Information City initiative employed the metaphor of the 'Information Superhighway', its invocation has been used primarily to describe the potential of the development of an ICT infrastructure for economic growth, competitiveness and employment generation in the city. However, as the project has developed, the growth in the media's interest in all things Internet related, including the social and political implications of this technology, has fuelled the perception that the Manchester initiative should articulate its own democratic ideal. One of those who has been involved with the Manchester initiative from the outset is Dave Carter of MCC's Economic Development Department. Carter acknowledged that 'the main scenario being debated is an essentially optimistic one where the Information Superhighway will be able to support a wide range of new services which will empower citizens and provide for their full participation in an emerging digital democracy' (Carter, 1995a: 1) and warned of the dangers that are inherent in this view, namely, that technology will serve to reinforce existing economic inequalities. Carter looks to the integration of regional, national and international learning networks

> to provide the basis for a potentially powerful counter-balance to

vested interests, in terms of corporate and state authority, which can be proactive in taking an advocacy role in relation to consumer, citizen and wider democratic interests.

(ibid.: 2)

Carter is enthusiastic about the initiative generally and keen to get across MCC's commitment to democratic as well as economic regeneration, Clem Herman of the Women's EVH shares Carter's analysis of the role of democracy in the initiative:

> It's certainly becoming more of a priority – where we saw it starting was less about democracy and the involvement in politics, that's something that comes later, but what we saw from the beginning was a generalised view of democracy.
>
> (Herman, 1995)

Other individuals involved with the project do not share the increased concern with the democratic potential of the Manchester HOST initiative. Andy Robinson, from Chorlton EVH, remains sceptical: 'you look at the people who express and interest in the Internet – it's generally people – young, white, male – and I don't know who's talking about democracy' (Robinson, 1995). In a report prepared for MCC (Shearman, 1994), it was acknowledged that the development of public information services in the US had demonstrated how telematics could become part of the culture of the people living in the city and how, as a result of this, 'the development of public access multimedia points across the city . . . would be an important element of overall strategy' (ibid.), yet, to date, there are no concrete plans to pilot such public access points. Elsewhere in the UK, local authorities have taken this route and projects such as those in Newham (Newham Council, 1995), East London and Cambridge have used digital technology to enable citizens to access information services from public kiosks. Democracy in terms of political participation has not been clearly articulated until recently, and the development of the articulation of this concept within the project seems to verify Guthrie and Dutton's thesis that rather than one individual's or certain individuals' ideal of democracy driving the project, there has been an interplay between a series of interacting influences so that this articulation is neither unilateral nor static. The organic nature of the project in Manchester is due in part to the funding arrangements which make long-term planning and ambitious proposals for expansion and development difficult, and also in part to the lack of political direction from MCC. While changes in technology and the explosion of interest in the Internet and a subsequent fall in the price of devices such as the

Manchester: democratic implications of an economic initiative? 161

modem, which are essential to being online, have influenced the project, it is changes in the political/social environment that are crucial to the articulation of democracy within the Manchester initiative. The 'electoral politics game' (Dutton and Guthrie, 1991: 292) which refers to the need of local officials to ensure re-election, and while this force has not been an overt factor in the development of the Manchester initiative, it is probable that the recent media attention devoted to the Information Superhighway and the Labour Party's enthusiastic embracing of social and democratic merits of ICTs will have awakened local officials generally to the electoral and media gains to be won.

The Manchester approach raises a number of much broader issues about the presumed failings of the political and democratic system. The most commonly cited evidence that democracy is in crisis is the decline of citizen participation in the central mechanisms of democracy – elections – and the cause of this decline is more often than not ascribed to a sense of alienation consisting of distrust of the political class and apathy with regard to political issues (Barber, 1984). Such analyses rest upon a number of assumptions; first, that the lack of electoral participation is the result of dissatisfaction, rather than a level of comfort, with the operation of democratic mechanisms; second, that participatory democracy is an ideal model of political organisation; and third, that this model of democracy is attainable through the facilitation of communication between certain groups in society, generally, the citizens and their representatives. It is upon this set of assumptions that many civic networking experiments and projects have been built. The ability of citizens to engage with each other and with their representatives in debate about issues of a public and political nature is a desirable end goal, but the emphasis upon a vertical interactive participation and the formalised recording of opinions is too narrow a focus for the achievement of this aim. This democracy can best be described as a kind of 'MacDemocracy', characterised by numerous outlets (public access points), a homogenised product (one debate in one unified public sphere) and an emphasis on efficiency (high-speed and low-cost delivery of information and services).

The Manchester City initiative did not employ the language of democratic revolution such as has been utilised at a national and supranational level and in similar city-based initiatives in the US; the work being undertaken through the Manchester initiative, including the HOST services and the Electronic Village Halls, is helping to foster a climate in which the needs of the information-poor have been acknowledged and, in some cases, privileged. Democracy requires, first and foremost, the skills to understand the political information under deliberation and the incentive to make use of or acquire these skills, i.e., the need for citizens to feel that they have a stake in the outcome of deliberative democracy. The attraction to direct democracy is rooted in a false notion of political community as simply the coming together of citizens with their representatives in one single physical or virtual space, yet, without the social conditions that provide people with a stake in the outcome of political deliberation, no amount of high-tech wizardry will convert the pushing of a button or the dialling of a telephone number into an act of deliberation. This substitution of instantaneous reaction for measured response to a single question or set of questions could, rather than facilitating a return to some Golden Age of Athenian democracy, 'rather spell the deathknell of democracy' (ibid.).

How then can we usefully discuss the role of ICTs in relation to democracy without falling into the trap of accepting unconditionally the values implicit in the Information Superhighway metaphor and the overdependence upon a narrow conception of democracy? I would suggest we look to current debates around Habermas's description of the bourgeois public sphere and, in particular, the project of feminist academics (Fraser, 1993) to reconceive the public sphere. Fraser has argued that Habermas effectively dismisses the ideas of social equality as a prerequisite for political democracy by bracketing or suspending such inequalities for individuals in this sphere. In the light of this analysis the EVHs can be seen to have served as 'unbracketing' mechanisms, whereby, in making explicit the social and economic inequalities of their target population, they reject the principle of their suspension. The discussion of the regeneration of the public sphere is an important project which asks critical questions regarding the nature and extent of public life and the ways in which individual citizens interact with this sphere. The public sphere can provide an impetus for the imagination so long as it is free of the nostalgic romanticism with which Habermas has described the establishment of a bourgeois public sphere (Dahlgren, 1991). This question requires us to think beyond the application of ICTs and look more broadly at the communicative structures within which these initiatives are taking place, and the political and economic context of their evolution. The Manchester initiative, partly as a result of its economic focus, has not employed an idealised version of democracy nor has it associated itself with the establishment of a bourgeois public sphere, and this absence of democratic theory from its strategy for the future of the Information City initiative renders the project vulnerable to assertions that electronic networks can breed a new type of communicative citizen who is able to overcome architectural,

Manchester: democratic implications of an economic initiative? 163

geographical and economic displacement with access to online communities (Rheingold, 1995) or that

> rooting cyberspace in the social realities of neighbourhood organisations increases the odds that the needs and priorities of potential have not areas will be aggregated and expressed effectively. It is the activism of these kinds of grassroots organisations that eventually will push top-down NII policy in democratic directions.
>
> (Miller, 1996: 248)

What the Manchester initiative has achieved is the laying of the foundations for the provision of opportunities for citizens to communicate socially and politically in line with Fraser's notion of a reformulated public sphere. However, the majority of the visions for the 'information age' as articulated by politicians and the media, will remain overly optimistic as they continue to privilege the technology over the role of human needs (Forester, 1992).

CONCLUSIONS

Despite increasing awareness by local business people and local government representatives that telecommunications play an important role in the restructuring of the relationships between cities, enterprises and global economic networks, there has been a 'notable failure to analyse in detail the policy processes that are shaping these projects and policies or the wider sets of relations between telecommunications and urban policies at the local, national and supranational levels within which they develop' (Graham, 1995: 358). The Manchester Information City initiative has not linked into the national policy debate, and attempts to consolidate regional interests have been thwarted by the competition for funding between different regions (Walker, 1996), which acts to set different local and regional projects against each other rather than fostering a climate of co-operation and potential integration. Yet, a media-friendly debate about the social and political applications of ICTs has taken place at a national level and democracy has been a part of this debate. The potential of ICTs to open up new channels of communication between citizen and state has been seized upon in a series of national information infrastructure initiatives, and in the UK it has been the Labour Party which has embraced this concept with the publication of the document *Communicating Britain's Future* (Labour Party, 1995), which intoned the language and imagery of revolution. More specifically, the document states 'that technology can improve the UK's system of representative democracy by streamlining the flow of information from government, by making decision-takers more accountable, and by enhancing the opportunities for citizens to contribute to political decisions' (ibid.: 21).

Historically, the majority of writing on the subject of the development of ICTs and their democratic potential has fallen into a binary division between optimism and dystopia, with the optimistic strand of thought giving rise to the current political infatuation with technological development as a panacea for a range of social and economic ills. A debate constructed upon these fault-lines does little to foster an environment in which the implications of choosing to invest in a particular technology are fully explored. The hype which has been stirred up is muddying the waters of discussion and fuelling unreal expectations from the development of ICTs, rather than bringing them into the public sphere for considered debate. As Richard Sclove points out, the development of any new technology has broader social implications than those to which it was nominally intended, and these externalities are often overlooked in discussions of public policy and technology. Sclove asserts that 'all technologies are associated with manifold latent social effects and meanings, and that it is largely in virtue of these that technologies come to function as social structures' (Sclove, 1995: 20).

NOTES

1 http://www.poptel.org.uk/telecities/english/about.htm
2 Amsterdam, Barcelona, Birmingham, Bologna, Den Haag, Hull, Köln, Leeds, Lille, Manchester, Nantes, Nice, Nottingham.
3 Declaration of Manchester, 7–8 October 1993:
http://www.poptel.org.uk/telecities/english/dec-man.htm

REFERENCES

Barber, B. (1984) *Strong Democracy: Participatory Politics for a New Age*, London: University of California Press.
Bellamy, C. and J. Taylor (1994) 'Introduction: Exploiting IT in Public Administration: Towards the Information Polity', *Public Administration*, 72: 1–2.
Bertelsen, D. (1992) 'Media Form and Government: Democracy as an Archetypal Image in the Electronic Age', *Communication Quarterly*, 40 (4), Fall: 325–337.
Betteridge, J. (1996) 'Answering Back: The Telephone, Modernity and Everyday Life', unpublished manuscript, University of Westminster.
Blair, T. (1995) *Speech to the 21st Century Communications Conference*, Queen Elizabeth II Conference Centre, London, 18 July.
Carter, D. (1991) *Manchester and the Information Economy*, Manchester City Council.
—— (1995a) *Cities as Engines of Regional Economies: The Role of Information*

and Communications Technologies in Supporting Economic Regeneration and Urban Development, Manchester City Council
—— (1995b) Author interview with Dave Carter, Economic Development Department, Manchester City Council, 13 October.
Castells, M. (1989) *The Informational City*, Oxford: Basil Blackwell.
Chorlton EVH (1995) *Strategic Plan 1995–96 to 1997–98*, Manchester: Chorlton EVH.
Dahlgren, P. (1991) 'Introduction', in P. Dahlgren and C. Sparks (eds) *Communication and Citizenship*, London: Routledge.
—— (1993) 'Introduction', pp. 1–24 in P. Dahlgren and C. Sparks (eds) *Communication and Citizenship: Journalism and the Public Sphere*, London and New York: Routledge.
Ducatel, K. and P. Halfpenny (1993) 'Telematics for the Community? An Electronic Village Hall for East Manchester, *Environment and Planning C: Government and Policy*, II: 367–379.
Dutton, W. and K. Guthrie (1991) 'An Ecology of Games: The Political Construction of Santa Monica's Public Electronic Network', *Informatization and the Public Sector*, 1: 279–301.
Fishkin, J. (1992) 'Talk of the Tube: How to get Teledemocracy Right', *The American Prospect*, 11, Fall: 46–52.
Forester, T. (1992) 'Megatrends or Megamistakes? What Ever Happened to the Information Society?', *The Information Society*, 8: 133–146.
Fraser, N. (1993) 'Rethinking the Public Sphere: A Contribution to the Critique of Actually Existing Democracy', in C. Calhoun (ed.) *Habermas and the Public Sphere*, London: MIT Press.
Garnham, N. (1993) 'The Media and the Public Sphere', pp. 359–376 in C. Calhoun (ed.) *Habermas and the Public Sphere*, London: MIT Press.
Gore, A. (1994) *Speech to the Superhighway Summit*, Royce Hall, UCLA, Los Angeles, California, 11 January.
Graham, S. (1995) 'Cities, Nations and Communications in the Global Era', *European Planning Studies*, 3 (3): 357–380.
Herman, C. (1995) Interview with Clem Herman at the Women's EVH, 13 October.
Horrocks, I. and J. Webb (1994) 'Electronic Democracy: A Policy Issue for UK Local Government?', *Local Government Policy Making*, 21 (3): 22–30.
Hyatt, K. and B. Leach (1991) 'Disabled People On-Line: Information Technology, Telecommunications and Disabled People', report to Manchester City Council.
The Labour Party (1995) *Communicating Britain's Future*, London: Bell Press.
Leach, R., C. Girbash, S. Walker and S. Fenson (1990) *The Manchester HOST Computer Feasibility Study*, Manchester, Centre for Employment Research and Soft Solution Ltd.
Miller, S. (1996) *Civilizing Cyberspace: Policy, Power and the Information Superhighway*, New York: ACM Press.
Newham Council (1995) *Council and Police Lead Technology Project*, Newham Council Press Office.
O'Connel, C. and S. O'Tuama (1995) 'Towards a Theory of Urban Sustainability', *Sociedad Urbana*, 2, Spring.
Raboy, M. (1995) 'Access to Policy, Policies of Access', *The Public*, II (4): 51–61.
Rheingold, H. (1995) *The Virtual Community*, London, Minerva.

Robinson, A. (1995) Author interview with Andy Robinson, Chorlton Workshop EVH, 13 October.
Rogers, E., L. Collins-Jarvis and J. Schmitz (1994) 'The PEN Project in Santa Monica: Interactive Communication, Equality, and Political Action', *Journal of the American Society for Information Science*, 45 (6): 401–410.
Sawhney, H. (1995) 'Information Superhighway: Metaphors as Midwives', *Media Culture and Society*, 18 (2): 291–314.
de Sola Pool, I. (1983) *Technologies of Freedom*, Cambridge, MA and London: Harvard University Press.
Schulman, M. (1992) 'Communications in the Community: Critical Scholarship in an Emerging Field', p. 36 in J. Wasko and V. Mosco (eds) *Democratic Communications in the Information Age*, Canada: Garramond Press.
Sclove, R. (1995) *Democracy and Technology*, London: The Guildford Press.
Shearman, C. (1994) Advanced Information and Communications Technologies (ICT), Growth and Employment: Opportunities for the Manchester Economy, report to Manchester City Council.
Snider, J. (1994) 'Democracy On-Line: Tomorrow's Electronic Electorate', *The Futurist*, September–October: 15–19.
van de Donk, W. and P. Tops (1992) 'Informatization and democracy: Orwell or Athens? A Review of the Literature', *Informatization and the Public Sector*, 2: 169–196.
Van Dijk, J. (1977) 'Models of Democracy: behind the Design and Use of New Media in Politics', *Jarnost/The Public*, 3 (1): 43–57.
Walker, S. (1996) Interview with Steve Walker at the Centre for Economic Research, Manchester Metropolitan University, 11 January.

9 Electronic democracy and the public sphere
Opportunities and challenges

Roza Tsagarousianou

'Electronic democracy' as a means of improving the responsiveness and accountability of political institutions and enhancing citizen participation in the political process has captured the imagination of scholars, politicians and activists since the 1960s, when, armed with optimism and belief in the democratic potential of technology activists set up a wide variety of radical media (such as pirate radio stations). Since then, experimentation with remote computing, telephone conferencing technology and interactive cable television has given rise to a debate on the advantages – and potential dangers – that the application of these technologies in the political process might entail (Abramson, Arterton and Orren, 1988; Arterton, 1987; Laudon, 1977). Since the mid-1980s, the development of computer networks has substantially altered the terms of the debate on the use of new technologies in the democratic process. Until then, discussions on the plebiscitary or deliberative character of electronic democracy had focused primarily on interactive television. They paid only secondary attention to the possibilities of group communication inherent in the emerging computer-mediated communications systems.

In the 1980s, the rapid convergence of information and communications technologies and the development of computer networks have been thought to have the capacity to challenge the monopoly of existing political hierarchies over powerful communications media and perhaps the ability to revitalise citizen-based democracy (Rheingold, 1995: 14). Furthermore, they could amplify the power of grassroots groups to gather critical information, organise political action, sway public opinion and guide policy-making (Rheingold, 1996). More recently, public awareness of the potential of information and communications technologies has been supported by the high-profile embrace of the new technologies by such political figures as Al Gore, Bill Clinton, Newt Gingrich and American conservative Republican organisations such as the Progress and Freedom Foundation (1996) and, to a lesser extent, by the Commission of the European Union (Bangemann et al., 1994).

In the mid-1980s, several American local government authorities (such as Glendale, Pasadena, Santa Monica) were at the forefront of this shift in the envisaged uses of information and communications technologies. They primarily sought to improve contact between the local authority and the citizens, to upgrade delivery of services and, in the longer term, to encourage citizen participation in public affairs (Docter and Dutton, Chapter 7 this volume; Dutton and Guthrie, 1991; Guthrie and Dutton, 1992). Similarly, since the early 1990s a number of European local authorities such as Amsterdam, Bologna, Manchester (see Francissen and Brants, Chapter 2; Tambini, Chapter 5; Bryan, Chapter 8; all this volume) and civil society actors (see Schwartz, Chapter 6 this volume) rather than central governments have been engaged in experiments in electronic democracy. They frequently argued that by embracing information and communications technologies, they could resuscitate declining citizen participation in political life and give new vigour to local politics.

Most, although not all, experiments in electronic democracy (and all of those examined in *Cyberdemocracy*) share a number of common characteristics:

- they are perceived by the social actors initiating or participating in them as a means of reviving and reinvigorating democratic politics which for a variety of reasons is perceived to have lost its appeal and dynamism;
- they have been local or regional in their character, being related to more or less territorially bounded urban and suburban communities;
- they have been based on broadly similar technological infrastructures.

Apart from these general similarities among the cases examined in this book, the diversity of approaches to electronic democracy is significant and clearly reveals the polyvalence of the notion of democracy in general, and of electronic democracy in particular. It can be argued that these diverse perceptions of democracy arise from the diversity of political cultures that underpin different societies and localities, and the several national and transnational (e.g. European Union-related) policy frameworks within which these projects develop. *Cyberdemocracy* constitutes partly an attempt to set in a comparative context the projects examined in the volume and to begin to suggest ways of analysing the factors that have shaped the diversity as well as the similarities among them.

APPROACHES TO THE DEMOCRATIC PROCESS

Clearly, centrally designed local government-led initiatives differ enormously from the more spontaneous, civil society-led projects such as Neighborhoods Online, and to a certain extent the case of civic networking in Berlin and in Amsterdam on the one hand, or initiatives pursued despite the lack of political will from above or below as in the case of Network Pericles on the other. In top-down and bottom-up approaches, it is clear that specific objectives and aims have informed the projects and shaped them from early on, while in the latter case, of Network Pericles, an electronic democracy project that was created in a virtual social and political vacuum, aims have been rather vague and more specific objectives have yet to be defined, largely by the authorities which will embrace the project in question (see Tsagarousianou, Chapter 3 this volume).

In addition, there are clearly different definitions of the meaning and scope of electronic democracy in each project.[1] These range from mainly deliberative to more plebiscitary models, and from grassroots self-organisation and empowerment (such as Neighborhoods Online) to public information provision-centred projects (such as the Berlin City Information System). Clearly, these distinctions between different conceptualisations of democracy are more heuristic than 'real' as, in practice, as many of the contributions in this volume show, different city or civic projects combine different modes of citizen participation and service provision.

Amsterdam's Digital City, for example, combines a number of different communicative and civic functions, such as deliberation, public information, and some degree of support of grassroots groups. The IperBolE project of the Comune of Bologna supports citizens' deliberation, public information provision and, to a lesser extent, support of grassroots groups; the Santa Monica PEN project enables deliberation and public information provision; the Manchester Information City initiative promotes economic regeneration-related information dissemination as well as deliberation and civic information provision. In contrast, the official city of Berlin project is geared towards the provision of local authority and local area information, while Network Pericles has plebiscitary and deliberative aspects, and allows for limited information provision mainly. A different approach to the democratic process is taken by Neighborhoods Online, an Internet resource centre assisting citizens' groups working to improve conditions in communities and neighbourhoods, which therefore focuses on information provision and exchange, deliberation and civic networking.

It is striking that, although the initial promise of most electronic democracy projects was to develop and implement interactive local democracy which would enable citizens to express their views, opinions and preferences in binding or consultative polls, this promise has not been fulfilled – at least not to the extent initially anticipated by advocates of electronic democracy. The only exception is Network Pericles, which has given – at its planning stage, at least – a central position to the citizens' right to express their opinions through voting. Even so, it seems increasingly likely that electronic voting might become no more than a consultation exercise. This inability or unwillingness to explore to the full the potential for interactivity inherent in new technologies raises questions as to why these promises have not been honoured. Several possible reasons have been explored, such as technical limitations (which, however, are not insurmountable), financial restrictions, the lack of citizen access to the necessary technology or their negative predisposition toward the technologies utilised, the lack of political will and factors related to political culture.

ACCESS AND EXTENT OF SERVICE PROVISION

As Bowie (1990: 133) suggests, the terms and conditions for access to information technology 'increasingly define one's right of access to information *per se* . . . information that is particularly useful, relevant, timely information, is increasingly tied to complex electronic technology'. The argument that the growth of a privatised information infrastructure will lead to growing disparity between information haves and have-nots has been quite potent in the context of the debate on electronic democracy: the fear that electronic democracy projects might be oblivious of the social and economic inequalities among the citizenry and, therefore, the differential distribution of the hardware and skills necessary to participate in them, has led many participants in the debate to argue that only public provision in information infrastructure and public subsidy for information (and more generally, electronic democracy) services can ensure that the benefits of access to information will be distributed equitably and democratically (Garnham, 1990a, 1990b; Gillespie and Robbins, 1989; Schiller, 1984; Webster and Robins, 1986).

The 'access qua public good' argument raises a number of interesting questions regarding the application of new technologies in the political process:

- Can public service and universal service ethics that have recently been receiving serious blows in the areas of broadcasting and telecommunications have any place in the deployment of new technologies in

Electronic democracy and the public sphere   171

local democracy (in the broadest sense of the term) projects?
- What would be the problems that the application of public good principles in this field might entail?
- Who will carry the cost of rendering the network services accessible to the public?
- Will the right to access be complemented by ensuring that citizens develop the competence to use the services available to them and overcome, often socially conditioned, and class, gender, age and ethnicity-related, aversion to and distance from the technology and skills necessary?
- How are the rights to free speech/expression and concerns over the abuse of the city network balanced?

Not surprisingly, the answers to these questions differ from case to case. However, it should be pointed out that although recognition of access as a public good is present in different degrees in virtually all the projects examined in *Cyberdemocracy*, these issues are by no means resolved, as local authorities and citizens' networks have to operate within an economic culture and climate hostile to regulatory practices and to public authorities involvement in the market. Fears of inequitable distribution of the 'public good' of electronic democracy access are by no means unfounded, as the democratic initiatives examined in *Cyberdemocracy* are developing within the context of deregulation and privatisation of the telecommunications industry at a global level (see Introduction to this volume).

Although concerns regarding citizen access are shared among the majority of electronic democracy projects, each initiative is premised on different assumptions and has different aims regarding citizen access to the 'services' provided or the new technology-mediated democratic process. Neighborhoods Online, for example, has not addressed issues of universal access, mainly as its main emphasis is not on individual citizen access to its resources and services but rather on group networking. Bologna, on the other hand, has, from the outset, leaned considerably towards a policy of increasing citizen access to IperBolE, and Network Pericles is premised on the principle of universal access through public terminals and allows access from private terminals for some of its communicative functions only, but not for voting.

MODERATION, CENSORSHIP, FREEDOM OF SPEECH

Similarly, the issues of moderation and censorship are by no means resolved as delicate balances must be struck between the right to free speech, inextricably linked to democratic politics, and the need to avert abuse of access to public networks as well as to facilitate the use of the latter as vehicles for enhancing rather than inhibiting democratic communication. As it has been pointed out (see Docter and Dutton, Chapter 7 this volume), the perceived impersonal and ephemeral character of CMC may render users/participants oblivious to the need to maintain some degree of civility. The issue becomes even more complicated when freedom of speech and the related opportunities opened by the new technologies (such as encryption) allow specific political groups (such as German neo-nazis) to exploit public networks to their own benefit (see Schmidtke, Chapter 4 this volume). Again, different solutions have been resorted to in the context of different projects: Santa Monica's transition from free-form discussion groups to moderated 'city conference' settings indicates the city's concern over the abuse of access to the network and its obligation not to contravene the First Amendment sanctioning of the freedom of speech. As both concern over the abuse of public networks and appreciation of the speed and freedom of unmoderated communication seem to be equally significant for network users, the 'moderation versus freedom of speech' dilemma seems to be a central issue in electronic democracy and, as yet, an unresolved one.

ELECTRONIC DEMOCRACY: SOCIAL ACTORS AND POLITICAL CULTURE

Both the definition of democracy and access issues are linked with the particular ways in which electronic democracy projects came into being and develop. In each case, different actors (such as local authorities, grassroots movements, software, hardware and telecommunications companies, central governments, and even transnational bodies) with different interests and aspirations have negotiated and confronted each other in order to inform and influence the projects. An 'ecology of games' analysis sheds light on these complex processes of negotiation, co-operation and competition among the key actors in the process of shaping electronic democracy projects.

On the other hand, there appear to be some shared or similar goals among these projects (see Introduction to this volume). These goals or hopes are informing the ideology that sustains civic projects, albeit in a vague and occasionally ill-formulated way, as the perceived 'crisis of political communication' or of 'democracy' outlined in the Introduction is clearly the common target of these projects, on the evidence of the history of these attempts to rejuvenate local democracy.

Electronic democracy and the public sphere 173

A question that almost certainly arises when we are faced with the diversity of electronic democracy projects at the local level is: why have different projects utilising essentially the same technology taken significantly different courses? Throughout the book it has become evident that electronic democracy projects have been informed by different definitions of democracy, different aims and objectives. Of course, as has already been pointed out, this diversity among electronic democracy projects can be partly explained and better understood when the particular 'ecology of games' underlying each project becomes the object of investigation. In this way, by focusing on the motivation and objectives of the different social and political actors involved in these processes, we can account for some of the differences in the form and content of the electronic democracy projects in question. On the other hand, an ecology of games approach, however instructive, could not possibly account for 'deeper' political cultural factors that influence individual projects. It is clear that different political cultures (local, regional and national) set the broad parameters within which political and social action (ecology of games) can take place, and therefore, different socio-political environments rationalise and use information and communications technologies in their democratic projects in different ways.

Although we do not wish to suggest a rigid distinction between political culture and political action and practice, we would suggest that establishing an analytical distinction between the level of 'structure' (including political culture) and the level of action[2] might allow us to acknowledge both the restrictive and enabling roles that political culture plays in the political process of a society – and therefore in the process of development of electronic democracy projects – and, thus, to shed more light on the different ways in which similar technological infrastructures have given rise to electronic democracy projects.

In the case of Neighborhoods Online, for example, one can clearly see the influence of the American libertarian civic tradition even at a time when the civic networking movement is willing to enter into partnership with government (federal, state or local). One of the central aims of Neighborhoods Online is to empower citizens by encouraging the formation of citizens' groups and the development of citizens' initiatives. Thus, the organisation of grassroots movements and their engagement in dialogue and exchange of information inspired by a political culture that has been premised on citizen self-help and organisation have given to Neighborhoods Online its distinctive character (see Schwartz, Chapter 6 this volume).

In the case of the traditionally left-wing Italian region of Emilia, the Bologna project has been dominated by an intense debate on the definition of network access as a public good and a rhetoric of citizens' rights (see Tambini, Chapter 5 this volume). The Manchester Information City initiative, on the other hand, had been designed initially as a medium of economic regeneration, within the context of a culture of emphasis on economic (as opposed to civic) initiatives (see Bryan, Chapter 8 this volume). In addition, the local political culture, shaped in different degrees by a Labour Party and working-class cooperative culture has given to the project its progressive character. In the case of the Berlin City Information System, its development has been influenced by the post-war German political culture which was shaped by the experience of the Weimar Republic and its demise at the hands of the Nazis. Indeed the development of the Berlin City Information System project owes a lot to the post-war German mistrust towards 'populist strategies and an irrational decision-making process' (see Schmidtke, Chapter 4 this volume). The fear, deeply embedded in German political culture, of the democratic process getting out of control has reinforced a 'tutelary' notion of democracy that has also influenced official 'electronic democracy' projects. In the case of Santa Monica, it has been pointed out that the city has had a political culture supportive of participation in local politics (Docter and Dutton, Chapter 7 this volume) which has provided the impetus for the development of PEN while, finally, in the case of Network Pericles, a culture of citizen heteronomy has played a major role in the virtual lack of grassroots support for the implementation of electronic democracy.

SOCIALISING DEMOCRACY AND THE FIELD OF PUBLICNESS

In spite of the discourses of interactivity which underlie most 'electronic democracy' initiatives, most of them have in practice been executive-initiated, top-down and mostly based on giving more access to information. Politics in this form remains more of a model of convincing through the dissemination of information than of communication and discussion. In the US, presidential candidates, the Congress and federal, state and local administrations have embraced the use of electronic systems to serve a variety of objectives (Dutton, 1992) equated in public discourse with electronic democracy but bearing no democratic content.

Often, behind the rhetoric of electronic democracy, what is initiated is a very particular version of publicness, arranged around ordered forms of dissemination of information, in which official political channels decide on the definition of the problem and the content of the message and thus strongly influence the direction of the outcome. Therefore, when assessing the impact of electronic democracy initiatives such as those examined in *Cyberdemocracy*, one should examine the degree of 'socialisation' of the initiatives in question.

The extent to which the particular applications of information and communications technologies enlarged the participatory process, their success in introducing other than top-down ways of political participation and in delivering their promise to 'promote community-oriented participatory democracy' through two-way communication between citizens and public officials are by no means easy to determine.

The answers to these questions are by no means clear or simple. As the case of Berlin's City Information System shows, CMC is not necessarily interactive. Some aspects of the WWW (and of applications of networks technology, in general), including information on civic issues, are not engaging people in interactivity, while this volume has demonstrated that, despite the more or less common or similar rhetoric and official discourse of electronic democracy advocates, there is a considerable diversity of networks, from highly to minimally interactive ones.

To assess further the democratising potential and record of electronic democracy projects, the impact of the latter on the public sphere has to be assessed in order to determine to what extent the latter has been widened and opened up; it is clear that the success of electronic democracy projects will depend on their capacity to support and enable the introduction of new forms of 'publicness' within a public sphere dominated by privately owned and controlled media and the state.

The idea of modern representative democracy has been inextricably linked to the 'recognition of a living web of citizen-to-citizen communications' (Rheingold, 1995: 13–14), a realm of public debate and information exchange, the public sphere. The commercial mass media-dominated public sphere today is being challenged by the emergence of new forms of publicness created by social networks. Today, new technologies increasingly play a central role in the mediation of social networks. As a result, any socially grounded theory of the public sphere will have to take into account these social network structures and the communications systems that bind them (Friedland, 1996: 189). What is more, Dahlgren (1991) has argued that the availability of suitable computer and communications technologies to citizens' groups has started to give rise to dynamic alternative public spheres next to those of the corporate state and the existing mass media. As most of the studies included in this volume indicate, most electronic democracy projects have established some degree of interactivity (and interaction), especially among citizens and citizens' groups, and have sustained a degree of deliberative process.

On the other hand, little has been done to broaden access to electronic democracy networks and therefore to extend democratic practices and broaden the public sphere. Access to hardware and software remains a significant issue, while policies to overcome socially and culturally conditioned 'technophobia' (such as that which is gender- or class-related) have not even been on the agenda. What is more, this volume demonstrates that, in the case of local government-initiated projects, more often than not it is the public information and local government transactions functions of the networks that take precedence over their interactive features.

One thing is quite clear, however. Electronic democracy in its plebiscitary or deliberative permutations expressed in the different city projects examined in *Cyberdemocracy* cannot by itself democratise the communities which it serves. The creation of public spaces, the articulation of views and demands, the formation of citizens, requires much more energy and commitment and grassroots involvement in public debate.

It would be very difficult to answer these questions in a positive or negative way, precisely because of the complexity of the processes under way and partly because of the relatively early stage in the career of the projects examined in this volume. As it has been stressed elsewhere in this volume (Bryan, Chapter 8), an attempt to evaluate the democratic potential of electronic democracy projects by succumbing to the binary division between optimism and dystopia undermines our ability to comprehend their implications and potential.

NOTES

1 These reflect the broader debate on electronic democracy. In general, the debate on CMC and democracy has been dominated by two key frameworks: plebiscitary and deliberative (Arterton, 1987). In the plebiscitary framework it is envisaged that individuals directly express their opinions through an expanding electronic marketplace. Such a notion of electronic democracy was actively promoted in the 1970s and 1980s by proponents of expanded democracy (Barber, 1984; Williams, 1982), futurists (Naisbett, 1982; Toffler, 1980). and corporate cable television interests seeking municipal franchises. The plebiscitary vision is now also embraced by conservative populists (H. Ross Perot and Newt Gingrich), who see electronic communication as a democratic end in itself.

In contrast to plebiscitary democracy, deliberative models seek to strengthen representative democracy and to render it more participatory. Barber (1984: 273 ff.), for example, advocates the use of CMCs as a means of strengthening democracy, as a medium of civic education and enhanced participation of the citizens. Deliberative models have stressed the importance and desirability of citizens' participation in public discourse, although not necessarily advocating their involvement in solving the problems of social reproduction.

2 Rather than seeing action and structure as the counteracting elements of a dualism, they should be regarded as the complementary elements of a duality. 'Social structures are both constituted by human agency, and yet at the same time are the very medium of its constitution' (Giddens, 1976: 121).

REFERENCES

Abramson, J.B., F.C. Arterton and G.R. Orren (1988) *The Electronic Commonwealth: The Impact of New Media Technologies on Democratic Politics*, New York: Basic Books.
Arterton, F.C. (1987) *Teledemocracy: Can Technology Protect Democracy?*, Newbury Park, CA: Sage.
Bangemann, M. et al. (1994) *Europe and the Global Information Society: Recommendations to the European Council*, http://www.cec.lu/en/comm/20c/bange.html
Barber, B.R. (1984) *Strong Democracy: Participatory Politics for a New Age*, Berkeley, CA and Los Angeles, CA: University of California Press.
Bowie, N. (1990) 'Equity and Access to Information Technology', pp. 131–167 in *The Annual Review*, Institute for Information Studies.
Commission of the European Union (1995) *Action Plan*, http://www.infosoc/backg/action.html (10 February).
Dahlgren, P. (1991) 'Introduction', pp. 1–24 in P. Dahlgren and C. Sparks (eds) *Communication and Citizenship: Journalism and the Public Sphere*, London: Routledge.
Dutton, W.H. (1992) 'Political Science Research on Teledemocracy', *Social Science Computer Review*, 10(4): 505–523.
Dutton, W.H. and K. Guthrie (1991) 'An Ecology of Games: The Political Construction of Santa Monica's Public Electronic Network', *Informatization and the Public Sector*, 1 (4): 1–24.
Friedland, L.A. (1996) 'Electronic Democracy and the New Citizenship', *Media, Culture and Society*, 18: 185–212.
Garnham, N. (1990a) 'Contribution to a Political Economy of Mass Communication', pp. 20–55 in N. Garnham *Capitalism and Communication: Global Culture and the Economics of Information*, London and Newbury Park, CA: Sage.
—— (1990b) 'The Media and the Public Sphere', pp. 104–114 in N. Garnham *Capitalism and Communication: Global Culture and the Economics of Information*, London and Newbury Park, CA: Sage.
Giddens, A. (1976) *New Rules of Sociological Method: A Positive Critique of Interpretative Sociologies*, London: Hutchinson.
Gillespie, A. and K. Robins (1989) 'Geographical Inequalities: The Spatial Bias of the New Communications Technologies', *Journal of Communication*, 39 (3): 7–18.
Guthrie, K. and W.H. Dutton (1992) 'The Politics of Citizen Access Technology', *Policy Studies Journal*, 20 (4): 574–597.

Habermas, J. (1976) *Legitimation Crisis*, London: Heinemann.
Huntington, S. (1975) 'The United States', pp. 149–165 in M. Crozier *et al.* (eds) *The Crisis of Democracy*, New York: New York University Press.
Laudon, K. (1977) *Communications Technologies and Democratic Participation*, New York: Praeger.
Melucci A. (1989) *Nomads of the Present: Social Movements and Individual Needs in Contemporary Society*, Philadelphia: Temple University Press.
Meyrowitz, J. (1985) *No Sense of Place*, New York: Oxford University Press.
Murdock, G. and P. Golding, (1989) 'Information Poverty and Political Inequality', *Journal of Communication*, 39: 2.
Naisbett, J. (1982) *Megatrends: Ten New Directions Transforming Our Lives*, New York: Warner Books.
Negroponte, N. (1995) *Being Digital*, London: Hodder & Stoughton.
Neustadt, R.M. (1982) 'Politics and the New Media', pp. 47–70 in H.F. Didsbury, Jr. *Communications and the Future; Prospects, Promises, and Problems*, Bethesda, MD: World Future Society.
Offe, C. (1984) *Contradictions of the Welfare State*, London: Hutchinson.
Poster, M. (1990) *The Mode of Information: Poststructuralism and Social Context*, Cambridge: Polity.
Progress and Freedom Foundation (1996) http://www.pff.org
Rheingold, H. (1995) *The Virtual Community: Homesteading on the Electronic Frontier*, London: Minerva.
Rheingold, H. (1996) *Electronic Democracy Toolkit*, http://www.well.com/user/hlr/electrondemoc.html
Schiller, H. (1984) *Information and the Crisis Economy*, Norwood, NJ: Ablex.
Toffler, A. (1980) *The Third Wave*, New York: Bantam.
Toffler, A. and H. Toffler (1995) *Creating a New Civilization: The Politics of the Third Wave*, Atlanta, GA.
Webster, F. and K. Robins (1986) *Information Technology: A Luddite Analysis*, Norwood, NJ: Ablex.
Williams, F. (1982) *The Communications Revolution*, New York: New American Library.
Wright, R. (1995) 'Hyperdemocracy', *Time*, 23 January.

Index

access, a critical question 15
'access qua public good' argument 170–1
administration–citizen interaction, and Citycard 90
adult literacy groups 112
advocacy groups 117–18
agenda-setting 107
American Civil Liberties Union v. Reno 134, 135
Amsterdam 7, 30–1; City Talks 7, 21–2; *see also* Digital City, Amsterdam
Asymmetric Digital Subscriber Loop (ADSL) switching 2–3
authority–citizenry interface 100–1

Bangemann report 11, 14
BBC, report on future of 10–11
Berlin: administration, problems with new media 65–6; student protest helped by new media 77–8
Berlin in the Net 60–83; the 'City Information System (CIS)' 63–7, 174; civic initiatives 68–78; CMC not necessarily interactive 175; and freedom of speech 172; political parties and the Internet 67–8; threats to vision of an interactive democratic community 80–1; used by right-wing/racist groups 73–6
bias: Bologna 106, 107; of the media 7
billboards/webvertisements 28
BIOS-plan/BIOS-3 report, Netherlands 32–3, 37

Blair, Tony, and BT deal 10
Bologna (Comune): access to internal information 100–1; agenda-setting 96; citizen information 95–6; civic working and universal rights to connectivity 84–109; cyberdemocracy debate 87–90; discussion groups 96–7, 105–6; Transparency in Public Services (1990) 87
Bologna project 13, 174; aim of universal access 106; brief history of 86–7; goals of computer-mediated democracy 88; hardware 92, 93; PR literature 88–9; right to connectivity 85; software 91–2; specific debates 89–90
Bonaga, Stefano 84, 90
bulletin boards, Manchester HOST 154
Bunker BBS-Mail box 75
BVE-Net, Digital City, Amsterdam 28

cable television 9
cable TV, interactive 127
Calhoun, G. 54
Carter, D. 152–3, 159–60
censorship 171–2
Chorlton Workshop EVH 156; search for funding 156–7
CINECA (universities computing consortium) 87, *92*, 93
citizen groups: and alternative public spheres 175; Santa Monica 144–5

citizen initiatives 46, 56
citizen moderators 138, 146
citizens 171; electronic access to public information 127; 'individualisation' of 54; political involvement of 49; preferences measured by new technology 6; services to 128
citizens' charters 15, 153
'citizens' movement' 124
citizenship: actualisation of 56; exercise of rights, Network Pericles 53; theory 103
'City Conference', PEN system, Santa Monica 137–8
City Consultations (Amsterdam) 22
'City Information System (CIS)', Berlin 63–7
city initiatives, and national policy setting 13–14
City Talks (Amsterdam) 21–2
Citycard project, EU 86, 89, 90, 105
civic/citizen participation: Philadephia 121, 123; USA 111
civic networking 1, 13, 16, 61, 161, 169; see also IperBolE
civic networking movement 15, 152; ideology of 6–8; and technology developments 2–3
civil liberties, little heed paid to in Bologna 87–8
civil rights 103
civility, a concern, Santa Monica 146
clientelism, in Greek politics 43
CMC see computer-mediated communication
co-operation, failure of 4
commercial media, expansion of 5
Communicating Britain's Future, Labour Party 163–4
communications technologies: and generation of collective action 79–80; new 14, 78
Community Development Block Grant (CDBG) 111
community development corporations 111
community groups, isolated 112
community policing 112

Compuserve, and the 'sex' problem 35–6
computer networks, results of development of 167
computer skills, extension of by EVHs 157
computer-based communications 66, 79; collective action and civic participation 69–73; technologies 60, 62–3
computer-literacy, Bologna 98, 103
computer-mediated communication 1, 2, 6–8; citizen behaviour 145–6; collective action and civic participation, Berlin 69–72; constitutional status of 134–5
conferences/conferencing: citizen 53; electronic 128; PEN conferences 136–9, 144, 145–6, 147, 172; see also teleconferencing/citizen conferencing
connectivity, right to 84–6, 103
'Cupcards', Bologna 86
cybercitizenship, universal v. non-universal 103–7
cyberdemocracy: Bologna 1997: a compromise? 90–4, *95*; Bologna debate 87–90; images over-optimistic 81; political prospects for 73
cyberspace 60, 72, 78; access to, Germany 61–2; and the have nots 163; used for propaganda 75–6; world of 62–3
cyberspace politics, appeal of 72

DALI (Delivery Access to Local Information Services) 158
data digitisation 2
De Digitale Stad see Digital City, Amsterdam
debate/communication, unsatisfactory quality 132
decision-making: democratic, and new communication techniques 60–1; political, Network Pericles 46–7
democracy: Athenian 45–6, 53; back to the future of (Network

Pericles) 41–57; and development of new public spaces 55; direct, fear and mistrust of 66, 67, 174; equated with institutional stability 79; and the Manchester initiative 160–2; and the role of ICTs 162–3; virtual, rhetoric of 85–6 democratic communication, problem of 9
democratic paradox, Amsterdam 21, 38
democratic process, approaches to 169–70
democratic renewal, through new communication techniques 61
'Den Mother Notes' 135
Digital City, Amsterdam 7, 18–40, 169; access to 31, 37–8; aims and objectives 23, 24, 37; city life 24–6; future of 35; inhabitant profile 30; issues and problems 35–7; living in 28–31; organisation and decision-making 33–5; population proliferating 30; 'rules of the game' 36–7; short history of the future 20–4; talking in 31–3; themed squares 20, 26, 28; version 2.0 23–4, 25–6; working in 26–33
digital compression 2
dilemmas, for representative democracies 145–6
'Dimmi' initiative, Bologna 86
discussion groups: Bologna Comune 96–7, 105–6; Digital City 312
Ducatel, K. and Halfpenny, P. 157–8
Dutton, W. and Guthrie, K. 158, 160, 161

E-mail 12, 78, 137, 155; and IperBolE 94, 100; links to politicians, Germany 68; and Neighborhoods Online 114, 115, 121–3; network for Santa Monica city personnel 127; and the PEN system 137, 144
E-mail lists, Neighborhoods Online 121–2, 123
ecology of games 158, 172, 173
Economic and Social Research Council 10

editors, Internet, Bologna 105
elections 102; decline in participation in 20–1, 161; *see also* voters
'electoral politics game' 161
electronic access, public support for, Santa Monica 127
electronic citizenship, selectivity of 98–9
'electronic city hall' 128, 137
electronic communication, and the First Amendment 134
electronic democracy 1–2, 5, 85, 170; common characteristics and diversity of approaches 168; debates on general principle of 87–9; deliberative models 176–7n; differing definitions 169; European experiments 42; experiments, Amsterdam 21–2; interactivity of projects 175–6; little done to broaden access to 176; and Network Pericles 45–8, 52–7; and new forms of 'publicness' 175; plebiscitary framework 176n; and the public sphere 167–78; social actors and political culture 172–4; socialisation of the issues 174–6; themes, in context of the PEN project 140–6; why the project differences? 173–4
Electronic Highway, and Digital City 20, 21
electronic networks, role and design of 128–9
electronic participation: further development of 145; innovation in 126–8
electronic service delivery (ESD) 126, 141–2
Electronic Village Halls 153, 155–8
elitism, Digital City 31
EU/EC 2, 14; Citycard project 86, 89, 90, 105; 'First Reflections' report 11; Information Society project 11; liberalisation of telecommunications 11; Telecities project 1, 158
European Movement Netherlands 32

European village 52
EVH *see* Electronic Village Halls

First Amendment online 133–9; establishment of a guideline 133–5; interpersonal influence 135–6; moderated conferences 136–9
Fishkin, J. 5
flaming 32, 37, 100, 132, 139, 146
freedom of speech 36, 171–2; and civil networking 14
Freenets (US and Canada) 22, 23
Freeport (software progam) 25

Garnham, N. 159
Germany *see* Berlin in the Net
government-led initiatives, centrally designed 169
group communication 167
Guidi, Leda 85–6, 89, 91

Habermas, J. 60–1, 162
Herman, C. 160
Hewlett-Packard 128

ICT *see* information and communication technology(ies)
Industrial Areas Foundation 113
information, access to 6, 174; PEN a new channel 140–1; public provision for 170
information city 9, 162–3
information and communication technology(ies): application in the political process 41; for electronic service delivery 125–6; Manchester's use of 152–64; problems of 14–15; use of in direct democracy projects 57; use in the USA 168; *see also* PEN system, Santa Monica
information delivery systems 64
Information Superhighway 9, 10, 11, 12
information technology, access to and extent of service provision 170–1
information-poverty, problems of 103

infrastructure, of Digital Cities 25
inhabitants, registered, Digital City 28–30
Institute for the Study of Civic Values 113; 'Empowerment Zone Online' menu 120; and LibertyNet 115–18, 119–20
Internet 12, 15, 36, 147; culture of 9; democratising effect of 134; and electronic democracy 125–6; German political parties, homepages 67–8; and Neighborhoods Online 114, 119; and the PEN system 132–3; used by right-wing and racist groups 73–6
Internet access 77, 107; Bologna 85, 87, 89, 101, 106; Bridge Project, and LibertyNet 120–1; Germany 61–2; for non-profit groups, Philadelphia 118–19; to Santa Monica PEN system 131, 132
Internet for Bologna and Emilia *see* IperBolE
Internet providers, legal battle with Bologna comune 89
interpersonal influence, PEN system, Santa Monica 135–6
IperBolE 84, 87, *104*, 169; authority-citizenry interface 100–1; based on idea of universal suffrage 88; the BBC of the Internet? 106–7; citizen access 93, 171; city's read-only database 95–6; legal problems 101–2; 'netiquette' and content regulation 99–100; selectivity 98–9; subscriber services package 90–1; take-up 97–8; use of the network 94, *95*; user identity 102–3; users *98–9*

Kellner, D. 5
kiosks, Network Pericles 48–9, 50, 52, 53–4
knowledge sharing 38

Labour Party, and media ownership 11
legal issues/problems: Digital City

35–6; IperBolE 101–2; status of publicly owned electronic networks 134–5
'LibertyNet', Philadelphia 110; Neighborhoods Online 114–21
local authority–user/citizen interaction 46
local government, transparency improved 38
local participation, motivation of 157–8

'MacDemocracy' 161
mail-boxes, used by right-wing groups 73, 74
Manchester Advice Network 155
Manchester Bangladesh Association and Community Centre 156, 157
Manchester HOST 154–8; background and history 152–4; development of the information city 158–63; Telecities Network 158
Manchester Information City initiative 152–3, 163, 169; and democracy 159–60; a medium of economic regeneration 174; and politics 158–9; private–public partnership 159
marginal groups, empowered by PEN 142–3
Marshall, T.H. 103
Mayell, S. 135
media, and the crisis of political participation 3–5
media, new 5, 37, 61; Berlin student protest 77–8; collective action and civic participation 69–72; helps formation of collective identity 71–2, 74; impact on right-wing group activities 74–6; policy debate on 8–16; potential still undeveloped, Berlin 64–5, 80; rejuvenation of political citizenship 84–5; urbanisation of 63; USA, First Amendment protection 134
media systems, and democratic communication 4–5
message routing, Bologna 101

Miller, S. 163
moderation 171–2; v. freedom of speech issue 172
moderators: PEN system conferences 136–9; use of, Digital City 32–3

National Association of Neighborhoods 113
National Information Infrastructure (NII) Agenda for Action 6, 9–10
National Peoples' Action 113
National Technical University of Athens (NTUA), and Network Pericles 44, 45, 46
neighbourhood planning councils 112
neighbourhood town watch schemes 111–12
neighbourhoods' movement, USA 111–14
Neighborhoods Online (Philadelphia) 6, 110–11, 114–18; and American libertarian civic tradition 173; empowerment menu 118; Internet resource centre 169; moving to empowerment 123–4; networking 121–3; recruitment and training 118–21; and universal access 171; use of the Internet 114, 123; Website 114, 115–18, 121, 123
net culture, and state intervention 107
Netherlands: computer-mediated communication (CMC) 1; telematics in 21; see also Digital City, Amsterdam
netiquette 33, 36, 37, 39, 99
Network Pericles 43–57, 174; access, participation and citizenship 48–52; aim of 42; electronic democracy 45–8, 52–7, 169, 170; specific design aims 42–3; technology, democracy and communication 44–5; universal access to 171
network transmission protocols 3
networks 10; high-capacity 2
'new public management' 7–8

open environment 10

PC networks 2
PC users, and Network Pericles 49
PEN community, conflict within 131–2
PEN system, Santa Monica 169, 174; access and the Internet 131, 132–3; components of 128–9, *130*; conferences 136–9, 144, 145–6, 147, 172; diverse community of users 145; empowerment of some at the margin 142–3; history of 126–31, *148*; and the Internet 131, 132–3; limited diffusion of 131–3; most promising components 146–7; prospects 139–40; strict interpretation of First Amendment 133; utilization of 129–31
Philadelphia Council of Neighborhood Organizations 111, 112
Phillips, Ken 137
'pillarisation' 37
political community, false notion of, and democracy 162
political cultures, set parameters for political and social action 173
political ideologies, diminishing importance of 21
political organisations, virtual 144
political parties: decline in membership 3; Germany, and the Internet 67–8
politics: in Amsterdam's Digital City 20; apathy towards 4; Berlin, on the Internet 67–8; electoral 113; and IperBolE 100; negative attitude to 44; political mobilisation 69, 71, 73–6; publicness of process 56
polls, electronic, interactive 89
pressure groups and lobbies 4
privatisation and deregulation 3
Programme on Information and Communication Technologies (PICT) 10
public access multimedia points/terminals 160; IperBolE 88; poor in Digital City 31; Santa Monica 129, 145; user-friendly 49–50
public apathy, a dilemma 145
public debate, and political action 5
public domain development 37–9; in electronic society 24
public electronic network (PEN), Santa Monica *see* PEN system, Santa Monica
public information utilities (PIUs) 140
public service broadcasting 3, 4
public space(s) 54; creation of 176; diversified 61; new 55
public sphere(s) 4, 162, 163; dynamic, alternative 39; and electronic democracy 52–7, 167–78; socially-grounded theories of 54
'publicness' 174–5; new forms of 53; nodes of 56

racism: Berlin in the Net 73–6; Digital City 36
recall 46–7
'received wisdom', likely to be contested 7
referenda 46, 102; and polls 90; and surveys 89
resource mobilisation theory 69–70
right-wing groups 78; and democratic participation 80; Europe, information network 75; Germany, use of Internet 73–6
Robinson, A. 160

Santa Monica, public electronic network (PEN) 125–51, 169, 174
science/technology, decision-making/policy formulation 12
Sclove, R. 164
seamless interconnection 10, 54
service provision, efficiency of 7–8
social equality, and the new information/communication services 14–15
social rights 103
'soundbite media' 5

subsidy, Digital City 33

technology(ies): democratic potential 167; new 12–13
Telecities Network 158
telecommunications 15–16; deregulation and privatisation of 14–15; liberalisation of 11, 15; and the Manchester Initiative 163–4; provision, government policies 115–16
Telecommunications Act (1996: USA) 12
teleconferencing/citizen conferencing 47, 49, 53
teledemocracy 125
'Thread Police' 135
Thule Net 73–4, 75; aims to create a 'counter-public' 76
touch-screens 50
training provision: Electronic Village Halls 156; Neighborhoods Online 118–21

UK, Programme on Information and Communication Technologies (PICT) 10

urban landscapes, transformation of 1
Urban Programme grant, for Manchester initiative 153
urbanity 54–5
USA 1; improvement of citizen–local authority contact 41–2; inner cities and Neighborhoods Online 110
user surveys, Digital City 30

voice-command equipment 50
voluntary organisations 4
voter identity, secrecy of 52
voters, apathy 3, 44, 161
voting: electronic 46, 48, 103, 170; kiosks for 49
voting rights, distinguishing between 52

William Penn Foundation 115, 120
Wired, about the Net 7
Women's EVH 156, 157
World Wide Web 1, 25–6, 126
WWW servers, Bologna 93

Young, I.M. 54